T0213270

Lecture Notes in Computer Science 9993

Commenced Publication in 1973
Founding and Former Series Editors:
Gerhard Goos, Juris Hartmanis, and Jan van Leeuwen

More information about this series at http://www.springer.com/series/7412

Guorong Wu · Pierrick Coupé
Yiqiang Zhan · Brent C. Munsell
Daniel Rueckert (Eds.)

Patch-Based Techniques in Medical Imaging

Second International Workshop, Patch-MI 2016
Held in Conjunction with MICCAI 2016
Athens, Greece, October 17, 2016
Proceedings

 Springer

Editors
Guorong Wu
University of North Carolina at Chapel Hill
Chapel Hill, NC
USA

Brent C. Munsell
College of Charleston
Charleston, SC
USA

Pierrick Coupé
Bordeaux University
Bordeaux
France

Daniel Rueckert
Imperial College London
London
UK

Yiqiang Zhan
Siemens Healthcare
Malvern, PA
USA

ISSN 0302-9743   ISSN 1611-3349   (electronic)
Lecture Notes in Computer Science
ISBN 978-3-319-47117-4   ISBN 978-3-319-47118-1 (eBook)
DOI 10.1007/978-3-319-47118-1

Library of Congress Control Number: 2016953332

LNCS Sublibrary: SL6 – Image Processing, Computer Vision, Pattern Recognition, and Graphics

Printed on acid-free paper

This Springer imprint is published by Springer Nature
The registered company is Springer International Publishing AG
The registered company address is: Gewerbestrasse 11, 6330 Cham, Switzerland

Preface

The Second International Workshop on Patch-Based Techniques in Medical Imaging (PatchMI 2016) was held in Athens, Greece, on October 17, 2016, in conjunction with the 19th International Conference on Medical Image Computing and Computer Assisted Intervention (MICCAI).

The patch-based technique plays an increasing role in the medical imaging field, with various applications in image segmentation, image denoising, image super-resolution, computer-aided diagnosis, image registration, abnormality detection, and image synthesis. For example, patch-based approaches using the training library of annotated atlases have been the focus of much attention in segmentation and computer-aided diagnosis. It has been shown that the patch-based strategy in conjunction with a training library is able to produce an accurate representation of data, while the use of a training library enables one to easily integrate prior knowledge into the model. As an intermediate level between global images and localized voxels, patch-based models offer an efficient and flexible way to represent very complex anatomies.

The main aim of the PatchMI 2016 Workshop was to promote methodological advances in the field of patch-based processing in medical imaging. The focus of this was on major trends and challenges in this area, and to identify new cutting-edge techniques and their use in medical imaging. We hope our workshop becomes a new platform for translating research from the bench to the bedside. We look for original, high-quality submissions on innovative research and development in the analysis of medical image data using patch-based techniques.

The quality of submissions for this year's meeting was very high. Authors were asked to submit eight-pages LNCS papers for review. A total of 25 papers were submitted to the workshop in response to the call for papers. Each of the 25 papers underwent a rigorous double-blinded peer-review process, with each paper being reviewed by at least two (typically three) reviewers from the Program Committee, composed of 43 well-known experts in the field. Based on the reviewing scores and critiques, the 17 best papers were accepted for presentation at the workshop and chosen to be included in this Springer LNCS volume. The large variety of patch-based techniques applied to medical imaging were well represented at the workshop.

We are grateful to the Program Committee for reviewing the submitted papers and giving constructive comments and critiques, to the authors for submitting high-quality papers, to the presenters for excellent presentations, and to all the PatchMI 2016 attendees who came to Athens from all around the world.

October 2016

Pierrick Coupé
Guorong Wu
Yiqiang Zhan
Daniel Rueckert
Brent C. Munsell

Organization

Program Committee

Charles Kervrann	Inria Rennes Bretagne Atlantique, France
Christian Barillot	IRISA, France
Dinggang Shen	UNC Chapel Hill, USA
Francois Rousseau	Telecom Bretagne, France
Gang Li	UNC Chapel Hill, USA
Gerard Sanrom	Pompeu Fabra University, Spain
Guoyan Zheng	University of Bern, Switzerland
Islem Rekik	UNC Chapel Hill, USA
Jean-Francois Mangin	I2BM
Jerome Boulanger	IRISA, France
Jerry Prince	Johns Hopkins University, USA
Jose Herrera	ITACA Institute Universidad Politechnica de Valencia, Spain
Juan Iglesias	University College London, UK
Julia Schnabel	King's College London, UK
Junzhou Huang	University of Texas at Arlington, USA
Jussi Tohka	Universidad Carlos III de Madrid, Spain
Karim Lekadir	Universitat Pompeu Fabra Barcelona, Spain
Li Shen	Indiana University, USA
Li Wang	UNC Chapel Hill, USA
Lin Yang	University of Florida, USA
Martin Styner	UNC Chapel Hill, USA
Mattias Heinrich	University of Lübeck, Germany
Mert Sabuncu	Harvard Medical School, USA
Olivier Colliot	UPMC
Olivier Commowick	Inria, France
Paul Aljabar	KCL
Paul Yushkevich	University of Pennsylvania, USA
Qian Wang	Shanghai Jiao Tong University, China
Rolf Heckemann	Sahlgrenska University Hospital, Sweden
Shaoting Zhang	UNC Charlotte, USA
Shu Liao	Siemens
Simon Eskildsen	Center of Functionally Integrative Neuroscience
Tobias Klinder	Philips
Vladimir Fonov	McGill, Canada
Weidong Cai	University of Sydney, Australia
Yefeng Zheng	Siemens

Yong Fan   University of Pennsylvania, USA
Yonggang Shi   University of Southern California, USA
Zhu Xiaofeng   UNC Chapel Hill, USA
Hanbo Chen   University of Georgia, USA
Xi Jiang   University of Georgia, USA
Xiang Jiang   University of Georgia, USA
Xiaofeng Zhu   UNC Chapel Hill, USA

Contents

Automatic Segmentation of Hippocampus for Longitudinal Infant Brain
MR Image Sequence by Spatial-Temporal Hypergraph Learning   1
Yanrong Guo, Pei Dong, Shijie Hao, Li Wang, Guorong Wu,
and Dinggang Shen

Construction of Neonatal Diffusion Atlases via Spatio-Angular Consistency . . .   9
Behrouz Saghafi, Geng Chen, Feng Shi, Pew-Thian Yap,
and Dinggang Shen

Selective Labeling: Identifying Representative Sub-volumes for Interactive
Segmentation   17
Imanol Luengo, Mark Basham, and Andrew P. French

Robust and Accurate Appearance Models Based on Joint Dictionary
Learning: Data from the Osteoarthritis Initiative   25
Anirban Mukhopadhyay, Oscar Salvador Morillo Victoria,
Stefan Zachow, and Hans Lamecker

Consistent Multi-Atlas Hippocampus Segmentation for Longitudinal
MR Brain Images with Temporal Sparse Representation   34
Lin Wang, Yanrong Guo, Xiaohuan Cao, Guorong Wu,
and Dinggang Shen

Sparse-Based Morphometry: Principle and Application to Alzheimer's
Disease   43
Pierrick Coupé, Charles-Alban Deledalle, Charles Dossal,
Michèle Allard, and Alzheimer's Disease Neuroimaging Initiative

Multi-Atlas Based Segmentation of Brainstem Nuclei from MR Images
by Deep Hyper-Graph Learning   51
Pei Dong, Yangrong Guo, Yue Gao, Peipeng Liang, Yonghong Shi,
Qian Wang, Dinggang Shen, and Guorong Wu

Patch-Based Discrete Registration of Clinical Brain Images   60
Adrian V. Dalca, Andreea Bobu, Natalia S. Rost, and Polina Golland

Non-local MRI Library-Based Super-Resolution: Application
to Hippocampus Subfield Segmentation   68
Jose E. Romero, Pierrick Coupé, and Jose V. Manjón

X   Contents

Patch-Based DTI Grading: Application to Alzheimer's Disease
Classification   76
   Kilian Hett, Vinh-Thong Ta, Rémi Giraud, Mary Mondino,
   José V. Manjón, Pierrick Coupé,
   and Alzheimer's Disease Neuroimaging Initiative

Hierarchical Multi-Atlas Segmentation Using Label-Specific Embeddings,
Target-Specific Templates and Patch Refinement   84
   Christoph Arthofer, Paul S. Morgan, and Alain Pitiot

HIST: HyperIntensity Segmentation Tool   92
   Jose V. Manjón, Pierrick Coupé, Parnesh Raniga, Ying Xia,
   Jurgen Fripp, and Olivier Salvado

Supervoxel-Based Hierarchical Markov Random Field Framework
for Multi-atlas Segmentation   100
   Ning Yu, Hongzhi Wang, and Paul A. Yushkevich

CapAIBL: Automated Reporting of Cortical PET Quantification
Without Need of MRI on Brain Surface Using a Patch-Based Method   109
   Vincent Dore, Pierrick Bourgeat, Victor L. Villemagne, Jurgen Fripp,
   Lance Macaulay, Colin L. Masters, David Ames,
   Christopher C. Rowe, Olivier Salvado, and The AIBL Research Group

High Resolution Hippocampus Subfield Segmentation Using Multispectral
Multiatlas Patch-Based Label Fusion   117
   José E. Romero, Pierrick Coupe, and José V. Manjón

Identification of Water and Fat Images in Dixon MRI Using Aggregated
Patch-Based Convolutional Neural Networks   125
   Liang Zhao, Yiqiang Zhan, Dominik Nickel, Matthias Fenchel,
   Berthold Kiefer, and Xiang Sean Zhou

Estimating Lung Respiratory Motion Using Combined Global
and Local Statistical Models   133
   Zhong Xue, Ramiro Pino, and Bin Teh

Author Index   141

Automatic Segmentation of Hippocampus for Longitudinal Infant Brain MR Image Sequence by Spatial-Temporal Hypergraph Learning

Yanrong Guo[1], Pei Dong[1], Shijie Hao[1,2], Li Wang[1], Guorong Wu[1], and Dinggang Shen[1(✉)]

[1] Department of Radiology and BRIC,
University of North Carolina at Chapel Hill, Chapel Hill, NC, USA
dgshen@med.unc.edu
[2] School of Computer and Information,
Hefei University of Technology, Anhui, China

Abstract. Accurate segmentation of infant hippocampus from Magnetic Resonance (MR) images is one of the key steps for the investigation of early brain development and neurological disorders. Since the manual delineation of anatomical structures is time-consuming and irreproducible, a number of automatic segmentation methods have been proposed, such as multi-atlas patch-based label fusion methods. However, the hippocampus during the first year of life undergoes dynamic appearance, tissue contrast and structural changes, which pose substantial challenges to the existing label fusion methods. In addition, most of the existing label fusion methods generally segment target images at each time-point independently, which is likely to result in inconsistent hippocampus segmentation results along different time-points. In this paper, we treat a longitudinal image sequence as a whole, and propose a spatial-temporal hypergraph based model to jointly segment infant hippocampi from all time-points. Specifically, in building the spatial-temporal hypergraph, (1) the atlas-to-target relationship and (2) the spatial/temporal neighborhood information within the target image sequence are encoded as two categories of hyperedges. Then, the infant hippocampus segmentation from the whole image sequence is formulated as a semi-supervised label propagation model using the proposed hypergraph. We evaluate our method in segmenting infant hippocampi from T1-weighted brain MR images acquired at the age of 2 weeks, 3 months, 6 months, 9 months, and 12 months. Experimental results demonstrate that, by leveraging spatial-temporal information, our method achieves better performance in both segmentation accuracy and consistency over the state-of-the-art multi-atlas label fusion methods.

1 Introduction

Since hippocampus plays an important role in learning and memory functions of human brain, many early brain development studies are devoted to finding the imaging biomarkers specific to hippocampus from birth to 12-month-old [1]. During this period,

G. Wu et al. (Eds.): Patch-MI 2016, LNCS 9993, pp. 1–8, 2016.
DOI: 10.1007/978-3-319-47118-1_1

the hippocampus undergoes rapid physical growth and functional development [2]. In this context, accurate hippocampus segmentation from Magnetic Resonance (MR) images is important to imaging-based brain development studies, as it paves way to quantitative analysis on dynamic changes. As manual delineating of hippocampus is time-consuming and irreproducible, automatic and accurate segmentation method for infant hippocampus is highly needed.

Recently, multi-atlas patch-based label fusion segmentation methods [3–7] have achieved the state-of-the-art performance in segmenting adult brain structures, since the information propagated from multiple atlases can potentially alleviate the issues of both large inter-subject variations and inaccurate image registration. However, for the infant brain MR images acquired from the first year of life, a hippocampus typically undergoes a dynamic growing process in terms of both appearance and shape patterns, as well as the changing image contrast [8]. These challenges limit the performance of the multi-atlas methods in the task of infant hippocampus segmentation. Moreover, most current label fusion methods estimate the label for each subject image voxel separately, ignoring the underlying common information in the spatial-temporal domain across all the atlas and target image sequences. Therefore, these methods provide less regularization on the smoothness and consistency of longitudinal segmentation results.

To address these limitations, we resort to using hypergraph, which naturally caters to modeling the spatial and temporal consistency of a longitudinal sequence in our segmentation task. Specifically, we treat all atlas image sequences and target image sequence as whole, and build a novel spatial-temporal hypergraph model, for jointly encoding useful information from all the sequences. To build the spatial-temporal hypergraph, two categories of hyperedges are introduced to encode information with the following anatomical meanings: (1) the atlas-to-target relationship, which covers common appearance patterns between the target and all the atlas sequences; (2) the spatial/temporal neighborhood within the target image sequence, which covers common spatially- and longitudinally-consistent patterns of the target hippocampus. Based on this built spatial-temporal hypergraph, we then formulate a semi-supervised label propagation model to jointly segment hippocampi for an entire longitudinal infant brain image sequence in the first year of life. The contribution of our method is two-fold:

First, we enrich the types of hyperedges in the proposed hypergraph model, by leveraging both spatial and temporal information from all the atlas and target image sequences. Therefore, the proposed spatial-temporal hypergraph is potentially more adapted to the challenges, such as rapid longitudinal growth and dynamically changing image contrast in the infant brain MR images.

Second, based on the built spatial-temporal hypergraph, we formulate the task of longitudinal infant hippocampus segmentation as a semi-supervised label propagation model, which can unanimously propagate labels from atlas image sequences to the target image sequence. Of note, in our label propagation model, we also use a hierarchical strategy by gradually recruiting the labels of *high-confident* target voxels to help guide the segmentation of *less-confident* target voxels.

We evaluate the proposed method in segmenting hippocampi from longitudinal T1-weighted MR image sequences acquired in the first year of life. More accurate and consistent hippocampus segmentation results are obtained across all the time-points, compared to the state-of-the-art multi-atlas label fusion methods [6, 7].

2 Method

For labeling the longitudinal target images with T time-points $\{I_{O,t}|t = 1,\ldots,T\}$, the first step is to linearly align S longitudinal atlas image sequences $\{I_{s,t}|s = 1,\ldots,S; t = 1,\ldots,T\}$ into the target image space. Then, the spatial-temporal hypergraph is constructed as detailed in Sect. 2.1. Finally, hippocampus is longitudinally segmented through the label propagation based on the semi-supervised hypergraph learning, as introduced in Sect. 2.2.

2.1 Spatial-Temporal Hypergraph

Denote a hypergraph as $\mathcal{G} = (\mathcal{V}, \mathcal{E}, w)$, composed of the vertex set $\mathcal{V} = \{v_i|i = 1,\ldots,|\mathcal{V}|\}$, the hyperedge set $\mathcal{E} = \{e_i|i = 1,\ldots,|\mathcal{E}|\}$ and edge weight vector $w \in \mathcal{R}^{|\mathcal{E}|}$. Since each hyperedge e_i allows linking more than two vertexes included in $\mathcal{V}$, $\mathcal{G}$ naturally characterizes groupwise relationship, which reveals high-order correlations among a subset of voxels [9]. By encoding both spatial and temporal information from all the target and atlas image sequences into the hypergraph, a spatial-temporal hypergraph is built to characterize various relationships in the spatial-temporal domain. Generally, our hypergraph includes two categories of hyperedges: (1) the atlas-to-target hyperedge, which measures the patch similarities between the atlas and target images; (2) the local spatial/temporal neighborhood hyperedge, which measures the coherence among the vertexes located in a certain spatial and temporal neighborhood of atlas and target images.

Atlas-to-Target Hyperedge. The conventional label fusion methods only measure the pairwise similarity between atlas and target voxels. In contrast, in our model, each atlas-to-target hyperedge encodes groupwise relationship among multiple vertexes of atlas and target images. For example, in the left panel of Fig. 1, a central vertex v_c (yellow triangle) from the target image and its local spatial correspondences $v_7 \sim v_{12}$ (blue square) located in the atlases images form an atlas-to-target hyperedge e_1 (blue round dot curves in the right panel of Fig. 1). In this way, rich information contained in the atlas-to-target hyperedges can be leveraged to jointly determine the target label.

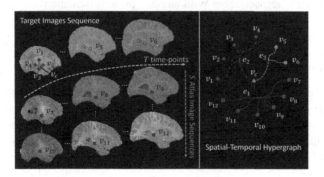

Fig. 1. The construction of spatial-temporal hypergraph.

Thus, the chance of mislabeling an individual voxel can be reduced by jointly propagating the labels of all neighboring voxels.

Local Spatial/Temporal Neighborhood Hyperedge. Without enforcing spatial and temporal constraints, the existing label fusion methods are limited in labeling each target voxel at each time-point independently. We address this problem by measuring the coherence between the vertexes located at both spatial and temporal neighborhood in the target images. In this way, local spatial/temporal neighborhood hyperedges can be built to further incorporate both spatial and temporal consistency into the hypergraph model. For example, *spatially*, the hyperedge e_2 (green dash dot curves in the right panel of Fig. 1) connects a central vertex v_c (yellow triangle) and the vertexes located in its local spatial neighborhood $v_1 \sim v_4$ (green diamond) in the target images. We note that $v_1 \sim v_4$ are actually very close to v_c in our implementation. But, for better visualization, they are shown with larger distance to v_c in Fig. 1. Temporally, the hyperedge e_3 (red square dot curves in the right panel of Fig. 1) connects v_c and the vertexes located in its local temporal neighborhood $v_5 \sim v_6$ (red circle), i.e., the corresponding positions of the target images at different time-points.

Hypergraph Model. After determining the vertex set $\mathcal{V}$ and the hyperedge set $\mathcal{E}$, a $|\mathcal{V}| \times |\mathcal{E}|$ incidence matrix H is obtained to encode all the information within the hypergraph $\mathcal{G}$. In H, rows represent $|\mathcal{V}|$ vertexes, and columns represent $|\mathcal{E}|$ hyperedges. Each entry $H(v, e)$ in H measures the affinity between the central vertex v_c of the hyperedge $e \in \mathcal{E}$ and each vertex $v \in e$ as below:

$$H(v, e) = \begin{cases} exp\left(-\frac{p(v) - p(v_c)_2^2}{\sigma^2}\right) & \text{if } v \in e \\ 0 & \text{if } v \notin e \end{cases} \tag{1}$$

where $\|.\|_2$ is the L_2 norm distance computed between vectorized intensity image patch $p(v)$ for vertex v and $p(v_c)$ for central vertex v_c. σ is the averaged patchwise distance between v_c and all vertexes connected by the hyperedge e.

Based on Eq. (1), the degree of a vertex $v \in \mathcal{V}$ is defined as $d(v) = \sum_{e \in \mathcal{E}} w(e)H(v, e)$, and the degree of hyperedge $e \in \mathcal{E}$ is defined as $\delta(e) = \sum_{v \in v} H(v, e)$. Diagonal matrices D_v, D_e and W are then formed, in which each entry along the diagonal is the vertex degree $d(v)$, hyperedge degree $\delta(e)$ and hyperedge weights $w(e)$, respectively. Without any prior information on the hyperedge weight, $w(e)$ is uniformly set to 1 for each hyperedge.

2.2   Label Propagation Based on Hypergraph Learning

Based on the proposed spatial-temporal hypergraph, we then propagate the known labels of the atlas voxels to the voxels of the target image sequence, by assuming that the vertexes strongly linked by the same hyperedge are likely to have the same label. Specifically, this label propagation problem can be solved by a semi-supervised learning model as described below.

Label Initialization. Assume $Y = [y_1, y_2] \in \mathcal{R}^{|\mathcal{V}| \times 2}$ as the initialized labels for all the $|\mathcal{V}|$ vertexes, with $y_1 \in \mathcal{R}^{|\mathcal{V}|}$ and $y_2 \in \mathcal{R}^{|\mathcal{V}|}$ as label vectors for two classes, i.e., hippocampus and non-hippocampus, respectively. For the vertex v from the atlas images, its corresponding labels are assigned as $y_1(v) = 1$ and $y_2(v) = 0$ if v belongs to hippocampus regions, and vice versa. For the vertex v from the target images, its corresponding labels are initialized as $y_1(v) = y_2(v) = 0.5$, which indicates the undetermined label status for this vertex.

Hypergraph Based Semi-Supervised Learning. Given the constructed hypergraph model and the label initialization, the goal of label propagation is to find the optimized relevance label scores $F = [f_1, f_2] \in \mathcal{R}^{|\mathcal{V}| \times 2}$ for vertex set $\mathcal{V}$, in which f_1 and f_2 represent the preference for choosing hippocampus and non-hippocampus, respectively. A hypergraph based semi-supervised learning model [9] can be formed as:

$$\arg \min_F \left\{ \lambda \cdot \sum_{i=1}^{2} f_i - y_i^2 + \Omega(F, H, W) \right\} \tag{2}$$

There are two terms, weighted by a positive parameter λ, in the above objective function. The first term is a loss function term penalizing the fidelity between estimation F and initialization Y. Hence, the optimal label prorogation results are able to avoid large discrepancy before and after hypergraph learning. The second term is a regularization term defined as:

$$\Omega(F, H, W) = \frac{1}{2} \sum_{i=1}^{2} \sum_{e \in \mathcal{E}} \sum_{v_c, v \in \mathcal{V}} \frac{w(e)H(v_c, e)H(v, e)}{\delta(e)} \times \left(\frac{f_i(v_c)}{\sqrt{d(v_c)}} - \frac{f_i(v)}{\sqrt{d(v)}} \right)^2 \tag{3}$$

Here, for the vertexes v_c and v connected by the same hyperedge e, the regularization term tries to enforce their relevance scores being similar, when both $H(v_c, e)$ and $H(v, e)$ are large. For convenience, the regularization term can be reformulated into a matrix form, i.e., $\sum_{i=1}^{2} f_i^T \Delta f_i$, where the normalized hypergraph Laplacian matrix $\Delta = I - \Theta$ is a positive semi-definite matrix, $\Theta = D_v^{-\frac{1}{2}} HWD_e^{-1} H^T D_v^{-\frac{1}{2}}$ and I is an identity matrix.

By differentiating the objective function (2) with respect to F, the optimal F can be analytically solved as $F = \frac{\lambda}{\lambda+1} (I - \frac{1}{\lambda+1} \cdot \Theta)^{-1} Y$. The anatomical label on each target vertex $v \in \mathcal{V}$ can be finally determined as the one with larger score: $\arg \max_i f_i(v)$.

Hierarchical Labeling Strategy. Some target voxels with ambiguous appearance (e.g., those located at the hippocampal boundary region) are more difficult to label than the voxels with uniform appearance (e.g., those located at the hippocampus center region). Besides, the accuracy of aligning atlas images to target image also impacts the label confidence for each voxel. In this context, we divide all the voxels into two groups, such as the high-confidence group and the less-confidence group, based on the predicted labels and their confidence values in terms of voting predominance from majority voting. With the help of the labeling results from high-confident region, the labeling for the less-confident region can be propagated from both atlas and the newly-added reliable target voxels, which makes the label fusion procedure more target-specific. Then, based on the refined label fusion results from hypergraph learning, more target voxels are labeled as high-confidence. By iteratively recruiting more and more high-confident target vertexes in the semi-supervised hypergraph learning framework, a hierarchical labeling strategy is formed, which gradually labels the target voxels from high-confident ones to less-confident ones. Therefore, the label fusion results for target image can be improved step by step.

3   Experimental Results

We evaluate the proposed method on a dataset containing MR images of ten healthy infant subjects acquired from a Siemens head-only 3T scanner. For each subject, T1-weighted MR images were scanned at five time-points, i.e., 2 weeks, 3 months, 6 months, 9 months and 12 months of age. Each image is with the volume size of $192 \times 156 \times 144$ voxels at the resolution of $1 \times 1 \times 1\,mm^3$. Standard preprocessing was performed, including skull stripping, and intensity inhomogeneity correction. The manual delineations of hippocampi for all subjects are used as ground-truth.

The parameters in the proposed method are set as follows. The patch size for computing patch similarity is $5 \times 5 \times 5$ voxels. Parameter λ in Eq. (2) is empirically set to 0.01. The spatial/temporal neighborhood is set to $3 \times 3 \times 3$ voxels. The strategy of leave-one-subject-out is used to evaluate the segmentation methods. Specifically, one subject is chosen as the target for segmentation, and the image sequences of the remaining nine subjects are used as the atlas images. The proposed method is compared with two state-of-the-art multi-atlas label fusion methods, e.g., local-weighted majority voting [6] and sparse patch labeling [7], as well as a method based on a degraded spatial-temporal hypergraph, i.e., our model for segmenting each time-point independently with only spatial constraint.

Table 1 gives the average Dice ratio (DICE) and average surface distance (ASD) of the segmentation results by four comparison methods at 2-week-old, 3-month-old,

Table 1. The DICE (average ± standard deviation, in %) and ASD (average ± standard deviation, in *mm*) of segmentation results by four comparison methods for 2-week-old, 3-month-old, 6-month-old, 9-month-old and 12-month-old data.

Time-point	Metric	Majority voting [6]	Sparse labeling [7]	Spatial-temporal hypergraph labeling	
				Degraded	Full
2-week-old	DICE	50.18 ± 18.15 (8e−3)*	63.93 ± 8.20 (6e−2)	64.09 ± 8.15 (9e−2)	64.84 ± 9.33
	ASD	1.02 ± 0.41 (8e−3)*	0.78 ± 0.23 (1e−2)*	0.78 ± 0.23 (1e−2)*	0.74 ± 0.26
3-month-old	DICE	61.59 ± 9.19 (3e−3)*	71.49 ± 4.66 (7e−2)	71.75 ± 4.98 (1e−1)	74.04 ± 3.39
	ASD	0.86 ± 0.25 (6e−3)*	0.66 ± 0.14 (5e−2)*	0.66 ± 0.15 (9e−2)	0.60 ± 0.09
6-month-old	DICE	64.85 ± 7.28 (2e−4)*	72.15 ± 6.15 (5e−3)*	72.78 ± 5.68 (4e−2)*	73.84 ± 6.46
	ASD	0.85 ± 0.23 (1e−4)*	0.71 ± 0.19 (3e−3)*	0.70 ± 0.17 (4e−2)*	0.67 ± 0.20
9-month-old	DICE	71.82 ± 4.57 (6e−4)*	75.18 ± 2.50 (2e−3)*	75.78 ± 2.89 (9e-3)*	77.22 ± 2.77
	ASD	0.73 ± 0.16 (9e−4)*	0.65 ± 0.07 (1e−3)*	0.64 ± 0.09 (9e−3)*	0.60 ± 0.09
12-month-old	DICE	71.96 ± 6.64 (8e−3)*	75.39 ± 2.87 (7e−4)*	75.96 ± 2.85 (1e−2)*	77.45 ± 2.10
	ASD	0.67 ± 0.10 (6e−3)*	0.64 ± 0.08 (2e−3)*	0.64 ± 0.07 (1e−2)*	0.59 ± 0.07

*Indicates significant improvement of spatial-temporal hypergraph method over other compared methods with p-value < 0.05

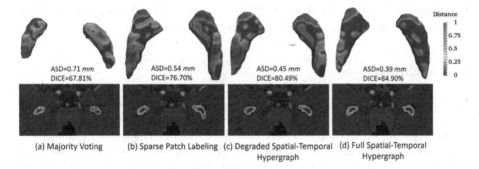

(a) Majority Voting   (b) Sparse Patch Labeling (c) Degraded Spatial-Temporal   (d) Full Spatial-Temporal
Hypergraph   Hypergraph

Fig. 2. Visual comparison between segmentations from each of four comparison methods and the ground truth on one subject at 6-month-old. Red contours indicate the results of automatic segmentation methods, and yellow contours indicate their ground truth. (Color figure online)

6-month-old, 9-month-old and 12-month-old data, respectively. There are two observations from Table 1. First, the degraded hypergraph with only the spatial constraint still obtains mild improvement over other two methods. Second, after incorporating the temporal consistency, our method gains significant improvement, especially for the time-points after 3-month-old. Figure 2 provides a typical visual comparison of segmenting accuracy among four methods. The upper panel of Fig. 2 visualizes the surface distance between the segmentation results from each of four methods and the ground truth. As can be observed, our method shows more blue regions (indicating smaller surface distance) than red regions (indicating larger surface distance), hence obtaining results more similar to the ground truth. The lower panel of Fig. 2 illustrates the segmentation contours for four methods, in which our method shows the highest overlap with the ground truth. Figure 3 further compares the temporal consistency from 2-week-old to 12-month-old data between the degraded and full spatial-temporal hypergraph. From the left panel in Fig. 3, it is observed that our full method achieves better visual temporal consistency than the degraded version, e.g., the right hippocampus at 2-week-old. We also use a quantitative measurement to evaluate the temporal consistency, i.e. the ratio between the volume of the segmentation result based on the degraded/full method and the volume of its corresponding ground truth. From the right panel in Fig. 3, we can see that all the ratios of full spatial-temporal

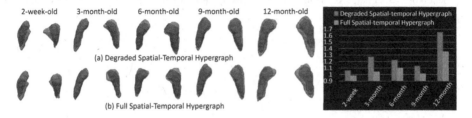

Fig. 3. Visual and quantitative comparison of temporal consistency between the degraded and full spatial-temporal hypergraph. Red shapes indicate the results of degraded/full spatial-temporal hypergraph methods, and cyan shapes indicate their ground truth. (Color figure online)

hypergraph (yellow bars) are closer to "1" than the ratios of the degraded version (blue bars) over five time-points, showing the better consistency globally.

4   Conclusion

In this paper, we propose a spatial-temporal hypergraph learning method for automatic segmentation of hippocampus from longitudinal infant brain MR images. For building the hypergraph, we consider *not only* the atlas-to-subject relationship *but also* the spatial/temporal neighborhood information. Thus, our proposed method opts for unanimous labeling of infant hippocampus with temporal consistency across different development stages. Experiments on segmenting hippocampus from T1-weighted MR images at 2-week-old, 3-month-old, 6-month-old, 9-month-old, and 12-month-old demonstrate improvement in terms of segmenting accuracy and consistency, compared to the state-of-the-art methods.

References

1. DiCicco-Bloom, E., et al.: The developmental neurobiology of autism spectrum disorder. J. Neurosci. **26**, 6897–6906 (2006)
2. Oishi, K., et al.: Quantitative evaluation of brain development using anatomical MRI and diffusion tensor imaging. Int. J. Dev. Neurosci. **31**, 512–524 (2013)
3. Wang, H., et al.: Multi-atlas segmentation with joint label fusion. IEEE Trans. Pattern Anal. Mach. Intell. **35**, 611–623 (2013)
4. Coupé, P., et al.: Patch-based segmentation using expert priors: application to hippocampus and ventricle segmentation. NeuroImage **54**, 940–954 (2011)
5. Pipitone, J., et al.: Multi-atlas segmentation of the whole hippocampus and subfields using multiple automatically generated templates. NeuroImage **101**, 494–512 (2014)
6. Isgum, I., et al.: Multi-atlas-based segmentation with local decision fusion: application to cardiac and aortic segmentation in CT scans. IEEE TMI **28**, 1000–1010 (2009)
7. Wu, G., et al.: A generative probability model of joint label fusion for multi-atlas based brain segmentation. Med. Image Anal. **18**, 881–890 (2014)
8. Jernigan, T.L., et al.: Postnatal brain development: structural imaging of dynamic neurodevelopmental processes. Prog. Brain Res. **189**, 77–92 (2011)
9. Zhou, D., et al.: Learning with hypergraphs: clustering, classification, and embedding. In: Schölkopf, B., Platt, J.C., Hoffman, A.T. (eds.) NIPS, vol. 19, pp. 1601–1608. MIT Press, Cambridge (2007)

Construction of Neonatal Diffusion Atlases via Spatio-Angular Consistency

Behrouz Saghafi[1], Geng Chen[1,2], Feng Shi[1], Pew-Thian Yap[1], and Dinggang Shen[1(✉)]

[1] Department of Radiology and BRIC, University of North Carolina,
Chapel Hill, NC, USA
dinggang_shen@med.unc.edu
[2] Data Processing Center, Northwestern Polytechnical University, Xi'an, China

Abstract. Atlases constructed using diffusion-weighted imaging (DWI) are important tools for studying human brain development. Atlas construction is in general a two-step process involving image registration and image fusion. The focus of most studies so far has been on improving registration thus image fusion is commonly performed using simple averaging, often resulting in fuzzy atlases. In this paper, we propose a patch-based method for DWI atlas construction. Unlike other atlases that are based on the diffusion tensor model, our atlas is model-free. Instead of generating an atlas for each gradient direction independently and hence neglecting inter-image correlation, we propose to construct the atlas by jointly considering diffusion-weighted images of neighboring gradient directions. We employ a group regularization framework where local patches of angularly neighboring images are constrained for consistent spatio-angular atlas reconstruction. Experimental results verify that our atlas, constructed for neonatal data, reveals more structural details compared with the average atlas especially in the cortical regions. Our atlas also yields greater accuracy when used for image normalization.

1 Introduction

MRI brain atlases are important tools that are widely used for neuroscience studies and disease diagnosis [3]. Atlas-based MRI analysis is one of the major methods used to identify typical and abnormal brain development [2]. Among different modalities for human brain mapping, diffusion-weighted imaging (DWI) is a unique modality for investigating white matter structures [1]. DWI is especially important for studies of babies since it can provide rich anatomical information despite the pre-myelinated neonatal brain [4]. But, application of atlases constructed from pediatric or adult population to neonatal brain is not straightforward, given that there are significant differences in the white matter structures between babies and older ages. Therefore, creation of atlases exclusively from neonatal population will be appealing for neonatal brain studies.

Various models have been used to characterize the diffusion of water molecules measured by the diffusion MRI signal [5]. The most common representation

© Springer International Publishing AG 2016
G. Wu et al. (Eds.): Patch-MI 2016, LNCS 9993, pp. 9–16, 2016.
DOI: 10.1007/978-3-319-47118-1_2

is the diffusion tensor model (DTM). However, DTM is unable to model multiple fiber crossings. There are other flexible approaches, such as multi-tensor model, diffusion spectrum imaging and q-ball imaging which are capable of delineating complex fiber structures. Most atlases acquired from diffusion MRI signal are DTM-based. In this work we focus on constructing a model-free atlas, based on the raw 4D diffusion-weighted images. This way we ensure that any model can later be applied on the atlas.

Usually construction of atlases involves two steps: An image registration step to align a population of images to a common space, followed by an atlas fusion step that combines all the aligned images. The focus of most atlas construction methods has been on the image registration step [7]. For the atlas fusion step, simple averaging is normally used. Averaging the images will cause the fine anatomical details to be smoothed out, resulting in blurry structures. Moreover, the outcome of simple averaging is sensitive to outliers. To overcome these drawbacks, Shi et al. [8] proposed a patch-based sparse representation method for image fusion. By leveraging over-complete codebooks of local neighborhoods, sparse subsets of samples will be automatically selected for fusion to form the atlas, and outliers are removed in the process. Also using group LASSO [6], they have constrained the spatial neighboring patches in T2-weighted atlas to have similar representations.

In constructing a DWI atlas, we need to ensure consistency between neighboring gradient directions. In this paper, we propose to employ a group-regularized estimation framework to enforce spatio-angular consistency in constructing the atlas in a patch-based manner. Each patch in the atlas is grouped together with the corresponding patches in the spatial and angular neighborhoods to have similar representations. Meanwhile, representation of each patch-location remains the same among selected population of images. We apply our proposed atlas selection method to neonatal data which often have poor contrast and low density of fibers. Experimental results indicate that our atlas outperforms the average atlas both qualitatively and quantitatively.

2   Proposed Method

2.1   Overview

All images are registered to the geometric median image of the population. The registration is done based on Fractional Anisotropy (FA) image by using affine registration followed by nonlinear registration with Diffeomorphic Demons [10]. The images are then upsampled to 1 mm isotropic resolution. For each gradient direction, each patch of the atlas is constructed via a combination of a sparse set of neighboring patches from the population of images.

2.2   Atlas Construction via Spatio-Angular Consistency

We construct the atlas in a patch-by-patch manner. For each gradient direction, we construct a codebook for each patch of size $s \times s \times s$ on the atlas. Each patch is represented using a vector of size $M = s^3$. An initial codebook (C) can include all the same-location patches in all the N subject images. However, in order to account for registration errors, we further include 26 patches of immediate neighboring voxels, giving us 27 patches per subject and a total of $\bar{N} = 27 \times N$ patches in the cookbook, i.e., $C = [p_1, p_2, \ldots, p_{\bar{N}}]$.

Each patch is constructed using the codebook based on K reference patches from the same location, i.e., $\{y_k | k = 1, \ldots, K\}$. Assuming high correlation between these patches, we measure their similarity by the Pearson correlation coefficient. Thus for patches p_i and p_j, the similarity is computed as:

$$\rho = \frac{\sum_{m=1}^{M}(p_{i,m} - \bar{p}_i)(p_{j,m} - \bar{p}_j)}{\sqrt{\sum_{m=1}^{M}(p_{i,m} - \bar{p}_i)^2}\sqrt{\sum_{m=1}^{M}(p_{j,m} - \bar{p}_j)^2}} \tag{1}$$

The group center of patches is computed as the mean patch, i.e., $\frac{1}{N}\sum_{i=1}^{N} p_i$. patches which are close to the group center are generally more representative of the whole population, while patches far from the group center may be outliers and degrade the constructed atlas. Therefore, we only select the K nearest (most similar) patches to the group center as the reference patches.

Each patch is constructed by sparsely representing the K reference patches using the codebook C. This is achieved by estimating the coefficient vector x in the following problem [9]:

$$\hat{x} = \arg\min_{x > 0} \left[\sum_{k=1}^{K} \|Cx - y_k\|_2^2 + \lambda \|x\|_1 \right], \tag{2}$$

where $C \in \mathbb{R}^{M \times \bar{N}}$, $x \in \mathbb{R}^{\bar{N} \times 1}$, $y_k \in \mathbb{R}^{M \times 1}$. The first term measures the squared L_2 distance between reference patch y_k and the reconstructed atlas patch Cx. The second term is the L_1-norm of the coefficient vector x, which ensures sparsity. $\lambda \geq 0$ is the tuning parameter.

To promote spatial consistency, we further constrain nearby patches to be constructed using similar corresponding patches in the codebooks. The coefficient vectors of the patches corresponding to 6-connected voxels are regularized in $G = 7$ groups in the problem described next. Each atlas patch corresponds to one of the groups. Let C_g, x_g, and $y_{k,g}$ represent the codebook, coefficient vector, and reference patch for the g-th group, respectively. We use $X = [x_1, \ldots, x_G]$ as the matrix grouping the coefficients in columns. X can also be described in terms of row vectors $X = [u_1; \ldots; u_{\bar{N}}]$, where u_i indicates the i-th row. Then, Eq. (2) can be rewritten as the following group LASSO problem [6]:

$$\hat{x} = \arg\min_{x \succ 0} \left[\sum_{g=1}^{G} \sum_{k=1}^{K} \|C_g x_g - y_{k,g}\|_2^2 + \lambda \|X\|_{2,1} \right], \tag{3}$$

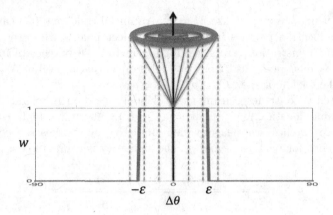

Fig. 1. The participation weight for each gradient direction is determined based on its angular distance from the current direction.

where $\|X\|_{2,1} = \sum_{i=1}^{\bar{N}} \|u_i\|_2$. To consider images of different gradient directions, $d = 1, \ldots, D$, we further modify Eq. (3) as follows:

$$\hat{X} = \arg\min_{X \succ 0} \left[\sum_{d=1}^{D} (w^d)^2 \sum_{g=1}^{G} \sum_{k=1}^{K} \left\| C_g^d x_g^d - y_{k,g}^d \right\|_2^2 + \lambda \left\| w^1 X^1, \ldots, w^D X^D \right\|_{2,1} \right].$$
(4)

where C_g^d, x_g^d, and $y_{k,g}^d$ denote the codebook, coefficient vector, and reference patch for the g-th spatial location and d-th gradient direction, respectively. Here, we have binary-weighted each representation task as well as regularization belonging to gradient direction d, with the participation weight w^d for direction d defined as (Fig. 1)

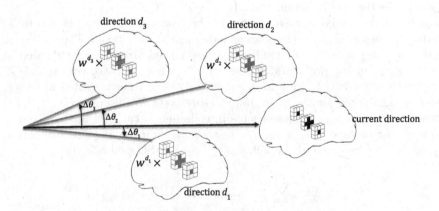

Fig. 2. Example patches in the spatial and angular neighborhood that are constrained to have similar representations.

$$w^d = \frac{1}{2}\text{sign}\left(\epsilon - \left|\cos^{-1} v^1 \cdot v^d\right|\right) + \frac{1}{2} \tag{5}$$

where ϵ is the angular distance threshold. According to Eq. (5), w^d is dependent on the angular distance between current orientation (v^1) and orientation d (v^d). This will allow an atlas patch to be constructed jointly using patches in both spatial and angular neighborhoods (Fig. 2). Eventually the atlas patch $\hat{p}^1$ at current direction is reconstructed sparsely from an overcomplete codebook $\phi = C_1^1$ obtained from local neighborhood in all subject images at current direction, using coefficients $\alpha = x_1^1$ obtained from Eq. (4). Thus $\hat{p}^1 = \phi\alpha$ (Fig. 3).

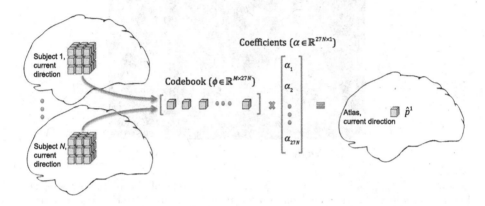

Fig. 3. Construction of a patch on the atlas by sparse representation.

3   Experimental Results

3.1   Dataset

We use neonatal brain images to evaluate the performance of the proposed atlas construction method. 15 healthy neonatal subjects (9 males/6 females) are scanned. The subjects were scanned at postnatal age of 10–35 days using a 3T Siemens Allegra scanner. The scans were acquired with size $128 \times 96 \times 60$ and resolution $2 \times 2 \times 2\text{mm}^3$ and were upsampled to $1 \times 1 \times 1\text{mm}^3$. Diffusion-weighting was applied along 42 directions with $b = 1000\,\text{s/mm}^2$. In addition, 7 non-diffusion-weighted images were obtained.

3.2   Parameter Settings

The parameters are selected empirically. The patch size was chosen as $s = 6$ with 3 voxels overlapping in each dimension. The number of reference patches is set to $K = 6$, the tuning parameter to $\lambda = 0.05$, and the angular distance threshold to $\epsilon = 22°$. Under this setting, the median number of neighbor directions for each gradient direction in our dataset is 2.

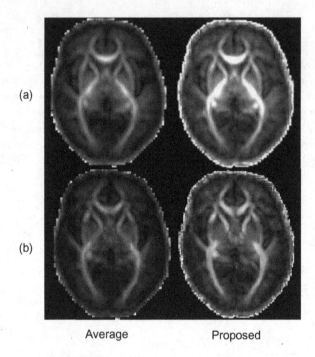

(a)

(b)

Average   Proposed

Fig. 4. (a) FA maps and (b) color-coded orientation maps of FA for the atlases produced by averaging method and our proposed method. (b) is best viewed in color. (Color figure online)

3.3 Quality of Constructed Atlas

Figure 4(a) shows the FA maps of the produced atlases using averaging and our method. The atlas produced using our method reveals greater structural details specially in the cortical regions. This is also confirmed from the color-coded orientation maps of FA shown in Fig. 4(b). We have also performed streamline fiber tractography on the estimated diffusion tensor parameters. We have applied minimum seed-point FA of 0.25, minimum allowed FA of 0.1, maximum turning angle of 45 degrees, and maximum fiber length of 1000 mm. We have extracted the forceps minor and forceps major based on the method explained in [11]. Figure 5 shows the results for forceps minor and forceps major in average and proposed atlases. As illustrated, our method is capable to reveal more fiber tracts throughout the white matter.

3.4 Evaluation of Atlas Representativeness

We also quantitatively evaluated our atlas in terms of how well it can be used to spatially normalize new data. For this, we used diffusion-weighted images of 5 new healthy neonatal subjects acquired at 37–41 gestational weeks using the same protocol described in Sect. 3.1. ROI labels from the Automated Anatomical

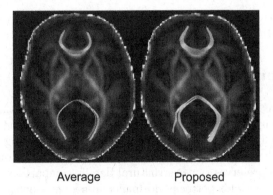

Average   Proposed

Fig. 5. Fiber tracking results for the forceps minor and forceps major, generated from average atlas (left) and our proposed atlas (right).

Labeling (AAL) were warped to the T2-image spaces of the individual subjects, and were then in turn warped to the spaces of the diffusion-weighted images to the respective $b = 0$ images. Spatial normalization was performed by registering each subject's FA map to the FA map of the atlas using affine registration followed by nonlinear registration with Diffeomorphic Demons [10]. The segmentation images were warped accordingly. For each atlas, a mean segmentation image was generated from all aligned label images based on voxel-wise majority voting. Aligned label images are compared to the atlas label image using Dice metric, which measures the overlap of two labels by $2\,|A \cap B|\,/(|A| + |B|)$, where A and B indicate the regions. The results shown in Fig. 6 indicate that our atlas

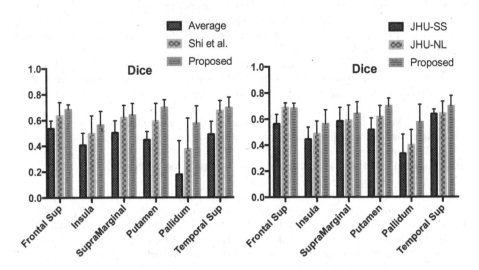

Fig. 6. The Dice ratios in the alignment of 5 new neonatal subjects by (Left) the average atlas vs. Shi et al. vs. proposed, (Right) JHU Single-Subject neonatal atlas vs. JHU Nonlinear neonatal atlas vs. proposed.

outperforms the average atlas, Shi et al.'s atlas using spatial consistency, JHU Single-subject (JHU-SS) and JHU Nonlinear (JHU-NL) neonatal atlases [7].

4   Conclusion

In this paper, we have proposed a novel method for DWI atlas construction that ensures consistency in both spatial and angular dimensions. Our approach construct each patch of the atlas by joint representation using spatio-angular neighboring patches. Experimental results confirm that, using our method, the constructed atlas preserves richer structural details compared with the average atlas. In addition, it yields better performance in neonatal image normalization.

References

1. Chilla, G.S., Tan, C.H., Xu, C., Poh, C.L.: Diffusion weighted magnetic resonance imaging and its recent trend: a survey. Quant. Imaging Med. Surg. **5**(3), 407 (2015)
2. Deshpande, R., Chang, L., Oishi, K.: Construction and application of human neonatal DTI atlases. Front. Neuroanat. **9**, 138 (2015)
3. Evans, A.C., Janke, A.L., Collins, D.L., Baillet, S.: Brain templates and atlases. Neuroimage **62**(2), 911–922 (2012)
4. Huang, H., Zhang, J., Wakana, S., Zhang, W., Ren, T., Richards, L.J., Yarowsky, P., Donohue, P., Graham, E., van Zijl, P.C., et al.: White and gray matter development in human fetal, newborn and pediatric brains. Neuroimage **33**(1), 27–38 (2006)
5. Johansen-Berg, H., Behrens, T.E.: Diffusion MRI: From Quantitative Measurement to In vivo Neuroanatomy. Academic Press, Cambridge (2013)
6. Liu, J., Ji, S., Ye, J.: Multi-task feature learning via efficient l 2, 1-norm minimization. In: Proceedings of 25th Conference on Uncertainty in Artificial Intelligence, pp. 339–348. AUAI Press (2009)
7. Oishi, K., Mori, S., Donohue, P.K., Ernst, T., Anderson, L., Buchthal, S., Faria, A., Jiang, H., Li, X., Miller, M.I., et al.: Multi-contrast human neonatal brain atlas: application to normal neonate development analysis. Neuroimage **56**(1), 8–20 (2011)
8. Shi, F., Wang, L., Wu, G., Li, G., Gilmore, J.H., Lin, W., Shen, D.: Neonatal atlas construction using sparse representation. Hum. Brain Mapp. **35**(9), 4663–4677 (2014)
9. Tibshirani, R.: Regression shrinkage and selection via the lasso. J. Roy. Stat. Soc. Ser. B (Methodol.) **58**, 267–288 (1996)
10. Vercauteren, T., Pennec, X., Perchant, A., Ayache, N.: Diffeomorphic demons: efficient non-parametric image registration. NeuroImage **45**(1), S61–S72 (2009)
11. Wakana, S., Caprihan, A., Panzenboeck, M.M., Fallon, J.H., Perry, M., Gollub, R.L., Hua, K., Zhang, J., Jiang, H., Dubey, P., et al.: Reproducibility of quantitative tractography methods applied to cerebral white matter. Neuroimage **36**(3), 630–644 (2007)

Selective Labeling: Identifying Representative Sub-volumes for Interactive Segmentation

Imanol Luengo[1,2]([⊠]), Mark Basham[2], and Andrew P. French[1]

[1] School of Computer Science, University of Nottingham, Nottingham NG8 1BB, UK
imanol.luengo@nottingham.ac.uk
[2] Diamond Light Source Ltd, Harwell Science & Innovation Campus,
Didcot OX11 0DE, UK

Abstract. Automatic segmentation of challenging biomedical volumes with multiple objects is still an open research field. Automatic approaches usually require a large amount of training data to be able to model the complex and often noisy appearance and structure of biological organelles and their boundaries. However, due to the variety of different biological specimens and the large volume sizes of the datasets, training data is costly to produce, error prone and sparsely available. Here, we propose a novel Selective Labeling algorithm to overcome these challenges; an unsupervised sub-volume proposal method that identifies the most representative regions of a volume. This massively-reduced subset of regions are then manually labeled and combined with an active learning procedure to fully segment the volume. Results on a publicly available EM dataset demonstrate the quality of our approach by achieving equivalent segmentation accuracy with only 5 % of the training data.

Keywords: Unsupervised · Sub-volume proposals · Interactive segmentation · Active learning · Affinity clustering · Supervoxels

1 Introduction

Automatic segmentation approaches have yet to have an impact in biological volumes due to the very challenging nature, and wide variety, of datasets. These approaches typically require large amounts of training data to be able to model the complex and noisy appearance of biological organelles. Unfortunately, the tedious process of manually labeling large volumes with multiple objects, which takes days to weeks for a human expert, makes it in-feasible to generate reusable and generalizable training data. To deal with this absence of training data, several semi-automatic (also called *interactive*) segmentation techniques have been proposed in the medical imaging literature. This trend has been rapidly growing over the last few years due to the advances in fast and efficient segmentation techniques. These approaches have been used to interactively segment a wide variety of medical volumes, such as arbitrary medical volumes [1] and organs [2]. However, segmenting large biological volumes with tens to hundreds of organelles

© Springer International Publishing AG 2016
G. Wu et al. (Eds.): Patch-MI 2016, LNCS 9993, pp. 17–24, 2016.
DOI: 10.1007/978-3-319-47118-1_3

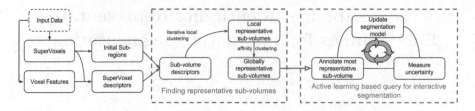

Fig. 1. Overview of our proposed pipeline

requires much more user interaction for which current interactive systems are not prepared. With current systems, an expert would need to manually annotate parts of most (or even all) the organelles in order to achieve the desired segmentation accuracy. To deal with the absence of training data and assist the human expert with the interactive segmentation task we propose a Selective Labeling approach. This consists of a novel unsupervised sub-volume[1] proposal method to identify a massively reduced subset of windows which best represent all the textural patterns of the volume. These sub-volumes are then combined with an active learning procedure to iteratively select the next most informative sub-volume to segment. This subset of small regions combined with a smart region-based active learning query strategy preserve enough discriminative information to achieve state-of-the-art segmentation accuracy while reducing the amount of training data needed by several orders of magnitude (Fig. 1).

The work presented here is inspired by the recent work of Uijlings et al. [3] (Selective Search) which extracts a reduced subset of multi-scale windows for object segmentation and has been proved to increase the performance of deep neural networks in object recognition. We adapt the idea of finding representative windows across the image under the hypothesis that a subset of representative windows have enough information to segment the whole volume. Our approach differs from Selective Search in the definition of what *representative windows* are. Selective Search tries to find windows that enclose objects, and thus, they apply a hierarchical merging process over the superpixel graph with the aim of obtaining windows that enclose objects. Here, we adopt a completely different definition of *representative windows* by searching for a subset of fixed-sized windows along the volume that best represent the textural information of the volume. This provides a reduced subset of volume patches that are easier to segment and more generalizable. Active learning techniques have been applied before in medical imaging [4,5], but they have been focused on querying the most uncertain voxels or slice according to the current performance of the classification model in single organ medical images. Our approach differs from other active learning approaches in medical imaging by: (1) It operates in the supervoxel space, making the whole algorithm several orders of magnitudes faster. (2) It first extracts a subset of representative windows which are used to loop the active learning procedure. Training and querying strategy is only applied in a

---

[1] The terms *sub-volume* and *window* will be used interchangeably along the document.

massively reduced subset of data, reducing computational complexity. (3) The queries for the user are fixed-sized sub-volumes which are very easy to segment with standard graphcut techniques. To summarize, the main contributions of the current work can be listed as follows:

1. A novel representative patch retrieval system to select the most informative sub-volumes of the dataset.
2. A novel active learning procedure to query the window that would maximize the model's performance.
3. Our segmentation framework, used as an upper bound measure, achieves similar performance to [6] while being much faster.

2   Segmentation Framework

To be able to segment large volumes efficiently, we adopt the supervoxel strategy introduced by Lucchi et al. [6] to segment mitochondria from Electron Microscopy (EM) volumes. Supervoxels consist of a group of neighbouring voxels in a given volume that share some properties, such as texture or color. Each of the voxels of the volume belong to exactly one supervoxel, and by adopting the supervoxel representation of a dataset, the complexity of a problem can be reduced two or three orders of magnitude. A supervoxel graph is created by connecting each supervoxel to its neighbours (the one it shares boundary with). Then, we extract local textural features from each voxel of the volume:

$$\mathbf{f} = \{G^{\sigma_1}, G_x^{\sigma_1}, G_y^{\sigma_1}, G_z^{\sigma_1}, G^{\sigma_5}, G_x^{\sigma_5}, G_y^{\sigma_5}, G_z^{\sigma_5}\}, \tag{1}$$

where G^{σ_x} represents the input volume convolved by a Gaussian filter of $\sigma = x$ and subscript indicates directional derivatives. Supervoxel descriptors ϕ_k (for supervoxel k) are then computed as Sigma Set [7] features of all the voxels belonging to them. These descriptors map the supervoxel covariance to a Euclidean space which has been proved to be a very efficient and robust for classification in sub-cellular volumes in [8]. To improve the accuracy and the robustness of the supervoxel descriptors, contextual information is added by appending for each supervoxel the mean ϕ of all its neighbors:

$$\psi_k = \left[\phi_k, \frac{1}{m} \sum_{i \in \mathcal{N}(k)} \phi_k\right] \tag{2}$$

Segmentation is then formulated as a Markov Random Field optimization problem defined over the supervoxel graph with labels $\mathbf{c} = \{c_i\}$:

$$E(\mathbf{c}) = \sum_{s_i \in SV} E_{data}(s_i, c_i) + \beta \sum_{(s_i, s_j) \in \mathcal{N}} E_{smooth}(c_i, c_j). \tag{3}$$

Here, the data fidelity term E_{data} is defined as the negative log likelihood of the output of an Extremely Random Forest [9] (ERF), with $T = 100$ trees, trained on the supervoxel features ψ_k. The pairwise potential E_{smooth} is also learn't from data (similar to [6]) with another ERF by concatenating the descriptors of every pair of adjacent supervoxels with the aim of modelling the *boundariness* of a pair of supervoxels. We refer the reader to [6] for more information about this segmentation model as it is used only as an upper bound and is out of the scope of this paper improving the framework.

3   Finding Representative Sub-volumes

Biological volumes are usually very large (here for example $1024 \times 768 \times 330$). In order to efficiently segment them, we provide a framework to extract most representative sub-volumes which can then be used to segment the rest of the volume. We start by defining a fixed size V_s for the sub-volumes, set empirically to preserve information whilst being easy to segment. In this work, we set $V_s = [100, 100, 10]$. Considering every possible overlapping window centered at each voxel of the volume would generate too many samples (around $200M$ voxels). Thus, we start by considering the set of proposed windows $w \in \mathcal{W}$ from N windows centered at each of the supervoxels of the image, as we already know these regions are likely to have consistent properties. We extract $10 \times 10 \times 10$ supervoxels which reduces the amount of windows by 3 orders of magnitude to roughly 200K. Next, in order to extract representative regions from the image we first need to define how to describe a region. To do so, we first cluster all the supervoxel descriptors ϕ_k in $B = 50$ bins to assign a *texton* to each supervoxel. The regional descriptor $\mathbf{r}_k$, assigned to the window proposal w_k centered at supervoxel k, is the $\ell1$-normalized histogram of supervoxel textons in that window. Thus, $\mathbf{r}_k$ encodes the different textural patches and the proportion of each of them present in each window. The descriptor is rotational invariant and very powerful discriminative descriptor for a region (Fig. 2).

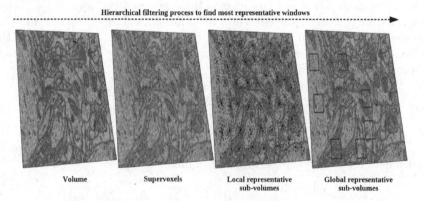

Fig. 2. Overview of the window proposal method. For visualization purposes a 2D slice is shown, but every step is performed in 3D.

3.1   Grouping Similar Nearby Sub-volumes

Once sub-volume descriptors are extracted, we perform a second local clustering. Similar to SLIC to create supervoxels but to cluster together nearby similar sub-volumes. To do so, we first sample a grid of V_s cluster centers $C_i \in \mathcal{C}$ uniformly across the volume and assign them to their nearest window w_k. For each window we use their position $\mathbf{p}_k$ in the volume and their descriptor $\mathbf{r}_k$. Then, the local k-means clustering iterates as follows:

1. **Assign each sub-volume to their nearest cluster center.** For each cluster C_i compute the distance to each of the windows in a neighbourhood. The neighbourhood is set to $2 \times V_s = [200, 200, 20]$.

$$d(C_i, k) = \left\| \mathbf{p}_{C_i} - \mathbf{p}_k \right\|_2 + \frac{\lambda}{\sqrt{2}} \left\| \sqrt{\mathbf{r}_{C_i}} - \sqrt{\mathbf{r}_k} \right\|_2 \qquad (4)$$

   where the first term represents the standard Euclidean spatial distance between windows and the second term is the Hellinger distance that measures the difference in appearance of the windows. Each window w_k is assigned to the neighbouring cluster C_i(label L_k) that minimizes the above distance.

2. **Update cluster centers.** The new cluster center is the assigned the window to minimizes the sum of differences with all the other windows, or in other words, the window that best represents all the others assigned to the same cluster:

$$C_i = argmin_{k \in \{k | L_k = i\}} \sum_{j \in \{j | L_j = i\}} d(k, j) \qquad (5)$$

The above update is very efficient and clusters nearby and similar windows into a even smaller set. After 5 iterations of the above procedure, the number of proposal windows $w_k \in \mathcal{W}$ is reduced from 200K to 3500 by only considering the windows that best describe their neighbouring windows $w_{C_i} \in \mathcal{W}$. Let us refer to this reduced set of windows as $\mathcal{R}$.

3.2   Further Refining Window Proposals

After filtering the window proposals that best represent their local neighbourhood, still a large number of possible sub-volumes remain. To further filter the most representative regions from $w_k \in \mathcal{R}$ we apply a affinity propagation based clustering [10]. Affinity propagation clustering is a message-passing clustering that automatically detects *exemplars*. The inputs for affinity clustering consist of an *affinity matrix* as the connection weights between data points and the *preference* of assigning each of the data points as *exemplars*. Then, through an iterative message-passing procedure the affinity propagation refines the weights between data points and the *preferences* until the optimal (and minimal) subset of *exemplars* is found. After local representative regions are extracted from Sect. 3.1, the pairwise similarity between all the remaining regions $w_k \in \mathcal{R}$ is extracted as

$$a(i, j) = intersection(\mathbf{r}_i, \mathbf{r}_j) \qquad (6)$$

to form the $M \times M$ affinity matrix A, where $A_{i,j} = a(i,j)$ is the similarity (only in appearance, measured by the *intersection* kernel) between all pairs of windows w_i and w_j. The *preference* vector P is set to a constant weighted by the ℓ_∞ norm of the appearance vector $P_i = \gamma \left(1 - \|\mathbf{r}_i\|_\infty\right)$. The ℓ_∞ norm of a vector returns the maximum absolute value of the vector. For a ℓ_1 normalized histogram is a good measure of how spread the histogram is. Thus, the weight $(1 - \ell_\infty)$ will encourage windows that contain wider variety of textural features to be selected. This is a desired feature, since we aim to extract a very small subset of window proposals for the whole volume, we would expect them to represent all the possible textural features of the volume or if not the training stage will fail to model unrepresented features. After the affinity propagation clustering, we now have a manageable set of <100 sub-volumes which together represent the global appearance of the whole volume. Let us denote this final subset of proposals as $\mathcal{P}$.

4   Querying the Next Most Informative Sub-volume

The active learning cycle starts once a minimal representative set of sub-regions $\mathcal{P}$ has been extracted and at least 1 window (containing both foreground and background) has been segmented. From there, the ERF model from Sect. 2 is trained and used to predict the labels of all the supervoxels belonging to all the windows in $\mathcal{P}$. Here, we average the probabilistic prediction of all the trees $t \in T$ of the ERF in order to model the probability of a supervoxel to belong to foreground or background. The uncertainty of its prediction is then estimated as the entropy. Then, the average uncertainty of all the supervoxels U_s in a window $w_k \in \mathcal{P}$ is defined as the average uncertainty in the predictions of all the supervoxels contained in that window. Similarly, the average uncertainty of *boundariness* U_e of all connected pair of supervoxels in a window is extracted from the other ERF trained to identify this property. The average window uncertainty is then defined as $U_w = U_s + \beta U_e$. The window with larger average uncertainty is selected as the next sub-volume to be segmented. As all the windows have been previously reduced to a minimal subset, the query strategy is very efficient and is able to return a globally representative sub-volume that would maximize the performance of the ERF classifier.

5   Experiments

In our experiments we used the publicly available EM dataset[2] used in [6]. The data set consists of a $5 \times 5 \times 5\,\mu$m section taken from the CA1 hippocampus region of the brain. Two $1024 \times 768 \times 165$ volumes are available where mitochondria are manually annotated (one for training and the other one for testing). We first validate the results of our segmentation pipeline by using one of the volumes for training while the other for testing. Table 1 shows results of different

---

[2] http://cvlab.epfl.ch/data/em.

Table 1. Performance of our segmentation pipeline in the testing dataset

	ERF_{raw}	ERF_{nh}	MRF_{nh}	MRF_{learnt}
Accuracy	0.975	0.984	0.987	0.991
DICE coefficient	0.751	0.825	0.851	0.871
Jaccard index	0.601	0.702	0.743	0.780

stages of our segmentation pipeline: (1) $\mathbf{ERF}_{raw}$ evaluates only the prediction of the ERF trained in the supervoxel features, (2) $\mathbf{ERF}_{nh}$ is the prediction of the ERF after aggregating neighboring supervoxel features, (3) $\mathbf{MRF}_{nh}$ is (2) refined with a contrast-sensitive MRF and (4) $\mathbf{MRF}_{learnt}$ is the full model with learned unary and pairwise potentials. Our model, used as an upper bound of the *maximum achievable accuracy* of the following experiment. It has similar segmentation performance to the one reported in [6], while being much faster (15 min of processing and training time vs 9 h).

Table 2 shows a benchmark of the quality and descriptive power of a reduced subset of our extracted windows. To evaluate the quality of our extracted windows, we simulate different user patterns. *Random User* will define the behaviour of a user selecting n random patches for training across the training volume. *Random Oracle* will select n random patches for training centered in a supervoxel that belongs to mitochondria (thus, assumes ground truth is known and simulates the user clicking in different mitochondria). *Selective Random* simulates a user choosing n windows at random from a reduced subset of windows $w_k \in \mathcal{P}$ obtained using our algorithm. And *Selective Labeling* will select the first window at random from $w_k \in \mathcal{P}$ (containing both background and foreground) while the next $n - 1$ will be selected by our active learning based query strategy. All different patterns are trained only on the selected windows of the training volume (with the full model) and tested in the whole testing volume. The 3 random patterns are averaged from 100 runs. It can be seen that our extracted windows without the active learning achieve similar performance to the random oracle (which assumes ground truth is known). This proves the quality of our windows as our unsupervised method is able to represent properly all the textural elements of the volume. With the active learning, our method outperforms all the

Table 2. DICE coefficient of the simulated retrieval methods. Percentages indicate fractions of total training data.

	Random user	*Random oracle*	*Selective random*	*Selective labeling*
3 sub-volumes ($<1\%$)	0.305	0.671	0.652	0.788
5 sub-volumes (1%)	0.533	0.736	0.740	0.792
10 sub-volumes (2%)	0.608	0.762	0.761	0.810
30 sub-volumes (5%)	0.691	0.805	0.803	0.841

others and is able to obtain similar performance to the baseline trained in the whole volume (Table 1) with much fewer training data (up to 5 %).

6 Conclusions and Future Work

We have presented a fully unsupervised approach to select the most representative windows of the volume, which combined with a novel active learning procedure obtain similar accuracy than fully automatic methods by using only 5 % of the data for training. The presented segmentation pipeline achieves similar performance to the state-of-the-art in a publicly available EM dataset, while being much faster and efficient. The results demonstrate that with the assistance of the proposed algorithm, a human expert could segment large volumes much faster and easier. It also makes the segmentation task much more intuitive by giving the user small portions of the volume, which are much easier to annotate. Extension to multi-label interactive segmentation is straight forward as all the methods here presented are inherently multi-label.

References

1. Karasev, P., Kolesov, I., Fritscher, K., Vela, P., Mitchell, P., Tannenbaum, A.: Interactive medical image segmentation using PDE control of active contours. IEEE Trans. Med. Imaging **32**, 2127–2139 (2013)
2. Beichel, R., et al.: Liver segmentation in CT data: a segmentation refinement approach. In: Proceedings of 3D Segmentation in the Clinic: A Grand Challenge, pp. 235–245 (2007)
3. Uijlings, J.R.R., van de Sande, K.E.A., Gevers, T., Smeulders, A.W.M.: Selective search for object recognition. IJCV **104**, 154–171 (2013)
4. Top, A., Hamarneh, G., Abugharbieh, R.: Active learning for interactive 3D image segmentation. In: Fichtinger, G., Martel, A., Peters, T. (eds.) MICCAI 2011. LNCS, vol. 6893, pp. 603–610. Springer, Heidelberg (2011). doi:10.1007/978-3-642-23626-6_74
5. Top, A., Hamarneh, G., Abugharbieh, R.: Spotlight: automated confidence-based user guidance for increasing efficiency in interactive 3D image segmentation. In: Menze, B., Langs, G., Tu, Z., Criminisi, A. (eds.) MICCAI 2010. LNCS, vol. 6533, pp. 204–213. Springer, Heidelberg (2011)
6. Lucchi, A., et al.: Supervoxel-based segmentation of mitochondria in EM image stacks with learned shape features. IEEE Trans. Med. Imaging **31**(2), 474–486 (2012)
7. Hong, X., Chang, H., Shan, S., Chen, X., Gao, W.: Sigma set: a small second order statistical region descriptor. In: CVPR 2009 (2009)
8. Luengo, I., Basham, M., French, A.P.: Fast global interactive volume segmentation with regional supervoxel descriptors. In: SPIE Medical Imaging, pp. 97842D–97842D. International Society for Optics and Photonics (2016)
9. Geurts, P., Ernst, D., Wehenkel, L.: Extremely randomized trees. Mach. Learn. **63**(1), 3–42 (2006)
10. Frey, B.J., Dueck, D.: Clustering by passing messages between data points. Science **315**(5814), 972–976 (2007)

Robust and Accurate Appearance Models Based on Joint Dictionary Learning Data from the Osteoarthritis Initiative

Anirban Mukhopadhyay[1]([⊠]), Oscar Salvador Morillo Victoria[2], Stefan Zachow[1,2], and Hans Lamecker[1,2]

[1] Zuse Institute Berlin, Berlin, Germany
anirban.akash@gmail.com
[2] 1000 Shapes Gmbh., Berlin, Germany

Abstract. Deformable model-based approaches to 3D image segmentation have been shown to be highly successful. Such methodology requires an appearance model that drives the deformation of a geometric model to the image data. Appearance models are usually either created heuristically or through supervised learning. Heuristic methods have been shown to work effectively in many applications but are hard to transfer from one application (imaging modality/anatomical structure) to another. On the contrary, supervised learning approaches can learn patterns from a collection of annotated training data. In this work, we show that the *supervised joint dictionary learning technique* is capable of overcoming the traditional drawbacks of the heuristic approaches. Our evaluation based on two different applications (liver/CT and knee/MR) reveals that our approach generates appearance models, which can be used effectively and efficiently in a deformable model-based segmentation framework.

Keywords: Dictionary learning · Appearance model · Liver CT · Knee MR · 3D segmentation

1 Introduction

Deformable model-based methods are widely used in medical image analysis for performing anatomical segmentation. These methods consist of two main parts, a cost function representing the appearance model and a Statistical Shape Model (SSM) based regularizer. One of the most common representation of deformable models are point clouds or (e.g. triangle) meshes. In this representation, the cost function a.k.a. 'detector' associated with each point (henceforth called *landmark point*) of the model is used to predict a new landmark location, followed by a deformation of the model towards the targeted positions. SSM based regularizer is used to ensure a smooth surface after deformation. This paper is mainly focused on the general design of cost function.

Many applications rely on heuristically learnt landmark detectors. Even though these detectors are highly successful in particular application scenarios

© Springer International Publishing AG 2016
G. Wu et al. (Eds.): Patch-MI 2016, LNCS 9993, pp. 25–33, 2016.
DOI: 10.1007/978-3-319-47118-1_4

[6,7], they are hard to transfer and generalize [5]. Systematic learning procedures can successfully resolve the aforementioned issues. E.g. Principal Component Analysis (PCA) on the Gaussian smoothed local profiles have been introduced as a learning-based cost function (henceforth called *PCA*) in the classical Active Shape Model (ASM) segmentation method [3]. However, this method is not very robust in challenging settings [8]. A more advanced approach is using normalized correlation with a globally constrained patch model [4] and sliding window search with a range of classifiers [2,11]. Most recently, Lindner et al. have proposed random-forest regression voting (RFRV) as the cost function [8]. Even though its performance is considered state of the art in 2D image analysis, memory and time consumption issues currently renders RFRV impractical in 3D scenarios.

The ability to learn generic appearance model independent of modalities during training and efficient and effective sparse representation calculation during testing, make Dictionary Learning (DL) an interesting choice to encounter the 3D landmark detection problem. In this work we adopt the method of Mukhopadhyay et al. [9] to sparsely model the background and foreground classes in separate dictionaries during training, and compare the representation of new data using these dictionaries during testing. However, unlike the focus of [9] in developing a sel-sufficient 2D+t segmentation technique for CP-BOLD MR segmentation, in this work the DL framework of [9] is exploited within the cost function premise by introducing novel sampling and feature generation strategy.

The non-trivial development of a special sampling strategy and gradient orientation-based rotation invariant features, exploits the full potential of Joint Dictionary Learning (JDL) as a *general and effective landmark prediction method* applicable to deformable-model based segmentation across different anatomies and 3D imaging modalities. According to our knowledge, although DL has been used previously as a 2D deformable model regularizer [14], *this is the first time*, when DL is employed as a 3D landmark detector.

The proposed landmark detection method is tested on 2 challenging datasets with wide inter subject variability namely High Contrast Liver CT and MR of Distal Femur. To emphasize the strength of JDL, structure of the learning framework is kept unchanged, i.e. parameter are not changed or adapted across applications, and the results are compared with that of ASM.

2   Method

Our proposed Joint Dictionary Learning (JDL) cost function for iterative segmentation is described here in details.

2.1   Active Shape Model

ASMs combine local appearance-based landmark detectors with global shape constraints for model-based segmentation. An SSM is trained by applying principal component analysis (PCA) on a number of aligned landmark points. This results in a linear model that encodes shape variation in the following way: $x_l = T_\theta(\bar{x}_l + M_l b)$, where x_l is the mean position of landmark $l \in \{1 \ldots L\}$, M_l is a set of modes for variation and b are the SSM parameters. T_θ measures the global transformation to align the landmark points. During segmentation of a new image, landmarks are aligned to optimize an overall quality of fit $Q = \sum_{l=1}^{L}(C_l(T_\theta(\bar{x}_l + M_l b)))$ s.t. $b^T S_b^{-1} b \leq M_t$. C_l is the cost function for locally fitting the landmark point l. S_b is the covariance matrix of the SSM parameters b and M_t is a threshold (98 % samples of multivariate Gaussian distribution) on the Mahalanobis distance. In this work, we have shown Dictionary Learning as an effective way of systematically modeling the cost function from a set of annotated training images.

2.2 Joint Dictionary Learning

This section describes the way Dictionary Learning is utilized as a landmark detector. In particular, Foreground and Background dictionaries are learnt during training. During testing, a weighted sum of approximation error is utilized for representing the cost function. Details of the method is described below.

Training: Given a set of 3D training images and corresponding ground truth landmarks, our goal is to learn a joint appearance model representing both foreground and background. Two classes (C) of matrices, Y^B and Y^F are samples from the training images for containing the background and foreground information respectively. Information is collected from image patches: cubic patches are sampled around each landmark point of the 3D training images and 144-bin (12×12) rotation invariant SIFT-style feature histograms (described in Sect. 2.3) are calculated for representing those patches.

Each column i of the matrix Y^F is obtained by taking the normalized vector of rotation invariant SIFT-style feature histograms at all the landmarks locations across all training images (similar features are obtained for matrix Y^B from the background locations aligned along the normals of landmarks) as shown in Fig. 1. JDL takes as input these two classes of training matrices, to learn two dictionary classes, D^B and D^F. These Dictionaries are learnt using K-SVD algorithm [1]. In particular, the learning process is summarized in Algorithm 1.

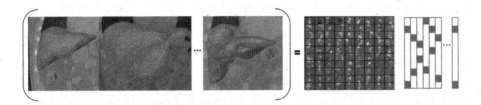

Fig. 1. Foreground dictionary learning using JDL. See text for details.

Algorithm 1. Joint Dictionary Learning (JDL)

Input: Training patches for background and the landmarks: Y^B and Y^F
Output: Dictionaries for background and the landmarks: D^B and D^F
1: **for** C={B,F} **do**
2:      Compute Y^C
3:      Learn dictionaries with K-SVD algorithm

$$\underset{D^C, X^C}{\text{minimize}} \|Y^C - D^C X^C\|_2^2 \quad \text{s. t.} \quad \|X_i^C\|_0 \leq S$$

4: **end for**

Testing: During segmentation of a new image, at each iteration we gather a set of test matrices Y_l corresponding to each landmark l. Y_l is obtained by sampling cubic patches along the profile and generating SIFT-like features of these patches in the similar way as training (Sect. 2.3). The goal is to assign to each voxel on the profile of landmark a cost, i.e. establish if the pixel belongs to the background or the foreground as shown in Fig. 2.

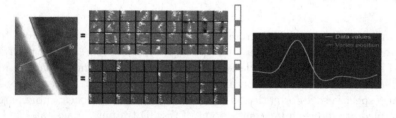

Fig. 2. Cost function: weighted sum of approximation errors from representations by background and foreground dictionaries.

To perform this procedure, we use the dictionaries, D^B and D^F, previously learnt with JDL. Orthogonal Matching Pursuit (OMP) [13] is used to compute, the sparse feature matrices $\hat{x}_{l,p}^B$ and $\hat{x}_{l,p}^F$. The cost is assigned based on the weighted sum of approximation errors. More precisely, for the cubic patch corresponding to profile voxel p of landmark l, a cost of $\lambda(1 - R_{l,p}^B) + (1 - \lambda)R_{l,p}^F$ is assigned, as detailed in Algorithm 2. The cost is motivated by the fact that for an "ideal" location, there will be high BG approximation error and low FG approximation error. The parameter λ balances the weight associated with approximation errors.

2.3   Sampling and Feature Description

The goal of sampling and rotation invariant feature description is to identify and characterize image patterns which are independent of global changes in anatomical pose and appearance. We have exploited our model-based segmentation strategy during sampling, by considering sample boxes aligned w.r.t. the surface normals. The advantages of this sampling strategy are twofold. During training,

---

Algorithm 2. Cost Function Calculation (CFC)

Input: Testing patches along profile of current landmark locations: $\{Y_{l,p}^T\}_{l=1}^L$, learnt Shape Model, Dictionaries for background and the landmarks: D^B and D^F

Output: Predicted Landmark location

1: **for** $l = 1...L$ **do**
2:   **for** $p =$ each location on the profile of current Landmark l **do**
3:     **for** C={B,F} **do**
4:       Compute $Y_{l,p}^T$
5:       $R_{l,p}^C = \|y_{l,p}^T - D^C \hat{x}_{l,p}^C\|_2^2$
6:     **end for**
7:     $P_{l,p} = \lambda(1 - R_{l,p}^B) + (1 - \lambda)R_{l,p}^F$
8:   **end for**
9: **end for**

---

all the foreground voxel patches can encode the boundary appearance and the background voxel patches can encode the completely inside/outside appearance. Whereas, during testing, the optimization along normal profile ensures that both foreground and background agrees on the final position. The main problem of this sampling strategy is that, the appearance of the sample strongly depends on the global rotation of the anatomy.

The problem of global rotation associated with sampling, is resolved during feature description. A 3D rotation invariant gradient orientation histogram derived from 3D SIFT [12] is used as a feature descriptor. In the first step, image gradient orientations of the sample are assigned to a local histogram of spherical coordinate H. In the next step, three primary orientations are retrieved from H in the following way: $\hat{\theta}_1 = argmax\{H\}$, $\hat{\theta}_2$ is the secondary orientation vector in the great circle orthogonal to $\hat{\theta}_1$ and with maximum value in H and $\hat{\theta}_3 = \hat{\theta}_1 \times \hat{\theta}_2$. Finally, The sample patch is aligned to a reference coordinate system based on these primary orientations, and a new 144-bins (12×12) gradient orientation histogram is generated to encode rotation invariant image features.

3 Results

The aim of the proposed method is to fully automatically detect the unique landmark locations from the dense annotation of 3D landmarks along the surface. In particular, we have considered 2 different anatomies acquired at 2 different modalities, to test the robustness of our proposed method: CT of livers and MR of distal femurs.

3.1 Data Preparation and Parameter Settings

The liver dataset consists of contrast enhanced CT data of 40 healthy livers, each with an approximate dimension of $256 \times 256 \times 50$. The corresponding surface of each liver is represented by 6977 landmark points. The distal femur MR dataset, obtained from the Osteoarthritis Initiative (OAI) database, available for public access at [10], consists of 48 subjects with severe pathological condition (Kellgren-Lawrence Osteoarthritis scale: 3). Each data has an approximate dimension of $160 \times 384 \times 384$. The corresponding distal femur surfaces are represented by 11830 landmarks each one.

For all experiments the mean shapes of respective dataset are used as initial shape. The experiment consists of a k-fold cross validation with $k = 10$ and 12 for the liver and the distal femur respectively. We have set a fixed sample box size of $5 \times 5 \times 5$, dictionary of size 500 with sparsity $S = 4$ and $\lambda = 0.5$. No additional parameters are adjusted during any of the following experiments.

3.2 Quantitative Analysis

To compare the performance of JDL with PCA, we have performed a local search in the following way. Starting from the mean shape at the correct pose, we have computed the cost of detection for each possible landmark position along the profile. Possible positions for each landmark are considered equidistantly in 15 positions along the profile of length ± 7.5 mm. As we are only interested on the performance of the landmark detector, each vertex is displaced solely based on the displacement derived from the cost of landmark detection, *without any SSM-based regularization*. The detection error for each vertex w.r.t. the ground-truth location is calculated using Euclidean Distance metric. To emphasize the superior performance of the proposed method in local search, we have compared JDL with PCA for both high contrast CT of liver as shown in Fig. 3 (left) and MR of distal femur in Fig. 3 (right). It is important to note that, JDL outperforms PCA in both cases. For high contrast CT of liver, 99 % of the landmarks are within 1 mm of the ground-truth for JDL, compared to 80 % for PCA. On the other hand, for distal femur MR, 90 % of the landmarks are within 1 mm of the ground-truth for JDL, compared to only 37 % for PCA.

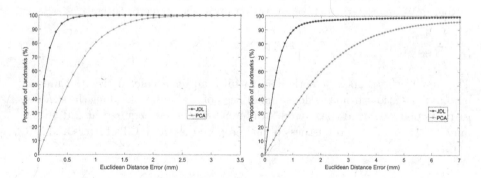

Fig. 3. Quantitative comparison: local search result starting from the mean shape at the correct pose for JDL and PCA on high contrast liver CT (left) and distal femur MR (right) datasets.

3.3   Qualitative Analysis

The features learnt by JDL are discriminative enough for representing the foreground separately from the background. In particular, a set of 144-bin feature histograms (rotation invariant gradient orientation) represented by patches of size 12×12, learnt for the foreground and background are shown in Fig. 4 to illustrate the quality of the learnt features. It is interesting to see that, the rotation invariant gradient information is more spread out for foreground in comparison to background, as modeled by these dictionaries, resulting in an overall brighter foreground dictionary w.r.t. the background one as shown in Fig. 4.

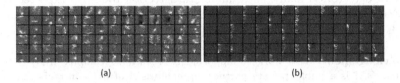

(a)   (b)

Fig. 4. Exemplar foreground (a) and background (b) dictionaries learnt from 144-bin feature vectors (12 × 12) of the distal femur MR.

The quality of JDL is emphasized further by plotting the mean detection error for each landmark as color map on the mean liver and mean distal femur surface in Fig. 5. For most of the points, low mean detection error ensures superior quality during segmentation. More importantly, Fig. 5 localizes areas more prone to landmark detection failure.

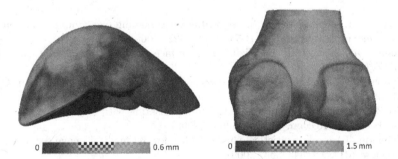

0 ▬▬▬▬▬▨▨▨▨▬ 0.6 mm   0 ▬▬▬▬▨▨▨▨▬ 1.5 mm

Fig. 5. Average accuracy for describing each landmark by JDL is superimposed as colormap on the mean liver (left) and distal femur (right) surface. (Color figure online)

4   Discussions and Conclusion

This study motivates us to rethink the standard cost function related assumptions of model-based segmentation for 3D images, especially regarding accommodation of several anatomies and modalities in a general framework. Deviating from heuristic learning techniques (hard to transfer and generalize across anatomies and modalities) towards systematic data-driven ones can benefit in multitude of ways: from operating with minimal manual setup to better handling of variability in image contrast, modalities and anatomies. In particular, by using JDL in 3D setting, we have shown that it is possible to address the scalability issues of Random Forest based landmark detectors in a similar situation. The performance of JDL is demonstrated in 2 challenging settings of liver CT and distal femur MR. Furthermore, the error prone areas for landmark detection is identified, which will be addressed in future to improve the performance. JDL can be an effective tool across challenging datasets where inter-acquisition and -anatomical variability prohibits the effectiveness of heuristic learning based landmark detectors. Finally, such landmark detection tools are expected to be instrumental in advancing the utility of fully automatic segmentation techniques towards clinical translation.

Acknowledgement. This work is supported by Forschungscampus MODAL Med-Lab. The OAI is a public-private partnership comprised of five contracts (N01-AR-2-2258; N01-AR-2-2259; N01-AR-2-2260; N01-AR-2-2261; N01-AR-2-2262) funded by the National Institutes of Health, a branch of the Department of Health and Human Services, and conducted by the OAI Study Investigators. Private funding partners include Merck Research Laboratories; Novartis Pharmaceuticals Corporation, Glaxo-SmithKline; and Pfizer, Inc. Private sector funding for the OAI is managed by the Foundation for the National Institutes of Health. This manuscript was prepared using an OAI public use data set and does not necessarily reflect the opinions or views of the OAI investigators, the NIH, or the private funding partners.

References

1. Aharon, M., et al.: K-SVD: an algorithm for designing overcomplete dictionaries for sparse representation. TSP **54**, 4311–4322 (2006)
2. Belhumeur, P.N., et al.: Localizing parts of faces using a consensus of exemplars. In: CVPR (2011)
3. Cootes, T.F., et al.: Active shape models - their training and application. CVIU **61**, 38–59 (1995)
4. Cristinacce, D., et al.: Automatic feature localisation with constrained local models. J. Pattern Recogn. **41**, 3054–3067 (2008)
5. Heimann, T., et al.: Statistical shape models for 3D medical image segmentation: a review. MIA **13**, 543–563 (2009)
6. Kainmueller, D., et al.: Shape constrained automatic segmentation of the liver basedon a heuristic intensity model. In: MICCAI Workshop 3D Segmentation in the Clinic: A Grand Challenge (2007)
7. Kainmueller, D., et al.: An articulated statistical shape model for accurate hip joint segmentation. In: EMBC (2009)
8. Lindner, C., et al.: Robust and accurate shape model matching using random forest regression-voting. PAMI **37**, 1862–1874 (2015)
9. Mukhopadhyay, A., Oksuz, I., Bevilacqua, M., Dharmakumar, R., Tsaftaris, S.A.: Data-driven feature learning for myocardial segmentation of CP-BOLD MRI. In: van Assen, H., Bovendeerd, P., Delhaas, T. (eds.) FIMH 2015. LNCS, vol. 9126, pp. 189–197. Springer, Heidelberg (2015)

10. http://www.oai.ucsf.edu/
11. Saragih, J.M., et al.: Deformable model fitting by regularized landmark mean-shift. IJCV **91**, 200–215 (2011)
12. Toews, M., et al.: Efficient and robust model-to-image alignment using 3D scale-invariant features. MIA **17**, 271–282 (2013)
13. Tropp, J.A., et al.: Signal recovery from random measurements via orthogonal matching pursuit. Trans. Inf. Theor. **53**, 4655–4666 (2007)
14. Zhang, S., et al.: Deformable segmentation via sparse representation and dictionary learning. MIA **16**, 1385–1396 (2012)

Consistent Multi-Atlas Hippocampus Segmentation for Longitudinal MR Brain Images with Temporal Sparse Representation

Lin Wang[1,2], Yanrong Guo[2], Xiaohuan Cao[2,3], Guorong Wu[2], and Dinggang Shen[2(✉)]

[1] School of Information Science and Technology,
Northwest University, Xi'an, China
[2] Department of Radiology and BRIC,
University of North Carolina at Chapel Hill, Chapel Hill, NC, USA
dgshen@med.unc.edu
[3] School of Automation, Northwestern Polytechnical University, Xi'an, China

Abstract. In this paper, we propose a novel multi-atlas based longitudinal label fusion method with temporal sparse representation technique to segment hippocampi at all time points simultaneously. First, we use groupwise longitudinal registration to simultaneously (1) estimate a group-mean image of a subject image sequence and (2) register its all time-point images to the estimated group-mean image consistently over time. Then, by registering all atlases with the group-mean image, we can align all atlases longitudinally consistently to each time point of the subject image sequence. Finally, we propose a longitudinal label fusion method to propagate all atlas labels to the subject image sequence by simultaneously labeling a set of temporally-corresponded voxels with a temporal consistency constraint on sparse representation. Experimental results demonstrate that our proposed method can achieve more accurate and consistent hippocampus segmentation than the state-of-the-art counterpart methods.

1 Introduction

The hippocampus plays a crucial role in memory and spatial navigation function of brain [1]. The structural change of hippocampus over time is highly related to many neurodegenerative diseases, such as Alzheimer's disease (AD). As a characteristic feature of AD, hippocampal atrophy is considered as a potential biomarker for the diagnosis and assessment of AD in magnetic resonance (MR) imaging based neuroscience studies [2, 3]. In order to measure the hippocampal atrophy over time, accurate quantization of hippocampal volumes from serial structural three-dimensional (3D) MR images is required. To this end, it is important to accurately and temporally consistently segment four-dimensional (3D+t) hippocampus from longitudinal structural MR images.

This work was supported in part by National Natural Science Foundation of China (No. 61503300) and China Postdoctoral Science Foundation (No. 2014M560801).

G. Wu et al. (Eds.): Patch-MI 2016, LNCS 9993, pp. 34–42, 2016.
DOI: 10.1007/978-3-319-47118-1_5

Many automatic segmentation methods have been proposed to segment 3D hippocampus independently from MR images of different time points [4–8]. In this case, hippocampus segmentation from longitudinal MR images is decomposed into a series of separate hippocampus segmentation from each 3D MR image. However, due to various reasons such as variant noises and hippocampal tissue contrast in the acquired longitudinal MR images, 3D segmentation methods, when applied to longitudinal MR images, have limited temporal consistency for segmented longitudinal hippocampi. To improve segmentation consistency from longitudinal MR images, several longitudinal segmentation methods have been proposed [9–12]. Wolz *et al.* [9] proposed a 4D graph-cut based method to simultaneously segment longitudinal MR images. By using a 4D graph to represent longitudinal MR data, the method segmented MR images at all time points by solving the min-cut/max-flow problem on the 4D graph. Chincarini *et al.* [12] presented a hippocampal segmentation method by integrating longitudinal information. They implemented longitudinal analysis with four progressive steps, and addressed the impact of these steps on longitudinal performance of hippocampal volume measurements for early detection of AD. However, due to large variance of noise level and intensity bias field across different time points in the longitudinal MR images, consistent hippocampus segmentation of serial MR images remains a challenging problem.

Accordingly, in this paper, we propose a 3D+t hippocampus segmentation method for longitudinal MR brain images, by integrating temporal sparse representation within the multi-atlas patch-based label fusion framework. First, we use the groupwise longitudinal image registration toolbox (GLIRT) [13] to simultaneously (1) estimate a subject-specific group-mean image and (2) register all time-point images of subject image sequence consistently to the estimated group-mean image. Then, by registering all atlas images to the estimated group-mean image, we can align all atlases longitudinally consistently to each time point of the subject image sequence. Thus, given the temporal correspondence in subject image sequence, we can form a 3D+t image patch at each location of subject brain. Then, we can use temporal sparse representation technique to simultaneously determine labels for all time points of the subject image sequence by propagating labels from all aligned atlas images. Experimental results on both simulated and real longitudinal MR images demonstrate that our proposed method can achieve more accurate and consistent hippocampus segmentation than the state-of-the-art multi-atlas label fusion methods, which often apply label fusion for each time point independently.

2   Method

Before describing our method in detail, we first introduce some mathematical descriptions. First, a longitudinal subject image sequence (also namely 3D+t subject image) is denoted as $\{T'_t\}_{t=1}^{N}$, where T'_t is a 3D image at time point $t(t \in \{1, \ldots, N\})$. Then, M 3D atlas images are denoted as $I'^{(1)}, \ldots, I'^{(M)}$, with their corresponding hippocampal label images denoted as $L'^{(1)}, \ldots, L'^{(M)}$. So, our goal is to segment 3D+t subject image, i.e., to automatically estimate a hippocampal label image sequence

$\{L'_t\}_{t=1}^N$ corresponding to the 3D+t subject image $\{T'_t\}_{t=1}^N$ as illustrated in Fig. 1, where L'_t denotes a 3D subject label image at time point $t (t \in \{1, \ldots, N\})$.

2.1 Temporal Sparse Representation

Unbiased Groupwise Registration. The first step in our method is to estimate temporal correspondences along different time points of the subject image sequence. Here, we use GLIRT [13] to achieve this goal. Unlike other pairwise registration methods, which need choose a reference template, the groupwise registration is free of template selection, and can thus build an unbiased subject-specific group-mean image and simultaneously register all time-point images to this group-mean image. Assuming $\{\varphi'_t\}_{t=1}^N$ as the deformation fields for N time points, the original 3D+t subject image $\{T'_t\}_{t=1}^N$ can be transformed to the group-mean image space as $\{T_t\}_{t=1}^N$, which is illustrated in Fig. 1. Here, $T_t = \varphi'_t(T'_t)$.

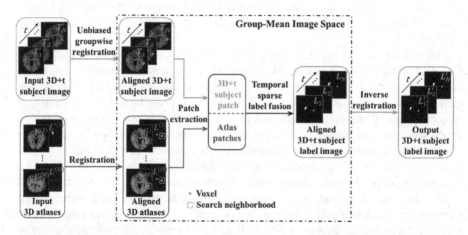

Fig. 1. Schematic diagram of the proposed 3D+t hippocampus segmentation method.

Furthermore, all 3D atlas images are registered to the estimated group-mean image, first by affine registration [14] with 12 degrees of freedom and then by deformable registration [15]. By following the same estimated *affine transformation matrix* and *deformation field*, the corresponding 3D hippocampal label image of each atlas can be also registered to the estimated group-mean image space. As shown in Fig. 1, $I^{(1)}, \ldots, I^{(M)}$ and $L^{(1)}, \ldots, L^{(M)}$ denote the M aligned 3D atlas images and their corresponding aligned 3D label images in the estimated group-mean image space, respectively.

Temporal Sparse Patch-Based Representation. For each voxel x in the group-mean image, its 3D+t subject patch can be extracted as $\{\alpha_{(x,t)}\}_{t=1}^N$, where $\alpha_{(x,t)}$ represents a 3D patch centered at voxel x of the aligned 3D+t subject image at time point t. Let $n(x)$ denote a spatial neighborhood of x. All candidate atlas patches within the search neighborhood $n(x)$ of the aligned atlas images $\{I^{(m)}\}_{m=1}^M$ are denoted as $\{\beta_z^{(m)}|z \in n(x), m = 1, \ldots, M\}$, along with their corresponding center voxel labels $\{l_z^{(m)}|z \in n(x), m = 1, \ldots, M\}$. The total number of atlas patches $\{\beta_z^{(m)}|z \in n(x), m = 1, \ldots, M\}$ used to label the 3D+t subject patch $\{\alpha_{(x,t)}\}_{t=1}^N$ is $Q = M \times |n(x)|$, where $|n(x)|$ denotes the cardinality of $n(x)$.

After rearranging $\beta_z^{(m)}$ and $\alpha_{(x,t)}$ into a d-dimensional column vector $b_z^{(m)}$ and $a_{(x,t)}$, respectively, where d is the number of voxels in each 3D patch, our temporal sparse representation can be formulated as a problem of finding optimal sparse representation for the 3D+t subject patch vector $\{a_{(x,t)}\}_{t=1}^N$ by using all atlas patch vectors $\{b_z^{(m)}\}_{m=1}^M$ as follows [6]:

$$
\{\hat{w}_{(x,t)}\}_{t=1}^N = \underset{\{w_{(x,t)}\}_{t=1}^N}{\arg\min} \left\{ \frac{1}{2} \sum_{t=1}^N \left\| B_x w_{(x,t)} - a_{(x,t)} \right\|_2^2 + \lambda_1 \sum_{t=1}^N \left\| w_{(x,t)} \right\|_1 + \right.
$$
$$
\left. \lambda_2 \sum_{t=1}^{N-1} \left\| w_{(x,t)} - w_{(x,t+1)} \right\|_1 \right\} \tag{1}
$$
$$
s.t. \quad w_{(x,t)} \geq 0, \forall t = 1, \ldots, N
$$

where $B_x \in \mathcal{R}^{d \times Q}$ denotes a dictionary matrix constructed by arranging $\{b_z^{(m)}\}_{m=1}^M$ column by column, $w_{(x,t)} \in \mathcal{R}^Q$ denotes a weight vector by arranging all non-negative weights $\{w_{(x,t),z}^{(m)}|w_{(x,t),z}^{(m)} \geq 0, z \in n(x), m = 1, \ldots, M\}$ into a column vector, and $w_{(x,t),z}^{(m)}$ is the representation coefficient of the patch vector $b_z^{(m)}$ of the m-th atlas image in constructing the patch vector $a_{(x,t)}$ of the subject image at time point t. The first term in Eq. (1) is the reconstruction discrepancy. The second term, which is equivalent to the ℓ_1-norm, enforces sparsity in $w_{(x,t)}$. The third term is the temporal fused smoothness term, used to constrain the temporal consistency of two successive sparse representation vectors ($w_{(x,t)}$ and $w_{(x,t+1)}$). λ_1 and λ_2 are the two weighting parameters used to balance the contributions from the second and third terms. The objective function in Eq. (1) can be solved by the fast proximal gradient method [16].

2.2 Multi-Atlas Based Label Fusion with Temporal Sparse Representation

Once the temporal sparse code $\{\hat{w}_{(x,t)}\}_{t=1}^N$ is estimated by solving the optimization problem in Eq. (1), the label at the voxel (x, t) of the aligned subject image T_t can be obtained by the multi-atlas based label fusion method by combining the center voxel labels $\{l_z^{(m)}|z \in n(x), m = 1, \ldots, M\}$ using the estimated temporal sparse code $\{\hat{w}_{(x,t)}\}_{t=1}^N$.

By following the same order of the dictionary matrix B_x, $\{l_z^{(m)}|z \in n(x), m = 1, \ldots, M\}$ is constructed as a label vector $l_x (l_x \in \mathcal{R}^{1 \times Q})$. Supposing there are P possible labels $\{L_1, \ldots, L_p, \ldots, L_P\}$ in the atlases, the label at the voxel (x, t) of the aligned subject image T_t can be determined by:

$$\hat{L}_{(x,t)} = \arg\max_{L_p, p=1,\dots,P}\left\{\sum_{j=1}^{Q} \hat{w}_{(x,t),j} \cdot \delta\big(l_{x,j}, L_p\big)\right\}, \forall t = 1,\dots,N \qquad (2)$$

where $\hat{w}_{(x,t),j}$ and $l_{x,j}$ are the j-th components of $\hat{w}_{(x,t)}$ and l_x, respectively, and the function $\delta\big(l_{x,j}, L_p\big)$ is equal to 1 if $l_{x,j} = L_p$ and 0 otherwise.

After determining the label $\hat{L}_{(x,t)}$ at each voxel (x, t) of aligned 3D+t subject image $\{T_t\}_{t=1}^{N}$, the aligned 3D+t subject label image $\{L_t\}_{t=1}^{N}$ in the group-mean image space can be obtained. Then, we can obtain the 3D+t subject label image $\{L'_t\}_{t=1}^{N}$ corresponding to the input 3D+t subject image $\{T'_t\}_{t=1}^{N}$ by transforming $\{L_t\}_{t=1}^{N}$ back to the subject image space by following $L'_t = \varphi'^{-1}_t(L_t)$, where φ'^{-1}_t is the inverse transformation field of φ'_t.

3 Experimental Results

In this section, we evaluate our proposed longitudinal (3D+t) hippocampus segmentation method on both simulated and real longitudinal MR brain image datasets. Specifically, 10 subjects with simulated atrophy in hippocampi, and 12 subjects with each subject having three MR images acquired at three time points in the Alzheimer's Disease Neuroimaging Initiative (ADNI) database (http://www.adni-info.org/) are used, respectively. All the images in both datasets are the T1-weighted MR images, which are processed to have the same size and same resolution of $256 \times 256 \times 256$ and $1 \times 1 \times 1\,\text{mm}^3$, respectively. The proposed method is compared to two state-of-the-art label fusion methods, namely nonlocal patch-based method (Non-local) [5] and sparse patch-based method (SPBM) [6]. To be fair, a similar unbiased groupwise registration is applied to the two comparison methods. That is, subject image is registered to the estimated group-mean image of subject image sequence by GLIRT, and all atlases are registered to the estimated group-mean image sequentially by affine registration and deformable registration. The final segmentations are evaluated in each subject's own space. In the following experiments, the patch size and search neighborhood size are both set to $3 \times 3 \times 3$, and the regularization coefficients λ_1 and λ_2 are both set to 0.001.

3.1 Experiments on Simulated Dataset

In the simulation experiments, 10 subjects with manual hippocampal labels at year 1 are used as the baseline data $(t = 1)$, and then used to simulate atrophy on the hippocampi. Each subject is simulated with three longitudinal MR images, where images at year 2 $(t = 2)$ and year 3 $(t = 3)$ are generated by an atrophy simulation model [17] to ensure shrinking hippocampal volumes along the temporal dimension. Thus, ten sets of simulated longitudinal data with about 5% of annual hippocampal volume shrinking are obtained. The total simulated atrophy rate of hippocampus in three years is 9.15%.

A leave-one-out strategy on the total 10 simulated subjects is adopted to compare the segmentation performances of Non-local, SPBM, and our proposed method. Specifically, in each leave-one-out experiment, one subject is selected as 3D+t *subject* image, and the rest 9 subjects are selected as 3D *atlases* (27 *atlases* in total). For both

Table 1. Mean and standard deviation of Dice ratio in hippocampus segmentation on simulated atrophy data (Unit: %).

Method	Left hippo	Right hippo	Overall
Non-local	81.27 ± 1.98	80.08 ± 2.82	80.69 ± 2.12
SPBM	80.80 ± 1.71	79.55 ± 2.43	80.19 ± 1.76
Proposed	82.71 ± 1.51*	81.86 ± 2.44*	82.30 ± 1.76*

*Indicates significant improvement over Non-local and SPBM methods ($p < 0.05$)

Non-local and SPBM methods, three time-point images in the 3D+t subject image are segmented independently. The mean and standard deviation of Dice ratios are shown in Table 1. We can observe that our proposed method receives significant improvement over both Non-local and SPBM methods in terms of Dice ratio according to the paired t-test ($p < 0.05$). Thus, our proposed method achieves the best segmentation accuracy.

Figure 2(a) shows the curves of the longitudinal loss of overall hippocampus volume in a typical subject by Non-local, SPBM, and our method. Figure 2(b) shows the averaged loss of overall hippocampus volume estimated by these three methods. The final estimated mean and standard deviation of loss of overall hippocampus volume is 11.84% ± 1.63% by Non-local, 12.31% ± 1.57% by SPBM, and 10.87% ± 1.21% by the proposed method. We can see that our proposed method is the closest to the ground truth, and also the most consistent in measuring longitudinal hippocampal volume changes, due to the use of temporal consistency constraint on sparse representation of multi-atlas based label fusion.

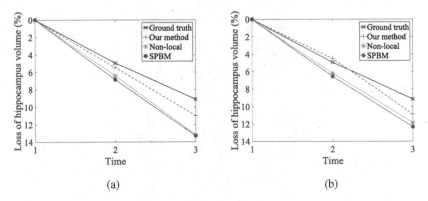

Fig. 2. Demonstration of loss of overall hippocampus volume through 3 time points. (a) Loss of longitudinal hippocampus volume for a typical subject, and (b) average loss of longitudinal hippocampus volumes for all subjects.

3.2   Experiments on Real Dataset

In the real experiments, we randomly select 12 subjects with each having 3 time points (baseline, 6 and 12 months) from ADNI dataset. The hippocampi of these MR images have been manually labeled, which are regarded as ground truth.

Table 2. Mean and standard deviation of Dice ratios and the average symmetric surface distance (ASSD) for automatic segmentations by Non-local, SPBM, and our proposed method.

	Method	Left hippo	Right hippo	Overall
Dice ratio (%)	Non-local	83.53 ± 2.99	82.37 ± 4.02	82.93 ± 2.97
	SPBM	82.32 ± 3.83	82.32 ± 2.64	82.31 ± 2.87
	Proposed	84.85 ± 2.30*	84.29 ± 2.34*	84.55 ± 2.22*
ASSD (mm)	Non-local	0.497 ± 0.072	0.524 ± 0.098	0.512 ± 0.067
	SPBM	0.520 ± 0.096	0.509 ± 0.057	0.515 ± 0.066
	Proposed	0.455 ± 0.049*	0.476 ± 0.063*	0.466 ± 0.053*

*Indicates significant improvement over Non-local and SPBM methods ($p < 0.05$)

We also adopt a leave-one-out strategy on the total 12 real subjects for experiments of hippocampus segmentation. The mean and standard deviation of Dice ratios and also the average symmetric surface distance (ASSD) of the hippocampus segmentation results by Non-local, SPBM, and our proposed method are shown in Table 2. We can observe that our proposed method achieves significant improvement over Non-local and SPBM methods in terms of both Dice ratio and ASSD according to the pair t-test ($p < 0.05$). Figure 3 shows the surface distances of the left hippocampus for a typical subject, between manual segmentations and automatic segmentations by Non-local, SPBM, and our proposed method. It is obvious that our proposed 3D+t hippocampus segmentation method achieves the best segmentation performance.

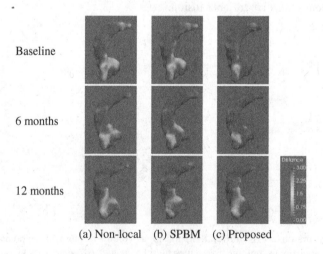

(a) Non-local   (b) SPBM   (c) Proposed

Fig. 3. Visualization of surface distances (in mm) for hippocampus segmentation results by three methods.

4   Conclusion

In this paper, we proposed an integrated *temporal sparse representation* and *multi-atlas patch-based label fusion* method for longitudinal (3D+t) hippocampus segmentation in the longitudinal MR images. To make the registration at different time points consistent to the subsequent data analysis, we registered the 3D+t subject image and all atlases to the group-mean image of 3D+t subject image by using GLIRT. Moreover, to respect the smooth change of longitudinal structure (i.e., hippocampus), we added a temporal fused smoothness term to the objective function of sparse representation, for enforcing small difference between two successive sparse representation vectors from adjacent time points. Experimental results demonstrated the improved segmentation accuracy and longitudinal consistency by our proposed method, compared to both Non-local and SPBM methods.

References

1. Bird, C.M., Burgess, N.: The hippocampus and memory: insights from spatial processing. Nat. Rev. Neurosci. **9**(3), 182–194 (2008)
2. Schuff, N., et al.: MRI of hippocampal volume loss in early Alzheimer's disease in relation to ApoE genotype and biomarkers. Brain **132**(4), 1067–1077 (2009)
3. Schröder, J., Pantel, J.: Neuroimaging of hippocampal atrophy in early recognition of Alzheimer's disease - a critical appraisal after two decades of research. Psychiatry Res.: Neuroimaging **247**, 71–78 (2016)
4. van der Lijn, F., et al.: Hippocampus segmentation in MR images using atlas registration, voxel classification, and graph cuts. NeuroImage **43**(4), 708–720 (2008)
5. Rousseau, F., Habas, P.A., Studholme, C.: A supervised patch-based approach for human brain labeling. IEEE Trans. Med. Imaging **30**(10), 1852–1862 (2011)
6. Zhang, D., Guo, Q., Wu, G., Shen, D.: Sparse patch-based label fusion for multi-atlas segmentation. In: Yap, P.-T., Liu, T., Shen, D., Westin, C.-F., Shen, L. (eds.) MBIA 2012. LNCS, vol. 7509, pp. 94–102. Springer, Heidelberg (2012)
7. Zarpalas, D., et al.: Gradient-based reliability maps for ACM-based segmentation of hippocampus. IEEE Trans. Biomed. Eng. **61**(4), 1015–1026 (2014)
8. Song, Y., Wu, G., Sun, Q., Bahrami, K., Li, C., Shen, D.: Progressive label fusion framework for multi-atlas segmentation by dictionary evolution. In: Navab, N., Hornegger, J., Wells, W.M., Frangi, A.F. (eds.) MICCAI 2015, Part III. LNCS, vol. 9351, pp. 190–197. Springer, Heidelberg (2015). doi:10.1007/978-3-319-24574-4_23
9. Wolz, R., et al.: Measurement of hippocampal atrophy using 4D graph-cut segmentation: application to ADNI. NeuroImage **52**(1), 109–118 (2010)
10. Leung, K.K., et al.: Automated cross-sectional and longitudinal hippocampal volume measurement in mild cognitive impairment and Alzheimer's disease. NeuroImage **51**(4), 1345–1359 (2010)
11. Guo, Y., Wu, G., Yap, P.-T., Jewells, V., Lin, W., Shen, D.: Segmentation of infant hippocampus using common feature representations learned for multimodal longitudinal data. In: Navab, N., Hornegger, J., Wells, W.M., Frangi, A.F. (eds.) MICCAI 2015, Part III. LNCS, vol. 9351, pp. 63–71. Springer, Heidelberg (2015). doi:10.1007/978-3-319-24574-4_8

12. Chincarini, A., et al.: Integrating longitudinal information in hippocampal volume measurements for the early detection of Alzheimer's disease. NeuroImage **125**, 834–847 (2016)
13. Wu, G., Wang, Q., Shen, D.: Registration of longitudinal brain image sequences with implicit template and spatial-temporal heuristics. NeuroImage **59**(1), 404–421 (2012)
14. Jenkinson, M., et al.: Improved optimization for the robust and accurate linear registration and motion correction of brain images. NeuroImage **17**(2), 825–841 (2002)
15. Vercauteren, T., et al.: Diffeomorphic demons: efficient non-parametric image registration. NeuroImage **45**(1), S61–S72 (2009)
16. Beck, A., Teboulle, M.: A fast iterative shrinkage-thresholding algorithm for linear inverse problems. SIAM J. Imaging Sci. **2**(1), 183–202 (2009)
17. Karacali, B., Davatzikos, C.: Simulation of tissue atrophy using a topology preserving transformation model. IEEE Trans. Med. Imaging **25**(5), 649–652 (2006)

Sparse-Based Morphometry: Principle and Application to Alzheimer's Disease

Pierrick Coupé[1,2(✉)], Charles-Alban Deledalle[3,4], Charles Dossal[3,4], Michèle Allard[5,6,7], and Alzheimer's Disease Neuroimaging Initiative

[1] CNRS, LaBRI, UMR 5800, PICTURA, 33400 Talence, France
pierrick.coupe@labri.fr
[2] University of Bordeaux, LaBRI, UMR 5800, PICTURA, 33400 Talence, France
[3] University of Bordeaux, IMB, UMR 5251, 33400 Talence, France
[4] CNRS, IMB, UMR 5251, 33400 Talence, France
[5] University of Bordeaux, INCIA, UMR 5287, 33400 Talence, France
[6] CNRS, INCIA, UMR 5287, 33400 Talence, France
[7] EPHE, Bordeaux, France

Abstract. The detection of brain alterations is crucial for understanding pathophysiological processes. The Voxel-Based Morphometry (VBM) is one of the most popular methods to achieve this task. Despite its numerous advantages, VBM is based on a highly reduced representation of the local brain anatomy since complex anatomical patterns are reduced to local averages of tissue probabilities. In this paper, we propose a new framework called Sparse-Based Morphometry (SBM) to better represent local brain anatomies. The presented patch-based approach uses dictionary learning to detect anatomical pattern modifications based on their shape and geometry. In our experiences, we compare SBM and VBM along Alzheimer's Disease (AD) progression.

Keywords: Voxel-based morphometry · Alzheimer's Disease · Dictionary learning · Abnormality detection · Patch-based processing

1 Introduction

In neurological diseases such as Alzheimer's Disease (AD), numerous studies suggest that some structures are affected by atrophy whereas others are relatively preserved. These brain abnormalities reflect pathophysiological processes, and are correlated with cognitive impairments and clinical symptoms. Thus, the analysis of the anatomical brain integrity in patients is an important challenge of current research in neurology. Automatic detection of such brain

Data used in preparation of this article were obtained from the Alzheimer's Disease Neuroimaging Initiative (ADNI) database (adni.loni.usc.edu). As such, the investigators within the ADNI contributed to the design and implementation of ADNI and/or provided data but did not participate in analysis or writing of this report. A complete listing of ADNI investigators can be found at: http://adni.loni.usc.edu/wp-content/uploads/how_to_apply/ADNI_Acknowledgement_List.pdf.

© Springer International Publishing AG 2016
G. Wu et al. (Eds.): Patch-MI 2016, LNCS 9993, pp. 43–50, 2016.
DOI: 10.1007/978-3-319-47118-1_6

abnormalities enables us to link anatomical substratum to cognitive performance or clinical symptoms. One of the classical methods used for automatic analysis of brain structures is voxel-based morphometry (VBM) [1]. VBM is an image processing framework enabling the identification of differences in the tissue density over the whole brain without *a priori* definition of a region of interest. Since its introduction, VBM has been successfully used in studies dedicated to a large variety of disorders. Despite its numerous advantages, VBM is based on a highly reduced representation of the local brain anatomy. Indeed, the complex local gray matter (GM) pattern is reduced to a local weighted average of GM probabilities through a Gaussian smoothing. While the importance of this smoothing step is well-known from a practical point of view [2], the use of a local average to represent complex anatomical patterns should be questioned. In this paper, we investigate the possibility of using a patch-based strategy to better represent the local brain anatomy. Recently, patch-based methods have demonstrated high performance in many neuroimaging applications such as anatomical structure segmentation [3,4] or automatic diagnosis [5,6]. As recently proposed for segmentation purposes [4], we use a dictionary learning process to construct a sparse representation of anatomical patterns. Unlike [4], this sparse modeling of the brain anatomy is used to detect abnormalities through a new framework called Sparse-Based Morphometry (SBM). As shown later, SBM is especially well-suited to detect local modifications in terms of their shape and geometry. However, the inherent patch normalization involved in sparse-coding approaches makes SBM insensitive to modifications of the mean GM density within a patch. Therefore, we propose to combine the capability of VBM to detect modifications of local average GM density with the high ability of SBM to capture subtle alterations of the local shape of GM patterns. As discussed in the following, VBM can be viewed as the comparison of the patch mean while SBM compares the patch geometry. The contribution of this paper is threefold: (i) we present the new concept of SBM susceptible to better represent the complexity of local anatomical patterns, (ii) we propose to combine VBM and SBM in order to simultaneously analyze modifications of the local mean GM density and alterations of the shape and geometry of local GM patterns, and (iii) we evaluate the proposed framework on the ADNI dataset.

2   Methods and Materials

Subjects Selection and Preprocessing. In this study we used a sample of the standardized ADNI1 collection [7]. By using the 818 baseline MRI scan at 1.5T, we created three groups of cognitively normal subjects (CN), one group of patients with AD, one group of subjects with Mild Cognitive Impairment (MCI) who progressed to AD (progressive MCI or pMCI) and one group of subjects with MCI who remained stable during the follow-up period (sMCI). All the groups have the same number of subjects ($N = 70$). In addition, to remove potential bias during our experiments, we randomly selected subjects from each group with the constraint of similar age and similar gender proportion between groups. See

Table 1. Demographic information about the considered groups

Group	Size	Gender (% female)	Age (SD)	MMSE (SD)
CN training	70	53%	76.3 (5.1)	29.0 (0.9)
CN testing	70	47%	76.1 (4.8)	29.0 (0.9)
sMCI	70	41%	76.3 (7.2)	27.2 (3.5)
pMCI	70	42%	75.8 (6.6)	26.1 (2.1)
AD	70	55%	76.6 (7.7)	23.0 (3.3)

Table 1 for details. As explained later, the CN (training) group is used to learn dictionaries (*i.e.*, to create a sparse representation of the normal brain anatomy) while the testing CN group is used to model the inter-subject variability. All the data were preprocessed with the Statistical Parametric Mapping 8 software (SPM8; http://www.fil.ion.ucl.ac.uk/spm) and the VBM8-toolbox (http://dbm. neuro.uni-jena.de/vbm.html) using default settings.

2.1 Sparse-Based Modeling of the Brain Anatomy

The proposed method estimates at each voxel the distribution of a scoring function measuring the degree of abnormality of a population at this location. The choice of the scoring function is the key to success for such an approach and thus it should be designed to be invariant to inter-subject variabilities inside the reference group while being discriminant to intra-group variabilities. In order to capture the local morphological structure of the brain, for each location in the MNI space, we use a 3D patch (i.e., a small rectangular windows) centered in a voxel v. The proposed scoring function measures the ability of this patch to be decomposed in a sparse way, i.e., as a linear combination of a small number of predefined patches. This family of predefined patches, called dictionary, is learned offline from the set of patches located at v in the training group. In this study, we then distinguish three groups G_1, G_2 and G_3. The first group G_1 composed of CN subjects is used to learn the dictionary (CN training). Distributions of the scoring functions are next computed independently on two other groups, a reference group G_2 composed of CN subjects (CN testing) and the group of interest G_3 (e.g., composed of AD patients). Since G_1 and G_2 are two groups composed of CN, the scoring function is expected to be statistically different for groups G_2 and G_3 where G_3 is abnormal compared to the control.

2.2 Sparse Brain Anatomy Representation Using Dictionary Learning

For each subject i of group G_1 and at each voxel v in the MNI space, a 3D patch is extracted, centered (subtraction of its mean), normalized (divided by its norm) and vectorized into a vector x^i. The dictionary D, that is a matrix whose columns are p patches, is next selected as the one minimizing the following quantity:

$$\min_{D,\alpha_i} \sum_{i=1}^{|G_1|} \frac{1}{2}\|x^i - D\alpha_i\|_2^2 + \lambda\|\alpha_i\|_1 \tag{1}$$

where λ is a positive parameter. The first term $\frac{1}{2}\|x^i - D\alpha_i\|_2^2$ ensures that each extracted patch x^i is not too far from its approximation $D\alpha_i$, while the second term $\|\alpha_i\|_1$ promotes that each extracted patch x^i can be indeed efficiently decomposed in a sparse way into the resulting dictionary D (i.e., such that α_i contains a large number of zero coefficients). At the end of the procedure, each column of D is a vectorization of a patch encoding one of the possible local morphological configurations of the brain in the training group G_1.

2.3   Group Comparison Using Sparse-Based Morphometry

As for the dictionary learning step, a patch is extracted at voxel v for each subjects of groups G_2 and G_3. This patch is also centered, normalized and vectorized. The following scoring function

$$f(x) = \min_{\alpha \in \mathbb{R}^p} \frac{1}{2}\|x - D\alpha\|_2^2 + \lambda\|\alpha\|_1$$

is then applied on each patch where D is the learned dictionary associated to voxel v. The empirical distribution of the scoring function $f(x)$ is next computed independently on each group. Thanks to the learning of an adapted dictionary on the CN training subjects of G_1, the dictionary D is expected to be flexible enough to reconstruct sparsely most of the patches of the CN testing group G_2 used as reference, hence leading to statistically low scoring values $f(x)$. On the contrary, at locations where the group of interest G_3 presents some abnormalities, a low approximation error $\frac{1}{2}\|x - D\alpha\|_2^2$ might not be reachable with low sparsity level, hence leading to statistically large values of $\|\alpha\|_1$ and $f(x)$. After applying a T-test on the distributions of $f(x)$ estimated at each voxel, our sparse-based morphological technique provides a map of degree of difference between the groups G_2 and G_3. Low values in this map can next be used to determine the voxels where G_3 seems to present some abnormalities.

Fusion of SBM and VBM. As usually done in sparse-based approaches, the patches are centered and normalized during the proposed SBM procedure. Therefore, the mean of the patches (i.e., the local GM density used for VBM) is not taken into account in SBM. We propose to fuse the SBM and VBM features in order to capture jointly the local anatomical geometry and the local tissue density. To this end, we propose to fuse the T-maps produced by SBM and VBM. The simple approach that takes the minimal p-value at each voxel is known to not produce p-values [8]. We use Bonferroni's method that is guaranteed to produce p-values from K p-values p_k using the fusion function F defined as:

$$F(p_1,\ldots,p_K) := K\min(p_1,\ldots,p_K) . \tag{2}$$

Implementation Details and Quality Metric. In our experiments the value of λ is not crucial and set to 0.15. The optimization of Eq. (1) is computed by alternating minimization on the dictionary D and the sequence (α_i) using SPAMS' toolbox (http://spams-devel.gforge.inria.fr/index.htm) [9]. In the following, the half patch sizes (HPS) are reported in mm. The number of atoms in the dictionary is set to 8. This number does not have a drastic impact on results according to our experiments. All images are displayed using the same p-value range from 10^{-2} to 10^{-8} and at the same coordinates in the MNI space. The methods are evaluated with two metrics. First, the abnormality ratio metric estimates the percentage of GM detected as abnormal (i.e., with p-value inferior to 0.01). Second, a merged p-value ($\tilde{p}$) metric reflects the level of significance in the area detected as abnormal. The p-values inferior to 0.01 are aggregated using the merging function [8] that produces a p-value (unlike the standard average):

$$M(p_1, \ldots, p_K) := \frac{2}{K}(p_1 + \ldots + p_K) \tag{3}$$

3 Results

3.1 Impact of the Patch Size and Number of Subjects

Table 2 presents the abnormality ratio and the merged p-value $\tilde{p}$ obtained for the considered patch sizes. The abnormality ratio increases when using bigger patch sizes and the fusion of SBM and VBM lead to similar or higher ratios. In terms of significance, SBM and the fusion provides lower $\tilde{p}$ than VBM. In addition, the fusion of VBM and SBM produces lower $\tilde{p}$ than SBM alone. We can note that a plateau is reached at $HPS = 15\,\mathrm{mm}$ for VBM and that the $\tilde{p}$ values are stable for SBM and the fusion. We therefore use this patch size in the following. Table 3 presents the abnormality ratio and the $\tilde{p}$ obtained for

Table 2. Abnormality ratios in % and merged p-values ($\tilde{p}$) in parentheses for each considered patch size. The presented results were obtained on 70 CN vs. 70 AD. The used threshold on the T-maps was set to 0.01.

	VBM	SBM	Fused
$HPS = 9\,\mathrm{mm}$	49.2 % (0.0032)	53.1 % (0.0027)	58.0 % (0.0027)
$HPS = 12\,\mathrm{mm}$	54.4 % (0.0028)	62.2 % (0.0022)	64.8 % (0.0021)
$HPS = 15\,\mathrm{mm}$	57.3 % (0.0025)	69.4 % (0.0019)	69.6 % (0.0018)

Table 3. Same as above but for each considered group size. The presented results were obtained on CN vs. AD using $HPS = 15\,\mathrm{mm}$.

	VBM	SBM	Fused
30 CN vs. 30 AD	29.8 % (0.0048)	47.5 % (0.0033)	46.4 % (0.0035)
50 CN vs. 50 AD	57.9 % (0.0028)	65.4 % (0.0023)	67.3 % (0.0021)
70 CN vs. 70 AD	57.3 % (0.0025)	69.4 % (0.0019)	69.6 % (0.0018)

Table 4. Same as above but for each considered testing group. The presented results were obtained with $HPS = 15\,\text{mm}$ and 70 subjects per group.

	VBM	SBM	Fused
sMCI	0.1 % (0.0170)	1.3 % (0.0132)	0.3 % (0.0147)
pMCI	34.5 % (0.0045)	53.7 % (0.0046)	51.2 % (0.0043)
AD	57.3 % (0.0025)	69.4 % (0.0019)	69.6 % (0.0018)

the considered group sizes. As expected, more significant differences are found between both groups when using a larger number of samples. Moreover, VBM is more affected by the reduction of the group size than SBM.

3.2   Early Detection of AD Signature

In this last experiment, we investigate the results provided by the methods on sMCI and pMCI groups. The pMCI group is expected to produce abnormalities close to the abnormalities detected in the AD group since the pMCI group is composed by patients converting to AD during the follow-up. The sMCI is expected to be closer to the CN group and can be viewed as an earlier stage of the AD compared to pMCI. Figure 1 shows the results of our abnormality detection approach on the considered groups (i.e., AD, pMCI, and sMCI). Table 4 presents the abnormality ratio and the $\tilde{p}$ obtained for each group. As expected, for all the methods, more abnormalities were detected in the AD group, followed by pMCI and sMCI. In all cases, SBM produces a higher abnormality ratio than VBM. Moreover, VBM produces a very low abnormality ratio for the sMCI group. These results seem to indicate that VBM is not sensitive enough to detect to subtle anatomical alterations present in the sMCI group. Consequently, the low abnormality ratio produced by VBM for the sMCI group impacts the fusion. For pMCI and AD groups similar results are obtained for SBM and fusion in terms of the abnormality ratio. However, fusion provides lower $\tilde{p}$ than SBM. In terms of anatomical difference, SBM finds significant differences for pMCI group in areas only detected for the AD group using VBM (e.g., medial frontal cortex and thalamus). VBM and SBM detect abnormalities in the posteriori cingulate cortex, while only SBM detects abnormality in the anterior cingulate cortex. Moreover, SBM found differences in the precuneus and the posterior cingulate cortex. Both structures have been shown to be impacted by AD in terms of anatomical atrophy [10], metabolism reduction [11] and functional alteration [12]. In addition, SBM and VBM detect abnormalities in the left entorhinal and parahippocampal cortex for the sMCI group with a larger extentfor SBM. It is interesting to note that these structures are known to be affected at the first stage of the pathology [13]. Finally, SBM is able to find subtle abnormalities in the medial frontal cortex in the sMCI group while such alterations are detected only in the AD group using VBM (see Fig. 1). This last result highlights the high sensitivity of SBM compared to VBM.

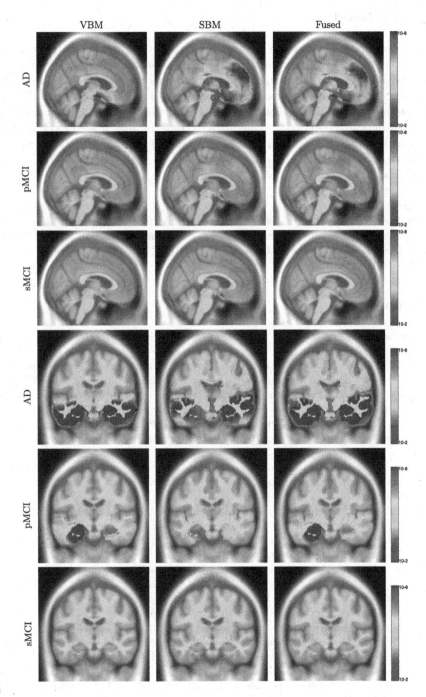

Fig. 1. Detection of abnormality in AD, sMCI and pMCI groups using $HPS = 15\,\mathrm{mm}$ and 70 subjects per group. The p-values of the T-maps are thresholded at 0.01.

4   Conclusion

In this paper, we proposed a new method to detect anatomical abnormalities called sparse-based morphometry. Based on local modeling of the normal anatomy using dictionary learning, SBM enables us to efficiently capture brain alterations in terms of their geometry and shape. In our experiments, SBM was shown to be more sensitive than VBM when using small groups or when studying early anatomical modifications caused by AD at the first stage of the pathology. We also presented a fusion strategy to combine VBM and SBM in order to take into account modifications of the local average GM density and to capture alterations of the local shape of GM patterns.

Acknowledgments. This study has been carried out with financial support from the French State, managed by the French National Research Agency (ANR) in the frame of the Investments for the future Program IdEx Bordeaux (HL-MRI ANR-10-IDEX-03-02), Clusters of excellence CPU and TRAIL (HR-DTI ANR-10-LABX-57) and the CNRS multidisciplinary project "Défi imag'In".

References

1. Ashburner, J., Friston, K.J.: Voxel-based morphometry–the methods. Neuroimage **11**(6), 805–821 (2000)
2. Shen, S., et al.: VBM lesion detection depends on the normalization template: a study using simulated atrophy. Magn. Resonan. Imaging **25**(10), 1385–1396 (2007)
3. Coupé, P., et al.: Patch-based segmentation using expert priors: application to hippocampus and ventricle segmentation. NeuroImage **54**(2), 940–954 (2011)
4. Tong, T., et al.: Segmentation of MR images via discriminative dictionary learning and sparse coding: application to hippocampus labeling. NeuroImage **76**, 11–23 (2013)
5. Coupé, P., et al.: Simultaneous segmentation and grading of anatomical structures for patient's classification: application to Alzheimer's disease. NeuroImage **59**(4), 3736–3747 (2012)
6. Liu, M., et al.: Ensemble sparse classification of Alzheimer's disease. NeuroImage **60**(2), 1106–1116 (2012)
7. Wyman, B., et al.: Standardization of analysis sets for reporting results from ADNI MRI data. Alzheimer's Dement. **9**(3), 332–337 (2013)
8. Vovk, V.: Combining p-values via averaging (2012). arXiv preprint arXiv:1212.4966
9. Mairal, J., et al.: Online dictionary learning for sparse coding. In: 26th AICML, pp. 689–696. ACM (2009)
10. Karas, G., et al.: Precuneus atrophy in early-onset Alzheimer's disease: a morphometric structural MRI study. Neuroradiology **49**(12), 967–976 (2007)
11. Ikonomovic, M., et al.: Precuneus amyloid burden is associated with reduced cholinergic activity in Alzheimer disease. Neurology **77**(1), 39–47 (2011)
12. He, Y., et al.: Regional coherence changes in the early stages of Alzheimer's disease: a combined structural and resting-state functional MRI study. Neuroimage **35**(2), 488–500 (2007)
13. Devanand, D., et al.: Hippocampal and entorhinal atrophy in mild cognitive impairment prediction of Alzheimer disease. Neurology **68**(11), 828–836 (2007)

Multi-Atlas Based Segmentation of Brainstem Nuclei from MR Images by Deep Hyper-Graph Learning

Pei Dong[1], Yangrong Guo[1], Yue Gao[2], Peipeng Liang[3],
Yonghong Shi[4], Qian Wang[5], Dinggang Shen[1(✉)],
and Guorong Wu[1(✉)]

[1] Department of Radiology and BRIC,
University of North Carolina at Chapel Hill, Chapel Hill, NC, USA
peidong1030@gmail.com, gyr0716@gmail.com,
{dgshen, guorong_wu}@med.unc.edu
[2] Department School of Software, Tsinghua University, Beijing, China
kevin.gaoy@gmail.com
[3] Department of Radiology, Xuanwu Hospital,
Capital Medical University, Beijing, China
ppliang1979@gmail.com
[4] School of Basic Medical Sciences, Digital Medical Research Center,
Fudan University/The Key Laboratory of MICCAI, Shanghai, China
yonghong.shi@fudan.edu.cn
[5] Med-X Research Institute of Shanghai Jiao Tong University, Shanghai, China
wang.qian@sjtu.edu.cn

Abstract. Accurate segmentation of brainstem nuclei (red nucleus and sub-stantia nigra) is very important in various neuroimaging applications such as deep brain stimulation and the investigation of imaging biomarkers for Parkinson's disease (PD). Due to iron deposition during aging, image contrast in the brainstem is very low in Magnetic Resonance (MR) images. Hence, the ambiguity of patch-wise similarity makes the recently successful multi-atlas patch-based label fusion methods have difficulty to perform as competitive as segmenting cortical and sub-cortical regions from MR images. To address this challenge, we propose a novel multi-atlas brainstem nuclei segmentation method using deep hyper-graph learning. Specifically, we achieve this goal in three-fold. *First*, we employ hyper-graph to combine the advantage of maintaining spatial coherence from graph-based segmentation approaches and the benefit of har-nessing population priors from multi-atlas based framework. *Second*, besides using low-level image appearance, we also extract high-level context features to measure the complex patch-wise relationship. Since the context features are calculated on a tentatively estimated label probability map, we eventually turn our hyper-graph learning based label propagation into a deep and self-refining model. *Third*, since anatomical labels on some voxels (usually located in uni-form regions) can be identified much more reliably than other voxels (usually located at the boundary between two regions), we allow these reliable voxels to propagate their labels to the nearby difficult-to-label voxels. Such hierarchical strategy makes our proposed label fusion method deep and dynamic. We evaluate our proposed label fusion method in segmenting substantia nigra

G. Wu et al. (Eds.): Patch-MI 2016, LNCS 9993, pp. 51–59, 2016.
DOI: 10.1007/978-3-319-47118-1_7

(SN) and red nucleus (RN) from 3.0 T MR images, where our proposed method achieves significant improvement over the state-of-the-art label fusion methods.

1   Introduction

The brainstem nuclei consist of two important gray matter structures: substantia nigra (SN) and red nucleus (RN). Automatic and accurate segmentation of these two structures has high impact in clinical practice, such as deep brain stimulation and current neuroimaging studies, which aim to find robust imaging biomarkers to quantitatively measure subtle and complex structural/functional differences related to Parkinson's disease (PD). Although morphological patterns of SN and RN are more observable in functional neuro-imaging (such as SPECT) and new quantitative MRI [1], segmenting brainstem nuclei from regular 1.5 T/3.0 T T1-weighted MR images is attractive in terms of healthcare cost and the availability of imaging instruments.

Segmentation of brainstem nuclei from MR images is challenging due to (**1**) large shape variations across individuals and (**2**) low image contrast at the brainstem. To address the first challenge, multi-atlas patch-based segmentation framework [2–4] is an effective solution, which assumes two voxels are likely to have the same anatomical label if their patch-wise appearances are similar. However, conventional patch-based methods have limited power to deal with the second challenge since low image contrast makes patch-wise similarity less reliable to guide label propagation from atlas images to the target subject image. Intuitively, the first remedy is to find other complementary feature representations, which can alleviate the issue of poor image quality in brainstem area. Second, as demonstrated in graph-cut approaches [5], optimizing label fusion toward the consensus of labeling results among a group of similar voxels can reduce the risk of mis-labeling compared to the voxel-by-voxel manner used in the current multi-atlas patch-based methods. In light of this, we reckon that the integration of multi-atlas segmentation framework and graph-cut technique is a potential solution to alleviate the second issue.

To that end, we introduce hyper-graph to leverage a novel multi-atlas brainstem nuclei segmentation method through deep hyper-graph leaning. Different from the conventional graph-based method that can only establish a pairwise relationship on a graph edge by connecting two vertices at a time, the hyper-graph can naturally capture group-wise relationship on a hyper-edge by linking multiple vertices [6]. Here in this paper, we use hyper-edge to partition the target subject image into a group of voxels, where subject voxels in the same hyper-edge have similar local anatomy. Meanwhile, we group each subject voxel and its matched voxels from atlas images into the same hyper-edge. Thus, the high-order information (beyond the conventional voxel-to-voxel relationship) within each hyper-edge encodes not only the multiple subject-to-atlas relationships (*i.e.,* using the power of multi-atlas segmentation framework) but also spatial coherence constraint (*i.e.,* taking the advantage of graph-based segmentation method). Given the constructed hyper-graph, the label fusion is not confined in each subject voxel separately. Instead, hyper-graph learning, dedicated to minimizing the label discrepancy within each hyper-edge, is deployed to propagate the known anatomical labels from atlas images to the target subject image domain until all subject voxels reach the unanimous agreement on label fusion.

In order to further improve the accuracy and robustness, we propose deep hyper-graph learning for nuclei segmentation by using high-level context features and hierarchical label fusion strategy. Specifically, context features, which encode the spatial relationship of one structure to other structures, provide a complementary source of information to characterize the local anatomy in low signal-to-noise ratio regions. Since the contexts features are calculated from the tentatively estimated label probability map, we have the chance to refine the hyper-edges constructed using context features, and then iteratively correct the possible mis-labeling in hyper-graph learning. Moreover, enlighted by the hierarchical label fusion strategy in [7], we hierarchically select a set of the reliable voxels with high labeling confidence to propagate their confidently-determined labels to the nearby difficult-to-label voxels. Our proposed method has been comprehensively evaluated in segmenting SN and RN regions from T1-weighted MR images. The segmentation results show significant improvement in labeling accuracy, compared to the counterpart state-of-the-art methods [2, 4].

2 Method

The first step in our method is to register N atlas images $\{I_1, I_2, \ldots, I_N\}$ to the target subject image S. After that, all voxels, including all subject image voxels $P = \{p_i | i = 1, \ldots, |P|\}$ and voxels from all atlas images $Q = \{q_j | j = 1, \ldots, |Q|\}$, are treated as the vertices in the hyper-graph. In the following text, the subscripts i and j represent the indices for subject image voxel and atlas image voxel, respectively.

2.1 Unanimous Label Fusion by Hyper-Graph Learning

Conventional multi-atlas patch-based label fusion methods find the label for each subject image voxel $p_c \in P$ by comparing only the patch-wise similarity w.r.t. all possible atlas image voxels. The information flow in conventional methods can be illustrated by the simple graph shown in the middle-right of Fig. 1. In this example, three atlas voxels $q_1 \sim q_3$ (red circles) are matched with p_c (red box). Note that there is no connection among subject image voxels, although such neighboring information in the subject image is useful to maintain the spatial coherence.

Hyper-Edge Construction. In light of this, we propose to use hyper-graph to reveal such complex relationship and achieve unanimous label propagation for all subject voxels. Compared to the conventional graph edge which can only connect two graph vertices, each hyper-edge e allows to accommodate more than two vertices. In order to address the difficulty of low image contrast, we take advantage of hyper-edge to find more heuristics for label fusion in two folds: **(1) High-order self-similarity relationship.** Intuitively, we allow each subject image voxel p_c to find a set of spatially-close and anatomically-similar voxels in the subject image domain. As the purple dot contour shown in the bottom-right of Fig. 1, four subject voxels $p_1 \sim p_4$ fall in the same hyper-edge centered at p_c. Thus, we can partition the whole subject image into a group of voxels which is essentially one hyper-edge describing the high-order self-similarity relationship (beyond two voxels). **(2) Multi-channel subject-to-atlas**

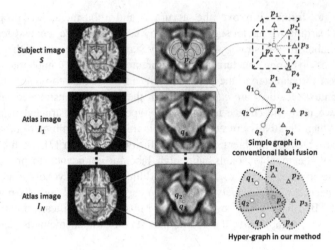

Fig. 1. Comparison of simple graph model in conventional methods and hyper-graph used in our method (with much richer information).

relationship. Existing methods can only use pre-defined similarity measurement, which is not adaptive to measure the complicated relationship between subject and atlas voxels at each location. In contrast, hyper-graph allows us to efficiently integrate diverse information from multiple channels by using various hyper-edges. For example, we can find a group of atlas image voxels (q_1 and q_2) which have similar patch-wise appearance as p_c and then form a hyper-edge as displayed in black dot contour in the bottom-right of Fig. 1. Given the tentative label probability map, we further extract context features for each voxel and form another hyper-edge in terms of context features centered at p_c, as shown in the bottom-right of Fig. 1 where p_c, q_2, and q_3 are included in the blue dot contour. Thus, many hyper-edges can be built to describe the complete characteristics of anatomical structure from different views. Compared to the simple information flow used in conventional label fusion methods, the hyper-graph (bottom-right of Fig. 1) contains much richer information to drive the label fusion.

Hyper-Graph Construction. In our method, the hyper-graph is denoted as $\mathcal{G} = (\mathcal{V}, \mathcal{E})$, where $\mathcal{V} = \mathcal{V}_P \cup \mathcal{V}_Q$ is the vertices set which includes all subject voxels P and atlas voxels Q. $\mathcal{E}$ denotes the set of hyper-edges constructed above. The information conveyed by various hyper-edges is encoded by an incidence matrix $\mathbf{H}_{|\mathcal{V}| \times |\mathcal{E}|}$. Each entry $h(v, e)$ in $\mathbf{H}$ measures the affinity degree between each vertex $v \in \mathcal{V}$ and the underlying center p_c in the hyper-edge $e \in \mathcal{E}$. Take the image appearance features as example, the degree of $h(v, e)$ can be defined as:

$$h(v, e) = \begin{cases} exp\left(-\frac{\Omega(\kappa(v)) - \Omega(p_c)_2^2}{\sigma^2}\right) & if \ v \in e \\ 0 & if \ v \notin e \end{cases} \tag{1}$$

where Ω is the operator of extracting intensity image patch at a given center. κ is an index function that maps each vertex $v \in \mathcal{V}$ to the spatial location in particular image. σ is used to control the strength of decay. Furthermore, we construct a $|\mathcal{E}| \times |\mathcal{E}|$ diagonal matrix $\mathbf{W}$ where each diagonal element $w(e)$ indicates the weight for particular hyper-edge e. Since there is no prior information on hyper-edges, we set $w(e) = 1$ ($\forall e \in \mathcal{E}$). Hence $\mathbf{W}$ is eventually an identity matrix. The degree of each vertex v is defined as $d(v) = \sum_{e \in \mathcal{E}} w(e)h(v,e)$, and the degree of hyper-edge is defined as $\delta(e) = \sum_{v \in \mathcal{V}} h(v,e)$. Thus, two diagonal matrices $\mathbf{D}_v$ and $\mathbf{D}_e$ can be formed with each entry along the diagonal using the vertex degree and hyper-edge degree, respectively.

Hyper-Graph Learning. After establishing the relationships among all the voxels through hyper-graph, the next step is to propagate anatomical labels from atlas vertices $\mathcal{V}_Q$ to subject image vertices $\mathcal{V}_P$. For convenience, let y_j denote the label on the atlas vertex $v_j \in \mathcal{V}_Q$, which has two values, '-1' for background and '1' of foreground (the underlying structure). We initially set the label y_i on the subject image vertex $v_i \in \mathcal{V}_P$ to '0', since the anatomical labels on the subject image are unknown. Furthermore, we arrange labels on all vertices into a column vector $\vec{Y} = \left[[y_i]_{i=1}^{|P|}, [y_j]_{j=1}^{|Q|} \right]^{\mathrm{T}}$.

The goal of label fusion is to jointly optimize relevance values $\vec{F} = \left[[f_i]_{i=1}^{|P|}, [f_j]_{j=1}^{|Q|} \right]^{\mathrm{T}}$ for all vertices, regardless from atlas or subject images, which suggests the preference of choosing background (<0) or foreground (>0). Thus, our label fusion method falls into the semi-supervised hyper-graph learning framework, i.e., the to-be-determined labels on the vertices from the subject image are influenced by the connected vertices from atlas images with known labels as well as subject voxels under labeling. The principle to propagate the labels is that the vertexes sitting in the same hyper-edge are likely to have the same label, by also keeping the minimal discrepancy of labels on the vertexes with known labels before and after label propagation. The objective function of hyper-graph learning is defined as:

$$\arg\min_{\vec{F}} \left\{ \|\vec{Y} - \vec{F}\|_2^2 + \lambda \cdot \Phi\left(\vec{F}, \mathbf{H}, \mathbf{W}, \mathbf{D}_e, \mathbf{D}_v\right) \right\} \tag{2}$$

The first term in Eq. 2 is called the fitting term, which requires the estimated relevance vector $\vec{F}$ and the initialization vector $\vec{Y}$ should have minimal discrepancy before and after label propagation.

The second term $\Phi\left(\cdot\right)$ is the graph balance term [8], defined as:

$$\Phi\left(\vec{F}, \mathbf{H}, \mathbf{W}, \mathbf{D}_e, \mathbf{D}_v\right) = \frac{1}{2} \sum_{e \in \mathcal{E}} \sum_{v,v' \subseteq e} \frac{w(e)h(v,e)h(v',e)}{\delta(e)} \left(\frac{f(v)}{\sqrt{d(v)}} - \frac{f(v')}{\sqrt{d(v')}} \right)^2 \tag{3}$$

which holds the constraint in each hyper-edge that two vertices v and v' in the same hyper-edge should have similar relevance value. The λ is a positive weighing parameter between the two terms. We can rewrite the graph balance term into $\Phi\left(\vec{F}, \mathbf{H}, \mathbf{W}, \mathbf{D}_e, \mathbf{D}_v\right) = \vec{F}^{\mathrm{T}}(\mathbf{I} - \mathbf{\Theta})\vec{F} = \vec{F}^{\mathrm{T}} \Delta \vec{F}$, where $\mathbf{\Theta} = \mathbf{D}_v^{-\frac{1}{2}}\mathbf{H}\mathbf{W}\mathbf{D}_e^{-1}\mathbf{H}^{\mathrm{T}}\mathbf{D}_v^{-\frac{1}{2}}$, $\mathbf{I}$ is the identity matrix, and Δ acts as a normalized hyper-graph Laplacian matrix. By differentiating the objective function with respect to $\vec{F}$, the optimal $\widehat{\vec{F}}$ can be computed by:

$$\widehat{\vec{F}} = (\mathbf{I} + \lambda(\mathbf{I} - \mathbf{\Theta}))^{-1}\vec{Y} \tag{4}$$

Given the estimated $\widehat{\vec{F}}$, the anatomical label on the subject image can be easily determined by the sign of the relevance value.

2.2   Hierarchical Label Propagation Mechanism

Some subject image voxels might have the higher confidence to be labeled than others due to better alignment of atlas images or locating in the uniform regions in the image. In light of this, we partition the vertices in $\mathcal{V}_P$ into two groups based on their difficulties in labeling. To achieve it, we use an existing label fusion method, such as the majority voting, to predict the label on each subject voxel as well as the confidence value in terms of the voting predominance. If the influence for voting one label dominates other labels, we assume the estimated label on the underlying subject voxel can be treated as ground-truth. Otherwise, we need to confirm the underlying voxel label by other heuristics. The advantage is that it allows label propagation from *not only* the atlas images *but also* some reliable regions of subject image, which are more specific to label fusion of subject image. After label fusion by hyper-graph learning, the refined labeling result brings more subject voxels with high labeling confidence. By iteratively selecting more and more subject vertices with high confidence and performing label fusion, we can gradually improve the label fusion result.

2.3   Deep Hyper-Graph Learning by Using High-Level Context Features

In Sect. 2.1, we only use the image appearance information to construct the hyper-graph. Due to low image contrast, low-level features derived from image intensity are not sufficient to steer hyper-graph learning. Other high-level features are of great necessity to alleviate the issue of poor image quality. To this end, we resort to context features which can encode spatial relationship of one structure to other structures. The anatomical structures are labeled with different colors, as shown in the blue box of Fig. 2. Thus, for each voxel, the label information from other surrounding voxels provides an additional clue to identify the underlying voxel in terms of its relationship to other structures. In order to make the context features more robust and efficient, we further construct the context feature profile (black dots in the red boxes of Fig. 2) in a multi-resolution manner, where we densely sample nearby the center (to represent the characteristics of local anatomy) and gradually reduce sampling outward (to capture the global scale information).

Given the context features, we can refine the segmentation result with more accurate self-similarity and atlas-subject relationship revealed in the hyper-graph. Since the context features of the subject image are extracted from the tentatively refined label

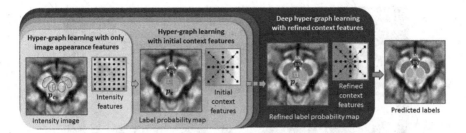

Fig. 2. Illustration of the deep hyper-graph learning leveraged by context features.

probability map, we can turn our label fusion method into a deep model. As shown in Fig. 2, the refined context features lead to more accurate segmentation results, as the label probability map (displayed in darker blue boxes) becomes clearer and clearer. In summary, by repeating **(1)** construction of hyper-graph with both low-level image features and high-level context features, **(2)** label fusion via hyper-graph learning and **(3)** update of the context features, we have the chance to correct mislabeling and hence improve the labeling accuracy.

3 Experiments

In the experiments, 11 MR images of PD subjects are used to evaluate the proposed label fusion method. Each subject has the SN and RN structures manually labeled by two radiologists. The image voxel size is $1 \times 1 \times 1 \, \text{mm}^3$. For all the experiments, the patch size is set to $5 \times 5 \times 5 \, \text{mm}^3$. The search neighborhood in constructing hyper-edges is set to $3 \times 3 \times 3 \, \text{mm}^3$. Parameter λ in Eq. 2 is 0.1.

To evaluate the performance of the proposed method, we adopted the leave-one-out cross-validation, where each subject was in turn used as a subject image and the remaining 10 subjects were used as atlas images. Our proposed deep hyper-graph patch labeling (DHPL) method is compared with two state-of-the-art methods: nonlocal mean patch-based label fusion method (NLM) [2], and sparse patch-based label fusion method (SPBL) [8]. Note, we compare our method with the best segmentation results by these counterpart methods.

Table 1 shows the mean and standard deviation of Dice ratios (DR) between manual segmentation and the estimated segmentation by three methods. Compared to the SPBL, our method can obtain overall 2.2 % and 1.3 % improvement ratio for SN and RN, respectively. Paired t-test further confirmed that our full method (DHPL)

Table 1. The mean and standard deviation of the Dice ratio by three methods.

	NLM	SPBL	DHPL
SN	72.2 ± 2.7 %*	73.0 ± 1.9 %*	75.2 ± 2.2 %
RN	82.2 ± 2.8 %*	83.0 ± 1.8 %*	84.3 ± 1.9 %

*Indicates significant improvement of our DHPL over other counterpart methods (p-value < 0.05)

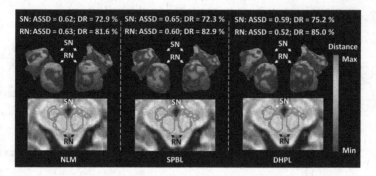

Fig. 3. Visual comparison of segmentation results by three label fusion methods on a typical subject. Automatic segmentations are shown in red contours and manual segmentations are shown in yellow contours in the bottom row. (Color figure online)

achieves the significant improvement in terms of DR over the two counterpart methods. Figure 3 further shows the average symmetric surface distance (ASSD) between the ground truth and estimated segmentation result by the three methods. Based on the color map shown in the right of Fig. 3, the segmentation result by our DHPL method is much closer to the ground truth than any other methods.

4 Conclusion

In this paper, we proposed a novel multi-atlas label fusion framework for brainstem nuclei segmentation for MR images using deep hyper-graph learning. The novelty of our method lies in three ways. First, we employed hyper-graph learning method to label anatomical regions, by taking its advantages of both maintaining the spatial consistency and coupling population priors from multiple atlases. Second, we harnessed high-level context features to steer the hyper-graph learning in order to overcome the poor image appearance. Here, we implemented our method in a deep and self-refining model by extracting context features from the tentatively estimated label probability map. Third, we allowed more and more reliable predicted subject voxel labels to guide label propagation to those difficult-to-label voxels, making our method *not only* deep *but also* dynamic. Experimental results show significantly enhanced better segmentation results using our proposed method compared to the state-of-the-art patch-based label fusion methods.

References

1. Ziegler, D.A., Augustinack, J.C.: Harnessing advances in structural MRI to enhance research on Parkinson's disease. Imaging Med. **5**, 91–94 (2013)
2. Coupé, P., Manjón, J.V., Fonov, V., Pruessner, J., Robles, M., Collins, D.L.: Patch-based segmentation using expert priors: application to hippocampus and ventricle segmentation. NeuroImage **54**, 940–954 (2011)

3. Wu, G., Kim, M., Sanroma, G., Wang, Q., Munsell, B., Shen, D.: Hierarchical multi-atlas label fusion with multi-scale feature representation and label-specific patch partition. NeuroImage **106**, 34–46 (2015)
4. Zhang, D., Guo, Q., Wu, G., Shen, D.: Sparse patch-based label fusion for multi-atlas segmentation. In: Yap, P.-T., Liu, T., Shen, D., Westin, C.-F., Shen, L. (eds.) MBIA 2012. LNCS, vol. 7509, pp. 94–102. Springer, Heidelberg (2012)
5. Shi, J., Malik, J.: Normalized cuts and image segmentation. IEEE Trans. Pattern Anal. Mach. Intell. **22**, 888–905 (2000)
6. Dong, P., Guo, Y., Shen, D., Wu, G.: Multi-atlas and multi-modal hippocampus segmentation for infant MR brain images by propagating anatomical labels on hypergraph. In: Wu, G., Coupé, P., Zhan, Y., Munsell, B., Rueckert, D. (eds.) Patch-MI 2015. LNCS, vol. 9467, pp. 188–196. Springer, Heidelberg (2015). doi:10.1007/978-3-319-28194-0_23
7. Zhang, D., Wu, G., Jia, H., Shen, D.: Confidence-guided sequential label fusion for multi-atlas based segmentation. In: Fichtinger, G., Martel, A., Peters, T. (eds.) MICCAI 2011, Part III. LNCS, vol. 6893, pp. 643–650. Springer, Heidelberg (2011)
8. Zhou, D., Huang, J., Schölkopf, B.: Learning with hypergraphs: clustering, classification, and embedding. In: Advances in NIPS, vol. 19, pp. 1601–1608 (2006)

Patch-Based Discrete Registration of Clinical Brain Images

Adrian V. Dalca[1](✉), Andreea Bobu[1], Natalia S. Rost[2], and Polina Golland[1]

[1] Computer Science and Artificial Intelligence Lab, EECS, MIT, Cambridge, USA
adalca@csail.mit.edu
[2] Department of Neurology, Massachusetts General Hospital,
Harvard Medical School, Boston, USA

Abstract. We introduce a method for registration of brain images acquired in clinical settings. The algorithm relies on three-dimensional patches in a discrete registration framework to estimate correspondences. Clinical images present significant challenges for computational analysis. Fast acquisition often results in images with sparse slices, severe artifacts, and variable fields of view. Yet, large clinical datasets hold a wealth of clinically relevant information. Despite significant progress in image registration, most algorithms make strong assumptions about the continuity of image data, failing when presented with clinical images that violate these assumptions. In this paper, we demonstrate a non-rigid registration method for aligning such images. The method explicitly models the sparsely available image information to achieve robust registration. We demonstrate the algorithm on clinical images of stroke patients. The proposed method outperforms state of the art registration algorithms and avoids catastrophic failures often caused by these images. We provide a freely available open source implementation of the algorithm.

1 Introduction

We propose a robust non-linear registration method for images with sparse slice acquisition. Medical image registration is a fundamental step in population studies and atlas-based analyses, and has been a topic of active research for many years. Most registration algorithms require research quality images with sufficiently high resolution. Unfortunately, in many clinical settings the acquired images have extremely sparse slices. The proposed method enables explicit modeling of spatially sparse images and facilitates analyses in a large class of image data. Such analyses are currently unavailable to clinical research due to challenges in alignment.

Throughout this paper we use the motivating example of a clinical imaging study of stroke patients where thousands of brain MR scans are acquired within 48 h of stroke onset. The in-plane resolution in these images is 0.85 mm, while the slice spacing is 5–7 mm, as illustrated in Fig. 1. The study aims to quantify the white matter disease burden and to analyze population trends, necessitating non-linear registration to a common coordinate frame, and segmentation of

© Springer International Publishing AG 2016
G. Wu et al. (Eds.): Patch-MI 2016, LNCS 9993, pp. 60–67, 2016.
DOI: 10.1007/978-3-319-47118-1_8

Fig. 1. An example clinical T2-FLAIR MRI of a stroke patient in axial (left), sagittal (center) and coronal (right) views. The slice spacing is much larger than is usually encountered in research scans, making registration a challenging task.

healthy tissue and pathology near the ventricles [13]. Analyses of such images are hindered by the wide slice spacing, presenting significant challenges for basic tasks such as registration, skull stripping, and bias correction. In this work, we focus on registration.

Non-linear registration methods developed for high resolution images often make continuity and smoothness assumptions [7] that are violated by clinically acquired images, as illustrated in Fig. 1. Specifically, most algorithms operate on image gradients. However, in volumes with wide slice spacing, the volume is no longer smooth, and the anatomical structure may change dramatically between subsequent slices. While for some images the registration may be adequate, in many cases it fails catastrophically. Some methods attempt to directly address this problem by designing processing pipelines and tuning respective parameters specific to a particular dataset [14]. Instead, we explicitly account for the sparse nature of the slices and avoid anatomical continuity assumptions.

Feature-based methods [8,11,15] present an alternative approach to voxel-wise registration algorithms by extracting sparse features or region summaries and using these features to guide the registration. Point set representations [3] use a representative selection of voxels to direct the registration. Unfortunately, the spatial sparseness of clinical images makes it difficult to extract meaningful and consistent features or point sets.

Our algorithm builds on discrete registration methods [5,6] that have been demonstrated recently as an alternative to gradient-based methods. The discrete registration approach models voxels of a moving image as nodes of a discrete Markov Random Field (MRF). Each node can move to a pre-specified number of voxels in each direction. Node potentials capture the agreement of intensities between the voxel in the moving image and the target voxel in the fixed image. Neighbouring voxels are encouraged to move together through pairwise potentials. The optimal registration is obtained via minimizing the energy of the MRF [5,6,12]. Since the same optimization can be used for a wide variety of potentials, the framework provides significant flexibility in adapting these terms to specific tasks. Discrete registration algorithms typically achieve similar results to state of the art gradient-based methods for research quality high resolution scans, and offer an alternative framework when image gradients cannot be computed reliably.

To address the challenges of clinical data, we design a general and robust patch-based discrete registration algorithm that captures the sparse structure characteristic of our problem. While most methods use single voxels to asses data similarity, we design an appropriate 3D patch-based similarity function surrounding each voxel. We demonstrate our approach on real clinical data from a study of stroke.

While a large number of software packages is available for continuous registration, very few tools have been developed for discrete registration, and are generally task-specific or proprietary [5,6]. To motivate and facilitate further research, we provide a flexible, fast, and open-source implementation of discrete deformable registration, and provide several voxel-based and patch-based data similarity functions at http://github.com/adalca/patchRegistration.

2   Methods

We let Ω be the set of all spatial locations, and aim to non-rigidly register a moving image $M = \{M_\mathbf{x}\}_{\mathbf{x} \in \Omega}$ to a fixed image $F = \{F_\mathbf{x}\}_{\mathbf{x} \in \Omega}$. For simplicity we assume both images have been interpolated to isotropic resolution and are of the same size. In our experiments we use affine registration with linear interpolation to align images into a common space as a pre-processing step. Although the method we develop below applies to the registration of data with any spatially missing data, in this paper we focus on registering a moving image with sparse slice acquisition to a high resolution atlas. In this section, we first review discrete deformable registration, then describe our treatment of sparse data within this framework, and finally discuss important implementation details.

2.1   Discrete Deformable Registration

Discrete registration is often modeled as a labeling problem using a Markov Random Field (MRF) [5,6]. Control points $\mathbf{x} \in \Omega$ of the moving image M are viewed as nodes arranged on a grid. For each node $\mathbf{x}$, a finite set of states $\mathcal{D}_\mathbf{x} = \{\mathbf{d}_\mathbf{x}\}$ represent discrete displacements $\mathbf{d}_\mathbf{x} \in \mathbb{Z}^3$ that node $\mathbf{x}$ can take. For example, a node could be allowed to move at most one voxel in each direction, resulting in 27 possible states.

The node potential $\Phi_\mathbf{x}(\mathbf{d}_\mathbf{x})$ measures the quality of each displacement $\mathbf{d}_\mathbf{x}$, most often in terms of similarity of image intensities $M(\mathbf{x})$ and $F(\mathbf{x} + \mathbf{d}_\mathbf{x})$. The pairwise potential $\Psi_{\mathbf{x},\mathbf{x}'}(\mathbf{d}_\mathbf{x}, \mathbf{d}_{\mathbf{x}'})$ encourages similar displacements for neighbouring nodes $\mathbf{x}$ and $\mathbf{x}'$. Registration aims to find the optimal displacement field by minimizing the MRF energy function

$$E(\mathcal{D}) = \sum_\mathbf{x} \Phi_\mathbf{x}(\mathbf{d}_\mathbf{x}) + \lambda \sum_{\mathbf{x},\mathbf{x}' \in \mathcal{N}(\mathbf{x})} \Psi_{\mathbf{x},\mathbf{x}'}(\mathbf{d}_\mathbf{x}, \mathbf{d}_{\mathbf{x}'}), \qquad (1)$$

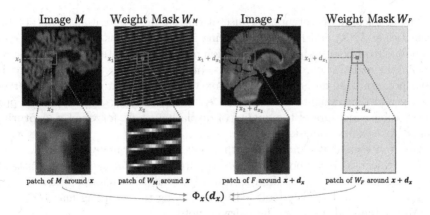

Fig. 2. Overview of the information captured by the unary potentials using 3D patches.

where λ is a parameter that trades off between the data and smoothness terms, and $\mathcal{N}(\mathbf{x})$ is the set of neighbors of node $\mathbf{x}$. While efficient MRF optimization methods have been a topic of active research [4,5,9], we find that using Loopy Belief Propagation [12] is sufficiently fast and accurate for our application.

2.2   Patch Based Discrete Registration

The node potential is most often based on a difference between image intensities $M(\mathbf{x})$ and $F(\mathbf{x} + \mathbf{d_x})$:

$$\Phi_{\mathbf{x}}(\mathbf{d_x}) = (M(\mathbf{x}) - F(\mathbf{x} + \mathbf{d_x}))^2. \tag{2}$$

In clinical datasets, where known voxels are sparse, we instead use patches to aggregate information from available voxels.

We introduce masks $W_M = \{W_{M_{\mathbf{x}}} \in [0,1]\}_{\mathbf{x} \in \Omega}$ and $W_F = \{W_{F_{\mathbf{x}}} \in [0,1]\}_{\mathbf{x} \in \Omega}$ that define the confidence in image intensities for each voxel. For example, in our clinical dataset, the moving weight mask describes the original locations of the original high-resolution slices in the interpolated clinical image (Fig. 2). Mask values vary between 0 and 1 due to interpolation effects of the affine transformations of the moving image M and the fixed image F.

All patches in our method share the same shape and size. We let $\{I(\mathbf{x} + \mathbf{z})\}_{\mathbf{z} \in \Omega_{\mathbf{x}}}$ define a patch of image I centered at voxel $\mathbf{x}$ with patch footprint $\Omega_{\mathbf{x}}$. We define the unary potential as the weighted patch distance

$$\Phi_{\mathbf{x}}(\mathbf{d_x}) = \frac{\sum_{\mathbf{z} \in \Omega_{\mathbf{x}}} W(\mathbf{x}, \mathbf{d_x}, \mathbf{z}) \left(M(\mathbf{x} + \mathbf{z}) - F(\mathbf{x} + \mathbf{d_x} + \mathbf{z})\right)^2}{\sum_{\mathbf{z} \in \Omega_{\mathbf{x}}} W(\mathbf{x}, \mathbf{d_x}, \mathbf{z})}, \tag{3}$$

where

$$W(\mathbf{x}, \mathbf{d_x}, \mathbf{z}) = W_M(\mathbf{x} + \mathbf{z}) W_F(\mathbf{x} + \mathbf{d_x} + \mathbf{z}). \tag{4}$$

The classical node potential (2) uses a single pair of potentially interpolated intensities at $M(\mathbf{x})$ and $F(\mathbf{x} + \mathbf{d_x})$, forcing implementations to either limit control points to only available high-resolution planes, or use interpolated intensities to drive the registration, resulting in sub-optimal alignment. Instead, our patch-based potential (3) relies more heavily on voxels whose intensity was observed directly and downweights the interpolated values (Fig. 2). This approach provides a robust measure of the quality of displacement $\mathbf{d_x}$ for voxel $\mathbf{x}$, capturing context for voxel $\mathbf{x}$ using known data.

We do not explicitly model slice thickness [10], as in many clinical datasets the slice thickness is unknown or varies by site, scanner or acquisition. Instead, we simply treat the original data as thin high resolution planes. When known, slice thickness can be easily modeled by modifying the sampling mask W.

We use the ℓ_2 distance as the pairwise potential:

$$\Psi(\mathbf{d_x}, \mathbf{d'_x}) = ||\mathbf{d_x} - \mathbf{d'_x}||_2^2. \tag{5}$$

Once $\Phi(\mathbf{d_x})$ and $\Psi(\mathbf{d_x}, \mathbf{d'_x})$ are defined and the parameter λ is set, we seek the optimal MRF labeling to obtain the desired displacement of each image voxel.

2.3 Implementation

We implemented a multi-resolution variant of the discrete registration algorithm described above. We prepare the moving clinical images at different scales by first down-sampling the original acquired slices for each scale, and then interpolating the data between slices. This approach maximizes the use of voxels with known intensity values.

To improve runtime, we implement several approximations. Specifically, we limit the number of states for each node to the top few states based on unary potentials, and remove nodes from the MRF based on the variance among their state potentials. Both pruning steps are controlled by model parameters. At the end of the registration step at each scale, the displacement field is linearly interpolated between nodes. We optimize parameter settings on a held-out subset of images described below. In this experiment, we varied the parameter λ to trade off the importance of the data and smoothness terms, as well as the spacing of the control points.

We use Loopy Belief Propagation to minimize energy function (1). When run on a single quad-code 2.7 GHz, 32 Gb of RAM registering two images takes approximately 120 min. Our implementation accepts for any patch definition and weight pattern and includes several built-in patch similarities. Developed to be highly modifiable and extensible, the code is freely available at http://github. com/adalca/patchRegistration.

3 Results

We demonstrate the performance of our algorithm on clinically acquired stroke images. The stroke study aims to quantify periventricular white matter disease burden, requiring particularly accurate registration around the ventricles.

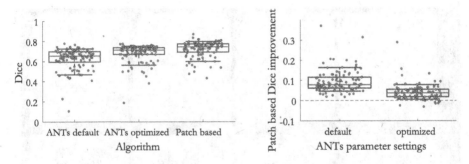

Fig. 3. Results on the stroke clinical dataset. For each setting, the measurements are shown in gray. The red line and cross represent the median and mean value respectively, box edges show 25th and 75th percentiles, and black whiskers show 10th and 90th percentiles. Left: Ventricle Dice measure for the ANTs algorithm with default and optimized parameters, and the patch based method. Right: Dice improvement achieved by patch based registration compared to ANTs, for both default and optimized parameters, respectively. Our method improves registration for all subjects when compared to default ANTs settings, and for 92 % of the subjects when compared to optimized ANTs settings. (Color figure online)

Data and Processing. To evaluate the algorithm, we randomly selected 100 T2-FLAIR brain MR scans from the stroke patient cohort for evaluation. Our clinical scans are severely anisotropic (0.85×0.85 mm in-plane, slice separation of 6mm, variable TR and TE). All subjects are linearly interpolated to isotropic resolution and intensity corrected by matching the intensity of the white matter across subjects. Finally, the subjects are affinely registered to a T2-FLAIR atlas. All subjects have manual delineation of the ventricles created for this evaluation.

Parameters. We choose patch registration parameters found to be optimal in a subset of 18 held-out scans, separate from those used in the experiments. We varied the parameter λ and the spacing of the control points. We set $\lambda = 0.1$ and an optimal grid spacing of 3 mm, but find little variation in the results when using wider spacing. At each scale, each node can only move up to two voxels in each dimension. We keep the top 50 states (out of 125 possible states) for each node, and keep the top 50 % of nodes. We use a patch size large enough to include at least two observed slices in every patch, which for our experiments is 9 mm in the highest resolution scale and 3 mm in the lowest.

Experiments. We register each scan in the evaluation set to the atlas. We evaluate registrations by propagating manual segmentations of the ventricles from the atlas to each subject through resulting warps and measuring volume overlap via the Dice metric [2]. We use the state of the art ANTs registration algorithm [1] as the baseline method for evaluation. Throughout our work with the clinical study, we found ANTs to be the most consistent at tackling the sparse data among all existing algorithms. We run ANTs with the default parameters, as well as parameters we identified by optimizing ANTs for stroke clinical images.

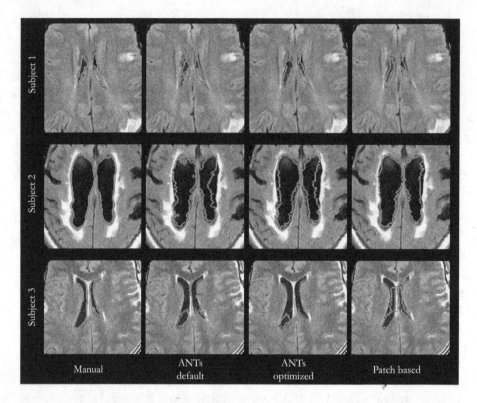

Fig. 4. Examples of serious registration failures of the ANTs algorithm. For the first two subjects, that patch based registration recovers successful registrations. For the third subject, the patch based registration yields dramatic improvement, but several areas can still be improved. Aside from low resolution, the image exhibits significant pathology, imperfect skull stripping, and suboptimal affine registration, all common in stroke subjects.

Patch based registration outperforms substantially the baseline ANTs algorithms in most subjects. Since the Dice measure varies significantly among subjects due to variable ventricle shape and cerebral pathology, we also report statistics of patch based registration improvement over ANTs results (Fig. 3). Patch based registration yields an improved Dice score in 92 % of the subjects compared to optimized ANTs results, with a mean improvement of 4.1 dice points. It also yields significant improvement (more than 5 Dice points) in 31 % of the subjects where ANTs often resulted in serious registration errors (Fig. 4). Overall, the presented algorithm shows consistent improvement across the dataset.

4   Conclusion

Clinical images present significant challenges for many computational analyses, yet hold the wealth of clinically relevant information. We combine three-dimensional patch information with the discrete registration framework to robustly drive registration of such images. The three-dimensional patches explicitly model the sparsely available image information to achieve robust registration. We demonstrate the algorithm on images with sparsely acquired slices in clinical scans of stroke patients. The proposed method outperforms the state of the art registration algorithms and avoids significant failures often observed in the alignment of these images. Our implementation is freely available and accepts images of varying resolution.

References

1. Avants, B.B., Tustison, N.J., Song, G., Cook, P.A., Klein, A., Gee, J.C.: A reproducible evaluation of ANTs similarity metric performance in brain image registration. Neuroimage **54**(3), 2033–2044 (2011)
2. Dice, L.R.: Measures of the amount of ecologic association between species. Ecology **26**(3), 297–302 (1945)
3. Gao, Y., Tannenbaum, A.: Image processing and registration in a point set representation, p. 762308 (2010)
4. Glocker, B., Komodakis, N., Tziritas, G., Navab, N., Paragios, N.: Dense image registration through MRFs and efficient linear programming. Med. Image Anal. **12**(6), 731–741 (2008)
5. Glocker, B., Sotiras, A., Komodakis, N., Paragios, N.: Deformable medical image registration: setting the state of the art with discrete methods*. Ann. Rev. Biomed. Eng. **13**, 219–244 (2011)
6. Heinrich, M.P., Jenkinson, M., Brady, M., Schnabel, J.A.: MRF-based deformable registration and ventilation estimation of lung CT. IEEE Trans. Med. Imaging **32**(7), 1239–1248 (2013)
7. Hill, D.L.G., Batchelor, P.G., Holden, M., Hawkes, D.J.: Medical image registration. Phys. Med. Biol. **46**(3), R1 (2001)
8. Johnson, H.J., Christensen, G.E.: Consistent landmark and intensity-based image registration. IEEE Trans. Med. Imaging **21**(5), 450–461 (2002)
9. Komodakis, N., Tziritas, G., Paragios, N.: Fast, approximately optimal solutions for single and dynamic MRFs. In: IEEE Conference on Computer Vision and Pattern Recognition, CVPR 2007, pp. 1–8. IEEE (2007)
10. Manjón, J.V., Coupé, P., Buades, A., Fonov, V., Collins, D.L., Robles, M.: Nonlocal MRI upsampling. Med. Image Anal. **14**(6), 784–792 (2010)
11. Ou, Y., Sotiras, A., Paragios, N., Davatzikos, C.: Dramms: deformable registration via attribute matching and mutual-saliency weighting. Med. Image Anal. **15**(4), 622–639 (2011)
12. Pearl, J.: Probabilistic Reasoning in Intelligent Systems: Networks of Plausible Inference. Morgan Kaufmann, Los Altos (1988)
13. Rost, N.S., Fitzpatrick, K., Biffi, A., Kanakis, A., Devan, W., Anderson, C.D., Cortellini, L., Furie, K.L., Rosand, J.: White matter hyperintensity burden and susceptibility to cerebral ischemia. Stroke **41**(12), 2807–2811 (2010)
14. Sridharan, R., et al.: Quantification and analysis of large multimodal clinical image studies: application to stroke. In: Shen, L., Liu, T., Yap, P.-T., Huang, H., Shen, D., Westin, C.-F. (eds.) MBIA 2013. LNCS, vol. 8159, pp. 18–30. Springer, Heidelberg (2013)
15. Toews, M., Zöllei, L., Wells III., W.M.: Feature-based alignment of volumetric multi-modal images. In: Information Processing in Medical Imaging (2013)

Non-local MRI Library-Based Super-Resolution: Application to Hippocampus Subfield Segmentation

Jose E. Romero[1], Pierrick Coupé[2,3(✉)], and Jose V. Manjón[1]

[1] Instituto de Aplicaciones de las Tecnologías de la Información y de las Comunicaciones Avanzadas, Universitat Politècnica de València, Camino de Vera s/n, 46022 Valencia, Spain
[2] University of Bordeaux, LaBRI, UMR 5800, PICTURA, F-33400 Talence, France
pierrick.coupe@labri.fr
[3] CNRS, LaBRI, UMR 5800, PICTURA, F-33400 Talence, France

Abstract. Magnetic Resonance Imaging (MRI) has become one of the most used techniques in research and clinical settings. One of the limiting factors of the MRI is the relatively low resolution for some applications. Although new high resolution MR sequences have been proposed recently, usually these acquisitions require long scanning times which is not always possible neither desirable. Recently, super-resolution techniques have been proposed to alleviate this problem by inferring the underlying high resolution images from low resolution acquisitions. We present a new super-resolution technique that takes benefit from the self-similarity properties of the images and the use of a high resolution image library. The proposed method is compared with related state-of-the-art methods showing a significant reconstruction improvement. Finally, we show the advantage of the proposed framework compared to classic interpolation when used for segmentation of hippocampus subfields.

1 Introduction

Magnetic resonance imaging (MRI) is a valuable tool in the study of many brain dysfunctions for different areas such as neurology and psychiatry. For instance, MRI enables to investigate specific structures such as the hippocampus. This structure is known to be an important biomarker for several pathologies like Alzheimer's disease [1]. However, the study of specific areas such as the hippocampus requires high-resolution images difficult to obtain in clinical practice. Interpolation based methods [2] have been used in the past to increase the apparent resolution. However, these techniques do not provide new information but just produce blurred versions of the corresponding high resolution images. The application of super-resolution techniques has demonstrated to improve image quality in MRI [3]. Nevertheless, these methods are usually based on multiple low-resolution acquisitions with small shifts that results in additional time and thus can be a limiting factor in clinical environments. Recently, single MRI super-resolution techniques have emerged as an efficient and accurate way to improve image resolution [4, 5]. These methods are often based on a nonlocal means

© Springer International Publishing AG 2016
G. Wu et al. (Eds.): Patch-MI 2016, LNCS 9993, pp. 68–75, 2016.
DOI: 10.1007/978-3-319-47118-1_9

framework [6] taking advantage of the intra-image pattern redundancy. Manjón et al. presented a method called Non-local Upsampling [4] that improved effectively the image resolution by using a constrained reconstruction process based on image regularity and inter-scale coherence constraints to produced physically plausible results. Coupe et al. [7] further extended this method by using a local adaptive regularization that made the process more efficient and accurate.

In this work we propose an extension of Local Adaptive SR (LASR) method [7] that uses an external HR image library to take advantage from the intra and inter-image pattern redundancy at the same time. The method is compared to related state-of-the-art methods and the impact of SR on hippocampus subfield segmentation is also evaluated.

2 Materials and Methods

As described in [4], MRI low resolution (LR) image voxels y can be related to the corresponding underlying high resolution (HR) voxels x through a simple degradation model:

$$y = DHx + n \tag{1}$$

where D is a decimation operator (defined as taking each Lth value starting from zero in each dimension), H is the convolution matrix (modeled as a 3D boxcar function), x is the underlying HR data, and n is random noise [4]. Therefore, the aim of any super-resolution method is to infer the HR x_i values within each y LR voxel using some internal or external image information together with some reconstruction constraints.

2.1 Non-local Upsampling

In [4], the authors presented the Non-local Upsampling method. This SR method is able to infer a HR image by taking benefit of the self-similarity properties on the MR images. The SR method proposed in this paper is an improvement of this method that improves the HR image reconstruction by using a library of HR images. Briefly, Non-local Upsampling method infers the HR image iteratively by alternating two steps: (1) regularization and (2) mean correction.

First, the regularization consist of the application of a 3D non-local means filter which enforces the regularity of the image by estimating the value of each voxel as a weighted average of nearby voxels by using their patch similarity (see Eqs. 2 and 3).

$$x_p^{t+1} = \frac{1}{C_p} \sum_{q \in \Omega} w(x_p^t, x_q^t) x_q^t \tag{2}$$

$$w(x_p^t, x_q^t) = \begin{cases} e^{-\frac{\left\| N(x_p^t) - N(x_q^t) \right\|^2}{h^2}}, & if \left| \mu_p^t - \mu_q^t \right| < 3h/\sqrt{N} \\ 0 & otherwise \end{cases} \tag{3}$$

Where x_p^t is the voxel located at the position p of the actual image at iteration t, w measures the similarity between $N(x_p^t)$ and $N(x_q^t)$, the patches around voxels p and q, Ω is a restricted search volume surrounding the voxel being processed, Cp is a normalization constant, h is a filtering parameter related to the degree of smoothing and N is the number of voxels in each patch. Equation (3) shows how the similarity between patches is estimated by preselecting patches with similar mean values μ_p^t.

Second, after the regularization step a mean correction step is necessary to enforce the inter-scale coherence (i.e. downsampled version of the inferred HR image has to be equal than the original LR image). To do so, Eq. (4) is applied.

$$\hat{x} = \hat{x} - NN(S(\hat{x}) - y) \tag{4}$$

where S is a downsampling operator that transforms actual reconstructed HR data to the original LR scale and NN is a nearest neighbor interpolation operation that interpolates LR data to HR scale. Due to the presence of noise, the constraint expressed in (4) cannot be directly used. To simplify the problem, LR data is first denoised using a non-local means filter [8] so the inter-scale constrain can be roughly met. For more details on the Non-local Upsampling method, we refer the reader to the original paper [4]. This process (regularization-correction) is repeated iteratively using decreasing values of the filter parameter h until no significant differences are found.

2.2 Library-Based Non-local Upsampling

One of the main limitations of the Non-local Upsampling method is the fact that only the information contained within the image itself is taken into account while inter-image pattern redundancy could be useful as shown in [5].

In this paper, we extend the Non-local Upsampling method by using a library of HR images that have the resolution desired after upsampling. Therefore, the training images and the image under study have to be preprocessed in a similar way. The steps included in this preprocessing are the following: (1) *Denoising:* The Spatially Adaptive Non-local Means (see [8]) Filter was applied to reduce the noise in the images. This filter is chosen because it is able to automatically consider stationary and spatially varying noise levels. (2) *Inhomogeneity correction:* The N4 bias field correction [9] was applied to correct intensity inhomogeneities across the image. (3) *MNI space affine registration:* The images are linearly registered to the Montreal Neurological Institute (MNI) space using the MNI152 template. This was done using the Advanced Normalization Tools (ANTs) [10]. (4) *Subvolume cropping:* A cropping step is applied as the region of interest is significantly smaller than the image volume to reduce the computational burden of the method limiting the process to the area of interest. This step can be omitted if we are interested in the whole volume. (5) *Subvolume Non-linear registration:* To achieve a better local anatomy matching between the target image and the image library the cropped volume of both (target and templates) is non-linearly registered to the cropped MNI152 atlas. The non-linear registration was performed using ANTs tool [10] using cross correlation similarity measure. (6) *Intensity normalization:* It is necessary to normalize the images in order to obtain the same intensity values across all subjects so similar patterns can be found among them by using an intensity based similarity metric. To this purpose, a simple mean and variance matching method was used so all the cases have the same mean and variance. This normalization needs only to be approximated since we will compensate any local difference during the reconstruction process as we will show later. (7) *BSpline interpolation*: This step is done to produce the initial estimation (only for the case to be upsampled not for the library cases).

Library-Based Upsampling. Once the library and the case to be upsampled are in the same geometric space and intensity range, we can apply the regularization-correction scheme but this time including the HR image library in the process (see Eq. 5).

$$x_p^{t+1} = \mu_p + \frac{1}{C_p}\left(\sum_{q\in\Omega} w(x_p^t, x_q^t)(x_q^t - \mu_q) + \sum_{i=1}^{K}\sum_{q\in\Omega} w_L(x_p^t, x_{q,i})(x_{q,i} - \mu_{q,i})\right) \quad (5)$$

$$w_L(x_p^t, x_{q,i}) = \begin{cases} e^{-\frac{\left\|(N(x_p^t)-\mu_p^t)-(N(x_{q,i})-\mu_{q,i})\right\|^2}{h^2}}, & if\left|\mu_p^t - \mu_{q,i}\right| < 3h/\sqrt{N} \\ 0 & otherwise \end{cases} \quad (6)$$

where K is the number of cases in the library, $x_{q,i}$ is the voxel q of the HR image I and μ_p, μ_q and $\mu_{q,i}$ are the mean value of a $3 \times 3 \times 3$ voxel patch around voxels p, q and q, i. Note that x^0 is initialized by BSpline interpolation.

The main difference between Eqs. 2 and 5 is the inclusion of a library of HR cases in the reconstruction process. While first term is aimed to regularize the image the second tries to bring new texture from proper examples in the library. To compensate for the different mean values of the patches from the library the mean of every patch is subtracted so only high frequency information is transferred from the HR images to the reconstructed image.

2.3   Multiatlas Non-local Label Fusion Segmentation

In order to measure the impact of the SR preprocessing on further image analysis, we decided to evaluate the ability of the SR to produce better segmentations. Specifically, we applied a recent non-local multi-atlas label fusion segmentation method that uses an adaptation of PatchMatch method called OPAL [11]. OPAL has an efficient strategy to find patch correspondences between two or more images, combines multiple matches and performs late label fusion with different scales and features.

3   Experiments and Results

For our experiments we used a public dataset consisting in 5 h cases with their corresponding manual hippocampus subfield segmentations[1] [12]. Each case consists of T1- and T2-weighted images at 0.3 mm resolution.

---

[1] Images obtained from http://cobralab.ca/atlases/Hippocampus.

These images were preprocessed as described in the previous section. Specifically, the native 0.3 mm images were registered to MNI space at 0.5 mm resolution, cropped, non-linearly registered and intensity normalized. To increase the size of the library left hippocampus cropped images were mirrored so the final library consists of 10 right hippocampus area images (10 for T1 and 10 for T2). We run two types of experiments:

1. *Reconstruction quality assessment*: In this experiment, the HR images were downsampled to have 1 mm resolution and later upsampled with the different methods to assess their quality.
2. *Segmentation accuracy assessment*: In this experiment, the different upsampling methods were evaluated in order to find out which was their impact on segmentation accuracy.

3.1 Superresolution Reconstruction Image Quality Assessment

For the first experiment, both T1 and T2 HR image libraries were used. A leave-two-out was used by removing from the library both hippocampi (left and right) belonging to the case being evaluated. We upsampled the 1 mm LR images to 0.5 mm resolution using 3 different methods, classic BSpline interpolation, LASR [7] and the proposed library-based SR method. Peak Signal to Noise Ratio (PSNR) was used to evaluate the results (Tables 1 and 2).

Table 1. Upsampling PSNR results of the 10 T1 cases. Best results in bold.

Method	Cases										
	1	2	3	4	5	6	7	8	9	10	Avg.
BSpline	26.06	27.22	30.98	28.46	28.83	27.69	29.26	29.06	28.27	26.83	28.27
LASR	27.72	28.40	32.50	30.01	29.92	29.05	30.00	30.58	29.97	29.51	29.77
Proposed	**30.89**	**29.96**	**34.41**	**32.28**	**31.72**	**31.01**	**31.83**	**32.18**	**31.50**	**30.80**	**31.66**

Table 2. Upsampling PSNR results of the 10 T2 cases. Best results in bold.

Method	Cases										
	1	2	3	4	5	6	7	8	9	10	Avg.
BSpline	29.95	30.13	29.64	29.38	30.23	29.82	31.12	30.47	29.31	29.54	29.96
LASR	31.64	31.44	31.72	30.85	31.62	32.02	32.75	32.29	31.36	31.93	31.76
Proposed	**32.98**	**32.60**	**32.58**	**31.74**	**32.96**	**33.65**	**34.15**	**33.60**	**32.07**	**32.62**	**32.89**

As can be noticed the proposed method obtained the best results in all the cases for both T1 and T2 libraries. The improvement of the proposed method over LASR was found to be significant (p < 0.001). In Fig. 1, an example of the SR results with the different methods is shown. Regarding the processing times, BSpline interpolation took 1 s to process, LASR around 20 s and the proposed method 5 min.

HR case   BSpline   LASR   Proposed

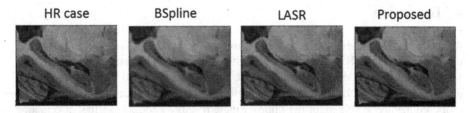

Fig. 1. Example of T1 SR results with the different methods. Note that both LASR and the proposed method produced a clearly better reconstruction than BSpline result (less blurry and more regular). Differences between LASR and the proposed method were not so obvious to assess visually (for example the white matter layer between hippocampus head and amygdala is better recovered by the proposed method).

3.2 Segmentation Accuracy Assessment

For the second experiment, we evaluated the accuracy improvement for a segmentation task obtained with the different upsampling methods. OPAL segmentation algorithm [11] was applied using default parameters to the original 10 HR T1 and T2 images (used as reference) and to the different upsampled results using BSpline, LASR and the proposed method over the images downsampled with a factor 2. Again, a leave-two-out was used by removing from the library both hippocampi (left and right) belonging to the case being evaluated. We used the DICE coefficient [13] to measure the segmentation accuracy. In Table 3 the segmentation results for the different subfields and for the whole hippocampus are shown.

Table 3. Segmentation results of the different methods compared (DICE). Best results in bold.

Method	Cases							
	T1 HR	T2 HR	T1 BSpline	T2 BSpline	T1 LASR	T2 LASR	T1 proposed	T2 proposed
CA1	0.6582	**0.7031**	0.6484	0.6826	0.6556	0.6935	0.6550	**0.6958**
CA2\CA3	**0.6725**	0.6261	0.6608	0.6061	0.6669	0.6176	**0.6681**	0.6195
CA4\DG	0.7035	**0.7538**	0.6932	0.7411	0.7020	0.7479	0.7019	**0.7499**
SR\SL\SM	0.4964	**0.5723**	0.4623	0.5401	0.4864	0.5539	0.4888	**0.5552**
Subiculum	0.5312	**0.6154**	0.5152	0.5830	0.5275	0.5980	0.5265	**0.6013**
Avg.	0.6124	**0.6541**	0.5960	0.6306	0.6077	0.6422	0.6081	**0.6443**
Whole	0.8752	**0.8843**	0.8701	0.8772	0.8742	**0.8817**	0.8738	0.8814

As expected, best results were found when using the T2 library. More importantly, we can clearly see how both SR methods improved significantly the segmentation results for both T1 and T2 cases compared to interpolation results. The proposed method improved subfield segmentation but not the whole hippocampus segmentation. Probably, SR helped to recover small details useful for subfield segmentation but not relevant to higher scale structures like the whole hippocampus.

4   Discussion

In this paper we presented a new super-resolution method that takes benefit from the use of an external HR image library to better reconstruct HR images from their corresponding LR counterparts. While LASR method was able to improve the image quality using the information within the image in form of a smart regularization, the proposed method is able to further improve these results by adding external information from similar examples in the library. More importantly, we have shown that both LASR and the proposed method are able to improve segmentation accuracy compared to simple BSpline interpolation and open the door to analyze retrospective LR data with a new insight. Although the improvement of the proposed method over LASR method is relatively small we have to note that we were using a small library (just 8 HR cases) and therefore we expect that using a larger library we will be able to represent more anatomical variability resulting in better results.

Acknowledgements. This research was partially supported by the Spanish grant TIN2013-43457-R from the Ministerio de Economia y competitividad. This study has been carried out with financial support from the French State, managed by the French National Research Agency (ANR) in the frame of the Investments for the future Program IdEx Bordeaux (ANR-10-IDEX-03-02, HL-MRI Project), Cluster of excellence CPU and TRAIL (HR-DTI ANR-10-LABX-57) and the CNRS multidisciplinary project "Défi imag'In".

References

1. Braak, H., Braak, E.: Neuropathological stageing of Alzheimer-related changes. Acta Neuropathol. **82**(4), 239–259 (1991)
2. Thévenaz, P., Blu, T., Unser, M.: Interpolation revisited. IEEE Trans. Med. Imaging **19**(7), 739–758 (2000)
3. Carmi, E., Liu, S., Alon, N., Fiat, A., Fiat, D.: Resolution enhancement in MRI. Magn. Reson. Imaging **24**(2), 133–154 (2006)
4. Manjón, J.V., Coupé, P., Buades, A., Fonov, V., Collins, D.L., Robles, M.: Non-local MRI upsampling. Med. Image Anal. **14**, 784–792 (2010)
5. Manjón, J.V., Coupé, P., Buades, A., Collins, D.L., Robles, M.: MRI superresolution using self-similarity and image priors. Int. J. Biomed. Imaging **2010**, 17 (2010)
6. Buades, A., Coll, B., Morel, J.-M.: A non-local algorithm for image denoising. In: Proceedings of IEEE Computer Society Conference on Computer Vision and Pattern Recognition (CVPR 2005), vol. 2, pp. 60–65 (2005)
7. Coupé, P., Manjon, J.V., Chamberland, M., Descoteaux, M.: Collaborative patch-based super-resolution for diffusion-weighted images. NeuroImage **83**, 245–261 (2013)
8. Manjón, J.V., Coupé, P., Martí-Bonmatí, L., Robles, M., Collins, L.: Adaptive non-local means denoising of MR images with spatially varying noise levels. J. Magn. Reson. Imaging **31**, 192–203 (2010)
9. Tustison, N.J., Avants, B.B., Cook, P.A., Zheng, Y., Egan, A., Yushkevich, P.A., Gee, J.C.: N4ITK: improved N3 bias correction. IEEE Trans. Med. Imaging **29**(6), 1310–1320 (2010)
10. Avants, B.B., Tustison, N., Song, G.: Advanced normalization tools (ANTS). Insight J. **2**, 1–35 (2009)

11. Giraud, R., Ta, V.-T., Papadakis, N., Manjón, J.V., Collins, D.L., Coupé, P., ADNI: An optimized PatchMatch for multi-scale and multi-feature label fusion. NeuroImage **124**, 770–782 (2016)
12. Winterburn, L., Pruessner, J.C., Chavez, S., Schira, M., Lobaugh, N., Voineskos, A.M., Chakravarty, M.: A novel in vivo atlas of human hippocampal subfields using high-resolution 3 T magnetic resonance imaging. NeuroImage **74**, 254–265 (2013)
13. Zijdenbos, A.P., Dawant, B.M., Margolin, R.A., Palmer, A.C.: Morphometric analysis of white matter lesions in MR images: method and validation. IEEE Trans. Med. Imaging **13** (4), 716–724 (1994)

Patch-Based DTI Grading: Application to Alzheimer's Disease Classification

Kilian Hett[1,2(✉)], Vinh-Thong Ta[1,2,3], Rémi Giraud[1,2,4,5], Mary Mondino[1,2],
José V. Manjón[6], Pierrick Coupé[1,2],
and Alzheimer's Disease Neuroimaging Initiative

[1] University of Bordeaux, LaBRI, UMR 5800 PICTURA, 33400 Talence, France
kilian.hett@labri.fr
[2] CNRS, LaBRI, UMR 5800, PICTURA, 33400 Talence, France
[3] Bordeaux INP, LaBRI, UMR 5800, PICTURA, 33600 Pessac, France
[4] University of Bordeaux, IMB, UMR 5251, 33400 Talence, France
[5] CNRS, IMB, UMR 5251, 33400 Talence, France
[6] Universitat Politècnia de València, ITACA, 46022 Valencia, Spain

Abstract. Early diagnosis is one of the most important challenges related to Alzheimer's disease (AD). To address this issue, numerous studies proposed biomarkers based on anatomical MRI. Among them, patch-based grading demonstrated state-of-the-art results when applied to T1-weighted MRI. In this work, we propose to use a similar framework on different diffusion parameters extracted from DTI. We also propose to use a fast patch-based search strategy to provide novel biomarkers for the early detection of AD. We intensively compare our new grading-based DTI features with basic MRI/DTI biomarkers and evaluate our method within a cross validation classification framework. Finally, we demonstrate that the proposed biomarkers obtain competitive results for the identification of the different stages of AD.

Keywords: Patch-based grading · Alzheimer's disease classification ·
DTI · DWI · Mild cognitive impairment

1 Introduction

Alzheimer's disease (AD) and its prodromal phase are the most prevalent neurodegenerative disorders for the elderly people. The neurodegeneration caused by AD leads to an irreversible decline of memory and cognition abilities. One of the most important challenges is to find relevant biomarkers that could help for

The Alzheimer's Disease Neuroimaging Initiative–Data used in preparation of this article were obtained from the Alzheimer's Disease Neuroimaging Initiative (ADNI) database (adni.loni.usc.edu). As such, the investigators within the ADNI contributed to the design and implementation of ADNI and/or provided data but did not participate in analysis or writing of this report. A complete listing of ADNI investigators can be found at: http://adni.loni.usc.edu/wp-content/uploads/how_to_apply/ADNI_Acknowledgement_List.pdf.

© Springer International Publishing AG 2016
G. Wu et al. (Eds.): Patch-MI 2016, LNCS 9993, pp. 76–83, 2016.
DOI: 10.1007/978-3-319-47118-1_10

early diagnosis and prognosis of AD. Such imaging biomarkers can make easier the design of clinical trials that would allow faster development of new therapies.

Over the last years, numerous works proposed new imaging biomarkers to perform early diagnosis of AD. Among them, MRI-based methods showed that the atrophy of medial temporal lobes is one of the most predictive biomarker candidates [1]. The volume of hippocampus (HC) is now considered as an important biomarker for mild cognitive impairment (MCI), the early stage of AD. HC-based biomarkers demonstrated state-of-the-art performances in AD classification as shown in several extensive comparisons (e.g., [2,3]). Recently, advanced patch-based grading within HC or over the whole brain were explored and demonstrated competitive performance [4–7]. These studies showed that patch-based grading methods are able to detect subtle hippocampal alterations several years before diagnosis [8] and can be useful to perform differential diagnosis [9].

Besides anatomical MRI, the use of DTI has been proposed to detect the first signs of microstructure alterations. Microstructural modifications are considered to occur before the atrophy measured by anatomical MRI. Therefore, we assume that DTI could be used as an earlier biomarker. DTI-based studies showed modifications of diffusion parameters in AD patients for structures such as corpus callosum, fornix, cingulum, hippocampus [10–13]. Moreover, it has been shown that HC mean diffusivity (MD) increase is related to pathology evolution [14] and thus could be used as an efficient biomarker of AD. Recently, more advanced methods using brain connectivity have been proposed to better capture white matter alterations [15,16]. These studies showed that brain connectivity is modified in the earliest stages of the pathologies.

Contributions: In this paper, we propose to apply the grading-based framework [4] on the different diffusion parameters extracted from DTI for AD classification. To reduce the computational burden, a fast patch-based search strategy is involved in the proposed method. In this work, we propose to compare the performances of basic DTI-based hippocampal features (e.g., mean MD) with hippocampal volume to demonstrate the efficiency of DTI biomarkers. Next, we study the performance of the proposed patch-based DTI grading compared to MRI grading. Finally, we demonstrate the efficiency of these new biomarkers to identify the different stages of AD.

2 Materials and Methods

2.1 Dataset

Data used in this work were obtained from the Alzheimer's Disease Neuroimaging Initiative (ADNI) dataset[1]. ADNI is a North American campaign launched in 2003 with aims to provide and test MRI, PET, clinical and neurological measures and other biomarkers. This dataset includes AD patients, MCI subjects and elderly controls (CN). Table 1 shows the distribution of the data for each group. The data include 60 CN, 110 MCI composed of 74 early mild cognitive impairment (eMCI), 36 late mild cognitive impairment (lMCI) and 48 AD.

---

[1] http://adni.loni.ucla.edu.

Table 1. Dataset description

Characteristic/group	CN	eMCI	lMCI	AD
Number of subjects	60	74	36	48
Age (years)	73.3 ± 5.9	72.9 ± 8.0	73.5 ± 6.7	75.2 ± 8.6
Gender (male/female)	31/29	45/29	22/14	28/20

Data Acquisition: For all subjects a whole brain MRI scanning and diffusion weighted imaging (DWI) on 3 Tesla GE Medical Systems scanners at 14 sites across North America was collected using the same protocol[2]. The DWI scans were composed of 46 separate angles, 5 T2-weighted images with no diffusion sensitization (b0 images) and 41 DWI ($b = 1000 \, s/mm^2$). The DWI protocol was chosen to optimize the signal-to-noise ratio in a fixed scan time [17].

MRI Processing: T1-weighted (T1w) images were processed using the vol-Brain system [18][3]. This system is based on an advanced pipeline providing automatic segmentation of different brain structures from T1w MRI. The preprocessing is based on: (a) a denoising step with an adaptive non-local mean filter [19], (b) an affine registration in the MNI space [20], (c) a correction of the image inhomogeneities [21], and (d) an intensity normalization [22]. Afterwards, MRI are segmented in the MNI space using non-local patch-based multi-atlas methods [23]. The obtained hippocampus are segmented with the EADC protocol [24] designed for AD studies.

DTI Processing: The preprocessing of the DWI images is based on: (a) a denoising step with a LPCA filter [25], (b) a correction of the head motion using an affine registration, and (c) an affine and a non-rigid registration to the T1w MRI in the MNI space [20]. Afterwards, a single tensor model [26] is estimated at each voxel using the Dipy software [27][4]. Next, we estimate the fractional anisotropy (FA), the axial diffusivity (AxD), the radial diffusivity (RD) and the mean diffusivity (MD) within the hippocampus structure with a mask provided by the volBrain system. These measures correspond to: the degree of diffusion anisotropy for the FA, the longitudinal diffusivity along the axonal fibers for the AxD, the diffusivity orthogonal to the axonal fibers for the RD and the mean diffusivity level in the three spatial directions for the MD.

2.2   Proposed Method

It is known that AD impacts specific brain areas especially the hippocampus. It has been shown that the hippocampal atrophy estimated on anatomical T1w MRI can help to classify the different stages of AD. However, a deterioration of

---

[2] https://adni.loni.usc.edu/wp-content/uploads/2010/05/ADNI2_GE_3T_22.0_T2. pdf.

[3] http://volbrain.upv.es.

[4] http://nipy.org/dipy/.

the microstructure should precede this atrophy measured with anatomical MRI. To capture these early alterations, we propose to apply the Scoring by Nonlocal Image Patch Estimator (SNIPE)[4] on DTI images. This patch-based method estimates a map of scores representing a CN/AD likeness that reflects the amount of anatomical alterations caused by AD. Previous works showed that SNIPE provides competitive results when applied on HC [6,8]. In this paper, we propose for each subject to apply SNIPE on MD, RD, AxD and FA maps as well as T1w images. To reduce the resulting computational burden, we use the Optimized PAtchMatch Label fusion (OPAL) method, which is a fast approximate of K-nearest neigbhors search strategy designed for large 3D template library. This approach enables to perform structure grading in few seconds. Therefore, we can quickly estimate grading maps for FA, MD, AxD and RD and T1w MRI. Finally, we use the mean scores within HC mask for each grading maps to identify the different stages of AD.

Fast Patch-Based Grading: Contrary to SNIPE that computes the distance of all the patches in a neighborhood surrounding the position of the considered voxel, the used of the OPAL strategy enables to directly obtain the good approximated candidates. The patch surrounding each voxel is used to estimate the anatomical pattern similarity between the considered subject i and a training library of templates – denoted L – composed of CN and AD patients. Once the set of the closest patches K_i is obtained with OPAL, the estimation of the grading value g can be computed for each voxel x_i as follows:

$$g(x_i) = \frac{\sum_{x_{j,t} \in K_i} w(x_i, x_{j,t}) p_t}{\sum_{x_{j,t} \in K_i} w(x_i, x_{j,t})}, \tag{1}$$

where $w(x_i, x_{j,t}) = e^{-\frac{d(P(x_i), P(x_{j,t}))^2}{h^2}}$ is the weight assigned to p_t in the grading value estimation. p_t corresponds to the pathological status of the template t, the value -1 is affected to an AD patient and 1 to a CN subject. The weight function w depends on the similarity between the patch $P(x_i)$ and $P(x_{j,t})$ centered on the voxels x_i and $x_{j,t}$, respectively. This similarity is estimated with a distance measure d. We use $h = \min_{x_{j,t}} d(x_i, x_{j,t}) + \epsilon$, with $\epsilon \to 0$. For the T1w images, the distance between two patches is provided by a zero mean normalized sum of squared differences (ZNSSD) defined as:

$$ZNSSD\left(P\left(x_i\right), P\left(x_{j,t}\right)\right) = \left\| \frac{P(x_i) - \mu_{P(x_i)}}{\sigma_{P(x_i)}} - \frac{P(x_{j,t}) - \mu_{P(x_{j,t})}}{\sigma_{P(x_{j,t})}} \right\|_2^2, \tag{2}$$

where μ and σ are the mean and the unbiased standard deviation of the considered patch, respectively. The advantage of the ZNSSD is to compute a robust inter-patches distance while addressing the local inhomogeneities problem. Contrary to anatomical MRI, DTI is a quantitative imaging. To preserve the quantitative information provided by each diffusion map we use the sum of squared differences (SSD) defined as:

$$SSD\left(P\left(x_i\right), P\left(x_{j,t}\right)\right) = \|P(x_i) - P(x_{j,t})\|_2^2, \tag{3}$$

Features Extraction: Mean value of each DTI map is measured within the hippocampus masks provided by the volBrain system in the MNI space. The hippocampus masks are used to compute the average grading values. Since the features are correlated with age, we performed a correction as done in [28].

Validation Framework: The classification process is performed in a leave-one-out cross validation procedure. A linear discriminant analysis (LDA) is used to classify each test subjects. The results of each experiment are compared in terms of area under curve (AUC) and accuracy (ACC). The AUC is estimated with the *a posteriori* probabilities provided by the LDA. We carried out several experiments: CN vs. AD, CN vs. MCI, AD vs. MCI and eMCI vs. lMCI.

Parameter Settings: The grading method is computed with a training library of 80 subjects composed of 40 AD and 40 CN templates. For each voxel that belongs to the HC area 100 patches are extracted from the training templates. The patch size is set to $5 \times 5 \times 5$ voxels.

3   Results

Figure 1 shows the hippocampus segmentation, the T1 and MD grading maps for the considered groups. For the grading images, the blue and the red colors correspond to the AD and the CN similarity, respectively. As shown in Fig. 1, grading values decrease in accordance to the different stages of AD and quantify impacts of the disease in each voxel. The T1w and MD grading maps show that for the CN subject, almost all the voxels are estimated as healthy while for the AD patient the majority of the voxels are detected to be impacted by AD. The results of the comparisons between basic biomarkers are summarized at the top of Table 2. HC volume provides the best accuracy for comparisons of CN vs. AD and CN vs. MCI with an ACC of 83.1 % and 63.9 %, an AUC of 88.4 % and 69.5 %, respectively. The DTI-based features provide best results for AD vs. MCI and eMCI vs. lMCI. For AD vs. MCI the mean MD provides 72.5 % of ACC and 75 % of AUC. For eMCI vs. lMCI the mean AxD provides 66.8 % of ACC and 68.9 % of AUC.

The lower part of Table 2 shows the results of the biomarkers based on grading. The grading-based biomarkers provide better results than the basic ones for all comparisons. The best result for the CN vs. AD is obtained by the T1w grading with 87.8 % of ACC and 93.4 % of AUC. The grading of this modality also provides the best results for the CN vs. MCI with an ACC of 64.1 % and an AUC of 71.3 %. The DTI-based grading features provide best ACC for AD vs. MCI and eMCI vs. lMCI. For AD vs. MCI the RD grading provides 76.5 % of ACC and 80 % of AUC. For eMCI vs. lMCI the MD grading provides 67.6 % of ACC and 71.8 % of AUC. It is interesting to note that results obtained with basic and grading-based features are in line. In fact, T1w-based features provide better results for AD vs. CN and CN vs. MCI while DTI-based features obtain

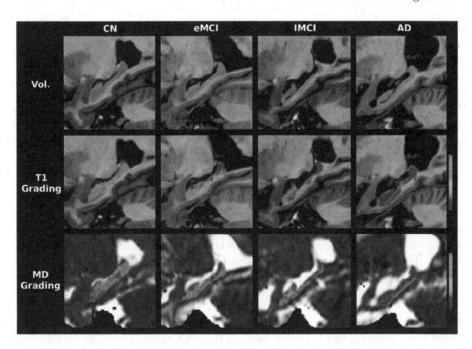

Fig. 1. From top to bottom: HC mask on the T1w images, T1w MRI grading and MD grading. For grading images blue and red colors correspond to the AD and the CN similarity, respectively. (Color figure online)

Table 2. Comparison of the considered biomarkers. Underlined results correspond to the individual basic or grading based features. Bold-faced values correspond to the best ACC over all the features. The results of each column correspond to the AUC/ACC in percentage.

Features	CN vs. AD	CN vs. MCI	AD vs. MCI	eMCI vs. lMCI
Volume	<u>88.4/83.1</u>	<u>69.5/63.9</u>	71.1/67.2	67.2/63.7
Mean FA	64.2/59.2	57.7/56.1	54.0/52.7	38.2/43.1
Mean MD	85.7/80.3	66.0/62.6	<u>75.0/72.5</u>	67.6/62.8
Mean AxD	83.5/81.4	63.5/58.0	74.3/70.2	<u>68.9/66.8</u>
Mean RD	86.2/79.2	66.5/62.3	74.8/70.5	66.0/61.5
T1 grading	**93.4/87.8**	**71.3/64.1**	82.0/73.4	68.7/66.2
FA grading	85.0/80.1	63.5/60.1	74.9/70.3	63.0/60.7
MD grading	90.6/86.5	68.8/60.7	80.4/76.3	70.4/65.8
AxD grading	91.1/85.8	68.7/59.6	80.2/73.1	**71.8/67.6**
RD grading	90.3/85.1	68.9/61.0	**80.0/76.5**	69.3/65.4

better results for AD vs. MCI and eMCI vs. lMCI. These results demonstrate the interest of DTI-based features to analyze AD evolution along eMCI, lMCI and AD stages. Recently, an advanced method based on brain connectivity has been evaluated on a similar dataset [16]. This approach obtained 78.5 % of ACC for the CN vs. AD while MD grading obtains 86.5 %. In addition, for the eMCI vs. lMCI, [16] obtained 63.4 % while AxD grading obtains 67.6 %. This demonstrates the competitive performance of the proposed DTI-based grading biomarkers.

4   Conclusion

In this work, we proposed a novel patch-based grading framework on different diffusion parameters extracted from DTI. The proposed method enables a fast feature extraction by using an optimized patch-based search strategy. We compare our new biomarkers with state-of-the-art MRI biomarkers and demonstrated that DTI grading provides efficient features for AD detection. Finally, we obtained competitive results to identify the different stages of AD. In a further work, we will study the complementarity of the grading based on T1w and DTI.

Acknowledgement. This study has been carried out with financial support from the French State, managed by the French National Research Agency (ANR) in the frame of the Investments for the future Program IdEx Bordeaux (ANR-10-IDEX-03-02), Cluster of excellence CPU and TRAIL (HR-DTI ANR-10-LABX-57) and the CNRS multidisciplinary project "Défi imag'In". This research was also supported by the Spanish grant TIN2013-43457-R from the Ministerio de Economia y competitividad, NIH grants P30AG010129, K01 AG030514 and the Dana Foundation.

References

1. Frisoni, G.B., et al.: The clinical use of structural MRI in Alzheimer disease. Nat. Rev. Neurol. **6**(2), 67–77 (2010)
2. Cuingnet, R., et al.: Automatic classification of patients with Alzheimer's disease from structural MRI: a comparison of ten methods using the ADNI database. NeuroImage **56**(2), 766–781 (2011)
3. Wolz, R., et al.: Multi-method analysis of MRI images in early diagnostics of Alzheimer's disease. PloS ONE **6**(10), e25446 (2011)
4. Coupé, P., et al.: Scoring by nonlocal image patch estimator for early detection of Alzheimer's disease. NeuroImage: Clin. **1**(1), 141–152 (2012)
5. Liu, M., et al.: Ensemble sparse classification of Alzheimer's disease. NeuroImage **60**(2), 1106–1116 (2012)
6. Tong, T., et al.: Multiple instance learning for classification of dementia in brain MRI. Med. Image Anal. **18**(5), 808–818 (2014)
7. Komlagan, M., et al.: Anatomically constrained weak classifier fusion for early detection of Alzheimer's disease. In: Wu, G., Zhang, D., Zhou, L. (eds.) MLMI 2014. LNCS, vol. 8679, pp. 141–148. Springer, Heidelberg (2014)
8. Coupé, P., et al.: Detection of Alzheimer's disease signature in MR images seven years before conversion to dementia: toward an early individual prognosis. HBM **36**(12), 4758–4770 (2015)

 9. Koikkalainen, J., et al.: Differential diagnosis of neurodegenerative diseases using structural MRI data. NeuroImage: Clin. **11**, 435–449 (2016)
10. Rose, S.E., et al.: Gray and white matter changes in Alzheimer's disease: a diffusion tensor imaging study. J. Magn. Resonan. Imaging **27**(1), 20–26 (2008)
11. Nir, T.M., et al.: Effectiveness of regional DTI measures in distinguishing Alzheimer's disease, MCI, and normal aging. NeuroImage: Clin. **3**, 180–195 (2013)
12. Wang, Z., et al.: Interhemispheric functional and structural disconnection in Alzheimers disease: a combined resting-state f MRI and DTI study. PloS ONE **10**(5), e0126310 (2015)
13. Jung, W.B., et al.: Automated classification to predict the progression of Alzheimer's disease using whole-brain volumetry and DTI. Psychiatr. Investig. **12**(1), 92–102 (2015)
14. Fellgiebel, A., et al.: Diffusion tensor imaging of the hippocampus in MCI and early Alzheimer's disease. J. Alzheimer's Dis. **26**(s3), 257–262 (2011)
15. Liu, Y., et al.: Diffusion tensor imaging and tract-based spatial statistics in Alzheimer's disease and mild cognitive impairment. Neurobiol. Aging **32**(9), 1558–1571 (2011)
16. Prasad, G., et al.: Brain connectivity and novel network measures for Alzheimer's disease classification. Neurobiol. Aging **36**, S121–S131 (2015)
17. Jahanshad, N., et al.: Diffusion tensor imaging in seven minutes: determining trade-offs between spatial and directional resolution. In: ISBI, pp. 1161–1164. IEEE (2010)
18. Manjón, J.V., et al.: volBrain: an online MRI brain volumetry system. In: Organization for HBM, vol. 15 (2015)
19. Manjón, J.V., et al.: Adaptive non-local means denoising of MR images with spatially varying noise levels. J. Magn. Reson. Imaging **31**(1), 192–203 (2010)
20. Avants, B.B., et al.: A reproducible evaluation of ANTs similarity metric performance in brain image registration. NeuroImage **54**(3), 2033–2044 (2011)
21. Tustison, N.J., et al.: N4ITK: improved N3 bias correction. IEEE Trans. Med. Imaging **29**(6), 1310–1320 (2010)
22. Manjón, J.V., et al.: NICE: non-local intracranial cavity extraction. Int. J. Biomed. Imaging **2014** (2014). Article ID 820205
23. Coupé, P., et al.: Patch-based segmentation using expert priors: application to hippocampus and ventricle segmentation. NeuroImage **54**(2), 940–954 (2011)
24. Boccardi, M., et al.: Training labels for hippocampal segmentation based on the EADC-ADNI harmonized hippocampal protocol. Alzheimer's Dement. **11**(2), 175–183 (2015)
25. Manjón, J.V., et al.: Diffusion weighted image denoising using overcomplete local PCA. PloS ONE **8**(9), e73021 (2013)
26. Basser, P.J., et al.: MR diffusion tensor spectroscopy and imaging. Biophys. J. **66**(1), 259 (1994)
27. Garyfallidis, E., et al.: Dipy, a library for the analysis of diffusion MRI data. Front. Neuroinform. **8**, 8 (2014)
28. Dukart, J., et al.: Age correction in dementia-matching to a healthy brain. PloS ONE **6**(7), e22193 (2011)

Hierarchical Multi-Atlas Segmentation Using Label-Specific Embeddings, Target-Specific Templates and Patch Refinement

Christoph Arthofer[(✉)], Paul S. Morgan, and Alain Pitiot

University of Nottingham, Nottingham, UK
lpxca2@nottingham.ac.uk

Abstract. Patch-based Multi-Atlas Segmentation methods typically transform a priori expert delineations of atlas images onto a new target image where they are fused based on local patch similarities. To improve efficiency and accuracy, we build a population template offline and a Target-Specific Template (TST) at runtime, which act as intermediate steps. At the regional level, we build a manifold for each label rather than globally, and from the deformation fields rather than from images, in order to better model the geometry of atlases and target with the aim to improve the similarity between TST and target. At the local level, we further refine the resulting weights in those areas prone to registration errors with patches sampled from the warped- and target-gray matter probability images. We evaluated our approach on the standard NIREP dataset for which it achieved state-of-the-art performance while being up to 16 times faster than competing approaches.

1 Introduction

Image segmentation plays an important role in the analysis of Magnetic Resonance Images (MRI) of the human brain and is a pivotal step to many neuroscience studies. Compared to both time-consuming and poorly reproducible manual delineation Multi-Atlas Segmentation (MAS) methods have shown to be precise and accurate alternatives. A MAS algorithm leverages a priori labelling information from previously acquired atlases each consisting of an MR intensity image and its corresponding label map, often obtained by means of expert manual delineation. These label maps are typically projected onto the target image by applying to them the spatial transformations estimated between the corresponding intensity images and the target. The resulting set of candidate segmentations can then be combined into a final segmentation with a label fusion algorithm. One way to account for registration errors and misalignment is by applying patch-based label fusion methods where for each voxel in the target a patch with a certain size around this voxel is compared to the corresponding local patches in all warped atlas images within a certain neighbourhood of the voxel of interest. While the number of necessary comparisons can be reduced by preselecting only similar patches and templates [2,12] the search can still be

© Springer International Publishing AG 2016
G. Wu et al. (Eds.): Patch-MI 2016, LNCS 9993, pp. 84–91, 2016.
DOI: 10.1007/978-3-319-47118-1_11

time-consuming. More importantly most top-performing MAS-based methods rely on the accurate alignment between each atlas and the target e.g. [3,14,18] which is usually done by estimating the non-linear spatial correspondences at runtime and is consequently computationally very expensive. For example Wang *et al.*'s joint label fusion and corrective learning MAS approach [14] and Doshi *et al.*'s method which utilizes ensembles of registration algorithms [3] to provide a more comprehensive atlas dictionary are highly ranked in the MICCAI 2012 [6] and 2013 MAS [9] challenges respectively. Although a high level of accuracy is reached they require the calculation of all pairwise non-linear deformation fields between atlases and target images with one or multiple registration methods. Just performing the registrations takes approximately 30 h per subject considering 15 atlases are non-linearly registered with SyN where each takes about 2 h on a standard PC. Others have focused on running speed, e.g. Coupe *et al.* whose approach [2] requires only linearly aligned atlases and was the fastest of the patch-based schemes implemented and tested by Wu *et al.* [17] but achieved the lowest performance. As pointed out in [8] most of the voxels incorrectly classified are in boundary areas.

One way to reduce the number of non-linear registrations at runtime is by creating an average population template from the atlases offline. The quality of the registration between target and template, and the segmentation accuracy depend on the similarity between the two images [11]. Consequently, an additional Target-Specific Template (TST) can be calculated at runtime from a selection of whole or parts of atlas images, to serve as intermediate step between the target and the population template [10]. This turns a potentially difficult template/target registration into two easier and more accurate task: (1) between the target and the TST, and (2) between the population template and the TST, which can be done explicitly, without the need for registration. The TST usually consists of a combination of the atlas intensity images most similar to the target. Those can be selected based on distances in image space, such as sum of squared differences or normalised mutual information [7], or, in more recent algorithms, on distances in manifold space [5]. Manifold distances not only make for more reliable TSTs [16] but also provide weighting factors for the fusion of the corresponding atlas label maps. The TST can be constructed from whole atlas images [4] or from parts of images [10]. The latter usually improves the similarity to the target since the TST is then assembled from those atlas parts locally most similar to the target rather than the atlas images globally most similar, with no guarantee that those would be the most similar for each label.

In order to reduce the number of direct pairwise non-linear registrations at runtime to two and reduce the number of patch comparisons while providing state-of-the-art accuracy we propose a novel hierarchical approach. Offline we construct a population template from pre-segmented atlas images and at runtime we non-linearly register the previously unseen target image to the template (Fig. 1.a). On the anatomical level, for each label, we then create a manifold embedding from the corresponding regions, extracted from the estimated atlas and target deformation fields (Fig. 1.b). The atlas regions are then ranked in order of similarity to the target region using their L^2 distances in manifold

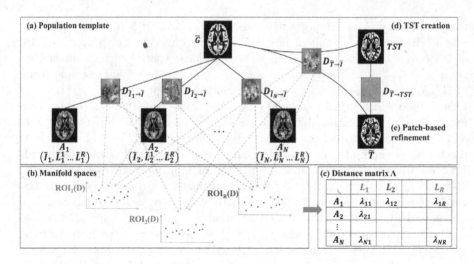

Fig. 1. Overview of our approach (please see text for detail)

space (Fig. 1.c). For each label the atlas images are then warped onto the target and a TST is constructed, to which the target is non-linearly registered. We then project the label maps onto the target by composing the deformation fields between the atlases and the population template, between the population template and the TST, and between the TST and the target (Fig. 1.d). The resulting candidate segmentations are fused using weights based on the rankings in manifold space. At the local level we apply patch-based refinement to voxels with a low probability, which is mostly the case in boundary regions and provides a second 'opinion' and another set of weights (Fig. 1.e). In addition to the probability values, we also use the intensity values of the target by comparing it to the intensity distribution determined from high-probability areas.

We detail our approach in the following section before presenting validation results on the NIREP[1] dataset [1] for which it reached state-of-the-art performance compared to registration- and patch-based methods while being up to 16 times faster.

2   Method

2.1   Pre-processing

Let us consider an a priori set of 3-D atlases $A = \{A_j = (I_j, \{L_j^r\}_{r=1...R})\}_{j=1...N}$, where each atlas consists of an intensity image I_j and R label maps $\{L_j^r\}_{r=1...R}$, with $L_j^r(x) = 1$ (maximum probability) if voxel x belongs to label r in atlas A_j and 0 otherwise. We also ensure that $\forall x, \sum_{r=1...R} L_j^r(x) \leq 1$, i.e. the label maps do not overlap.

Next, we skull-strip all atlas images, $\{I_j\}_j$ using Freesurfer and linearly register them with 12 degrees of freedom to a common space, that of the MNI152 MR

---

[1] www.nirep.org.

brain atlas, using FSL FLIRT4.1. We obtain a set of affinely registered images, $\{\widetilde{I_j}\}_j$, and the corresponding affine transformations. We then estimate tissue maps, $\{\widetilde{G_j}\}_j$, $\{\widetilde{W_j}\}_j$, and $\{\widetilde{C_j}\}_j$, with SPM's New Segment. Finally, we apply the affine transformations to the individual label maps to also bring them into the same MNI152 coordinate system: $\{\widetilde{L_j^r}\}_{r,j}$.

2.2 Estimating a Population Template

In a traditional MAS algorithm, an average population template built offline is used to establish the spatial correspondence between every new target image T and every atlas image, I_j. This is much more efficient than non-linearly regis-tering the $\{I_j\}_j$ to T at runtime, which would require as many registrations as there are atlases. Here we use SPM's groupwise registration algorithm DARTEL to iteratively create increasingly sharper population templates $\overline{I}$, $\overline{G}$, $\overline{W}$ and $\overline{C}$ from the set of affinely registered atlas intensity images and tissue maps. As a byproduct we also get a set of deformation fields $D = \{D_{\widetilde{I_j} \to \overline{I}}\}_{j=1...N}$ that precisely map each image and tissue maps to the corresponding population tem-plate. Note that DARTEL creates all three population templates concurrently, using the tissue maps to improve the accuracy of the process. Consequently, we get the same deformation fields between the atlas images and the image template as between the atlas tissue maps and their respective population templates.

2.3 Building a Target-Specific Template

We build our TST image from the atlas images combined in such a way as to satisfy the following two constraints: (a) the TST should be as similar to the target as possible, to make it easier to estimate an accurate non-linear mapping between them and (b) the mapping between atlas images and TST should be estimated directly, without the need for registration, for efficiency sake.

To satisfy constraint (a) we construct a TST locally similar to the target image by working at the label level, merging together regions in those atlas images selected for their similarity to the corresponding region in the target. We chose as similarity measure the L^2 distance in non-linear manifold embeddings of the deformation fields in those regions. Using deformation fields rather than image intensities makes for a similarity measure much less influenced by the intensity artefacts and inhomogeneities frequently found in MR images. And using label specific non-linear manifolds makes it possible to better take into account the local geometry of the atlas and target images.

Manifold Embedding. For each label r we build a non-linear manifold space from the corresponding region of the deformation fields estimated between the atlas images and the population template, and between the target and the pop-ulation template. This region, B_r, consists of the minimum set of all voxels with non-zero probability across the individual label maps $\{\widetilde{L_j^r}\}_r$, i.e. $B_r = \{x | \exists j \in [1, N], \widetilde{L_j^r}(x) > 0\}$. Note that this makes for potentially overlapping regions across labels, which has to be taken into account when assembling the TST and fusing the labels (see below). Following the recommendation of Duc *et al.* [5], we considered and empirically tested both LLE and Isomaps, and selected the latter as they exhibited the best overall results. The parameters were fine-tuned by systematically varying the number of neighbours and dimensions, as they did.

We extract the set of displacement vectors in the region from both the atlas deformation fields, $\{D_{\widetilde{I}_j \to \overline{I}}\}_{j=1\ldots N}$, and from the target deformation field, $D_{\widetilde{T} \to \overline{I}}$. The resulting sets of displacement vectors, $\{U_{\widetilde{I}_j}^r = \{D_{\widetilde{I}_j \to \overline{I}}(x) | x \in B_r\}\}_{j=1\ldots N}$ and $U_{\widetilde{T}}^r = \{D_{\widetilde{T} \to \overline{I}}(x) | x \in B_r\}$ respectively, are then mean corrected and we compute their pairwise L^2 distances to serve as input for the Isomap algorithm. For each label, we get a projection of $U_{\widetilde{T}}^r$ and of the $\{U_{\widetilde{I}_j}^r\}_j$ onto the lower dimensional manifold space. We can then calculate the L^2 distances between the target label projection and the atlas label projections and rank them. Overall, we get a distance matrix, Λ, with R columns, one per label, and N rows.

TST Construction. For each label r we warp the atlas intensity images $\widetilde{I}_{j_i}$ on the target $\widetilde{T}$ by composing $D_{\widetilde{I}_{j_i} \to \overline{I}}$ and $D_{\widetilde{T} \to \overline{I}}^{-1}$. This satisfies constraint (b) and results in a set of warped intensity images $\widehat{I_{j_i}}$, from which we extract the intensities in region B_r. Here we use the normalised manifold distances as weights for the candidate segmentations: $\omega_i^r = 1 - \frac{\lambda_i^r}{\sum_j \lambda_i^r}$ where $\sum_{j=1}^N (w_j^r) = 1$ to compute a weighted sum $H^r = \{\sum_{j=1}^N \omega_j^r \cdot \widehat{I_{j_i}}(x) \,|\, x \in B_r\}$. Finally, we assemble the TST by putting together the $\{H^r\}_r$: for those voxels which belong to more than one region, we average the intensity values of the H^r, for the others, we use the intensity value of the target image.

Figure 2 shows the same axial 2-D view cut through the 3-D gray matter tissue map of a participant from the NIREP dataset, the NIREP gray matter template, the participant's gray matter TST and the calculated deformation fields. Note how the TST is more similar to the target image than the population template $\overline{I}$, as evidenced by the visual comparison of both the images and of the magnitude of the deformation fields estimated between the target and the

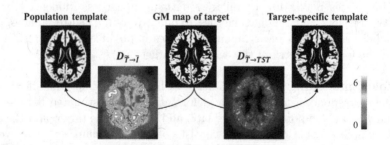

Population template   GM map of target   Target-specific template

$D_{\widetilde{T} \to \overline{I}}$ $D_{\widetilde{T} \to TST}$

Fig. 2. The advantages of a target specific template (see text for detail)

population template, $D_{\widetilde{T} \to \overline{I}}$ (bottom left) and between the target and the TST, $D_{\widetilde{T} \to \text{TST}}$ (bottom right).

2.4   Label Propagation and Regional Weighted Fusion

Equipped with a TST, we can now non-linearly register the affinely transformed target image $\widetilde{T}$ to it to get deformation field $D_{\widetilde{T} \to \text{TST}}$ using SPM's DARTEL in a non-iterative fashion, for maximum efficiency. Since the TST is very similar to $\widetilde{T}$, this non-linear registration should be very accurate.

For each label r we then warp all individual label maps, $\{\widetilde{L_j^r}\}_j$, onto the target by using the composed transformation $D_{\widetilde{T} \to \text{TST}} \circ D_{\text{TST} \to \overline{I}} \circ D_{\widetilde{I_j} \to \overline{I}}^{-1}$ and trilinear interpolation to get N candidate segmentations $\{\widehat{L_j^r}\}_{j=1 \ldots N}$.

We then use a local fusion strategy and compute the weighted sum of the candidate segmentations for each label, with the same weights we used for TST construction: $\widehat{L^r} = \sum_{j=1}^{N} \omega_j^r \cdot \widehat{L_j^r}$. We project those back onto the space of the input target image, by applying the inverse of the previously estimated affine transformation using trilinear interpolation.

2.5   Local Refinement and Thresholding the Probabilistic Segmentations

For all voxels x with a probability smaller than a predefined threshold $\widehat{L^r}(x) < \delta$ we recalculate their weights locally. We compare the patch around each of the selected voxels to the corresponding patches in the warped GM atlas images by calculating the sum of squared differences. Based on these results more accurate weights can be calculated similarly to the weight calculation in 2.2. For all voxels larger than the threshold the previously acquired weights are used.

Finally, we threshold them so they can be compared against ground truth delineations. We consider the intensity values of the target and similarly to Doshi et al.'s approach [3] we check whether the intensity of a voxel falls within the intensity distribution estimated from those areas of the target image with a probability of at least 90 % of the maximum probability: $Y = \{x | \widehat{L^r}(x) > 0.9 \cdot max(\widehat{L^r})\}$.

3   Results

We evaluated our method on the NIREP-NA0 dataset and compared its performance against results reported in the literature. Based on empirical tests we used 7 dimensions and a neighbourhood of size 7 for the Isomap embedding in all experiments. We set the threshold for the patch-based refinement to a probability of 0.4 and used a patch size of $7 \times 7 \times 7$.

The NIREP dataset comprises 16 T1-weighted MR images of the whole brain and their corresponding label maps with 32 manually annotated labels each. The dataset was randomly split up in multiple sets of 3 images for testing and 13 images for training. For each set a population template was created from the respective training images.

Our approach achieved a mean Dice coefficient of $81.26 \pm 1.85\%$ and required approximately 1.5 h per image with 32 ROIs.

This compares very favourably against the registration-based method by Doshi *et al.* [3], the top-performer on the MICCAI 2013 challenge. Their best result is $80.95 \pm 1.79\%$ and they required 14 pairwise non-linear registrations per target, 7 with each of the two registration methods (ANTS, DRAMMS), and used a similar intensity refinement method. In contrast our method required only two non-linear registrations per target.

We also outperform the recently published patch-based iterative approach by Wang *et al.* [15] who reached $77.45 \pm 3.39\%$. Wu *et al.* [17], who implemented three patch-based methods, their own as well as that by Coupe *et al.* [2] and by Rousseau *et al.* [12] reported Dice scores of $73.37 \pm 3.25\%$, $74.58 \pm 2.87\%$ and $76.33 \pm 2.25\%$ respectively, all inferior to ours. For a typical ROI, runtimes for those methods were 10 min, 28 min and 45 min respectively resulting in an approximate minimum runtime of 5.3 h and maximum of 24 h for all ROIs, which is in strong contrast to our 1.5h. The sparse patch-based method by Zhang *et al.* achieved 75.6% and the recently proposed forward and backward patch-based method by Sun *et al.* [13] reached 77.06%, both inferior to ours. The performance of our method is however slightly inferior to the results by Wu [18] with 82.7% who used pairwise deformable registrations and joint probabilities, but required 7.7 h per target. Similarly in [2] the use of ANTs and STAPLE, which are both very time-consuming, reached a Dice overlap of 82.3%.

4 Conclusion

We presented a novel multi-atlas segmentation approach using label-specific non-linear manifolds of deformation fields to build target-specific templates even more similar to the segmentation targets. This allows for a more accurate propagation of the labels with only 2 non-linear registrations at runtime. Furthermore it provides a first set of weights for the fusion which allows an already good estimate of the labels which requires only minimal refinement in boundary areas. This made it possible to achieve (a) efficiency, since it only requires 2 non-linear registrations at runtime and (b) accuracy since it displayed excellent performance in our validation tests. We are currently working on improvements to the label fusion algorithm and on a theoretically sound framework for the selection of the optimal number of atlases to be combined in the TST.

References

1. Christensen, G.E., Geng, X., Kuhl, J.G., Bruss, J., Grabowski, T.J., Pirwani, I.A., Vannier, M.W., Allen, J.S., Damasio, H.: Introduction to the non-rigid image registration evaluation project (NIREP). In: Pluim, J.P.W., Likar, B., Gerritsen, F.A. (eds.) WBIR 2006. LNCS, vol. 4057, pp. 128–135. Springer, Heidelberg (2006). doi:10.1007/11784012_16

2. Coupé, P., Manjón, J.V., Fonov, V., Pruessner, J., Robles, M., Collins, D.L.: Patch-based segmentation using expert priors: application to hippocampus and ventricle segmentation. NeuroImage **54**(2), 940–954 (2011)
3. Doshi, J., Erus, G., Ou, Y., Resnick, S.M., Gur, R.C., Gur, R.E., Satterthwaite, T.D., Furth, S., Davatzikos, C.: Muse: multi-atlas region segmentation utilizing ensembles of registration algorithms and parameters, and locally optimal atlas selection. NeuroImage **127**, 186–195 (2016)
4. Gao, Q., Tong, T., Rueckert, D., Edwards, P.: Multi-atlas propagation via a manifold graph on a database of both labeled and unlabeled images. In: Proceedings of SPIE 9035, pp. 90350A–90350A-7 (2014)
5. Duc, H.A.K., Modat, M., Leung, K.K., Cardoso, M.J., Barnes, J., Kadir, T., Ourselin, S.: Using manifold learning for atlas selection in multi-atlas segmentation. PLoS ONE **8**(8), e70059 (2013)
6. Landman, B.A., Warfield, S.K. (eds.) MICCAI 2012 Workshop on Multi-Atlas Labeling (2012)
7. Lötjönen, J.M., Wolz, R., Koikkalainen, J.R., Thurfjell, L., Waldemar, G., Soininen, H., Rueckert, D.: Fast and robust multi-atlas segmentation of brain magnetic resonance images. NeuroImage **49**(3), 2352–2365 (2010)
8. Ma, G., Gao, Y., Wu, G., Wu, L., Shen, D.: Nonlocal atlas-guided multi-channel forest learning for human brain labeling. Med. Phys. **43**(2), 1003–1019 (2016)
9. Marcus, D.S., Fotenos, A.F., Csernansky, J.G., Morris, J.C., Buckner, R.L.: Open access series of imaging studies: longitudinal MRI data in nondemented and demented older adults. J. Cogn. Neurosci. **22**(12), 2677–2684 (2010)
10. Ramus, L., Malandain, G., et al.: Multi-atlas based segmentation: application to the head and neck region for radiotherapy planning. In: MICCAI Workshop Medical Image Analysis for the Clinic-A Grand Challenge, pp. 281–288 (2010)
11. Rohlfing, T., Brandt, R., Menzel Jr., R., Maurer, C.R.: Evaluation of atlas selection strategies for atlas-based image segmentation with application to confocal microscopy images of bee brains. NeuroImage **21**(4), 1428–1442 (2004)
12. Rousseau, F., Habas, P., Studholme, C.: A supervised patch-based approach for human brain labeling. IEEE Trans. Med. Imaging **30**(10), 1852–1862 (2011)
13. Sun, L., Zu, C., Zhang, D.: Reliability guided forward and backward patch-based method for multi-atlas segmentation. In: Coupé, G., et al. (eds.) Patch-MI 2015. LNCS, vol. 9467, pp. 128–136. Springer, Heidelberg (2015). doi:10.1007/978-3-319-28194-0_16
14. Wang, H., Avants, B., Yushkevich, P.A.: Grand challenge on multi-atlas segmentation: a combined joint label fusion and corrective learning approach. In: Landman, B.A., Warfield, S.K. (eds.) MICCAI 2012, pp. 91–94. Springer, Berlin (2012)
15. Wang, Q., Wu, G., Kim, M.-J., Zhang, L., Shen, D.: Interactive registration and segmentation for multi-atlas-based labeling of brain MR Image. In: Yi, S., et al. (eds.) CCCV 2015. CCIS, vol. 546, pp. 240–248. Springer, Heidelberg (2015). doi:10.1007/978-3-662-48558-3_24
16. Wolz, R., Aljabar, P., Hajnal, J.V., Hammers, A., Rueckert, D.: Leap: learning embeddings for atlas propagation. NeuroImage **49**(2), 1316–1325 (2010)
17. Wu, G., Wang, Q., Daoqiang, S.: Robust patch-based multi-atlas labeling by joint sparsity regularization. In: MICCAI 2012 Workshop STMI, pp. 91–94 (2012)
18. Wu, G., Wang, Q., Zhang, D., Nie, F., Huang, H., Shen, D.: A generative probability model of joint label fusion for multi-atlas based brain segmentation. Med. Image Anal. **18**(6), 881–890 (2014)

HIST: HyperIntensity Segmentation Tool

Jose V. Manjón[1], Pierrick Coupé[2,3(✉)], Parnesh Raniga[4], Ying Xia[4],
Jurgen Fripp[4], and Olivier Salvado[4]

[1] Instituto de Aplicaciones de las Tecnologías de la Información y de las
Comunicaciones Avanzadas, Universitat Politècnica de València,
Camino de Vera s/n, 46022 Valencia, Spain
[2] Univ. Bordeaux, LaBRI, UMR 5800, PICTURA, F-33400 Talence, France
pierrick.coupe@labri.fr
[3] CNRS, LaBRI, UMR 5800, PICTURA, F-33400 Talence, France
[4] Australian e-Health Research Centre, CSIRO, Brisbane, QLD 4029, Australia

Abstract. Accurate quantification of white matter hyperintensities (WMH) from
MRI is a valuable tool for studies on ageing and neurodegeneration. Reliable
automatic extraction of WMH biomarkers is challenging, primarily due to their
heterogeneous spatial occurrence, their small size and their diffuse nature. In this
paper, we present an automatic and accurate method to segment these lesions that
is based on the use of neural networks and an overcomplete strategy. The proposed method was compared to other related methods showing competitive and
reliable results in two different neurodegenerative datasets.

1 Introduction

White matter hyperintensities (WMH) are regions of increased MR signal in
T2-Weighted (T2W) and FLuid Attenuated Inversion Recovery (FLAIR) images that
are distinct from cavitations. The role of WMH have been extensively studied in
normal ageing, cerebrovascular disease and dementia. The presence, topography and
volume of WMH is used as biomarkers for stroke, small vessel cerebrovascular disease
(CVD), dementia [1] and in multiple sclerosis (MS) [2]. In order to utilize WMH as a
biomarker of cerebrovascular health, they need to be segmented and quantified in terms
of volume and localization.

Manual segmentation of WMH is a demanding process requiring trained observers
and several hours per image for manual delineation by an expert. Moreover, manual
segmentation is prone to inter and intra-observer variability. With many large clinical
studies being conducted into ageing, cerebrovascular disease and dementia, the need
for robust, repeatable and automated techniques for the segmentation of WMH is
essential. Over the years, several methods have been proposed for the automated
segmentation of WMH in cerebrovascular disease and in multiple sclerosis.

Broadly, these methods can be classified into supervised and unsupervised.
Supervised methods require a training dataset where manual labels for the WMH are
available. Unsupervised methods rely on features and/or domain knowledge together
with clustering type approaches. Among them, the lesion growth algorithm
(LGA) available in the lesion segmentation toolbox (LST) is widely used [3]. LGA

© Springer International Publishing AG 2016
G. Wu et al. (Eds.): Patch-MI 2016, LNCS 9993, pp. 92–99, 2016.
DOI: 10.1007/978-3-319-47118-1_12

requires both T1W and FLAIR images to first compute a map of possible lesions and then to use these candidates as seeds to segment entire lesions. Also included in the LST toolbox, there is a newer method called lesion prediction algorithm (LPA) that only requires FLAIR images as input. Besides, the LTS toolbox, Weiss *et al.* [4] proposed a dictionary learning-based approach that segments lesions as outliers from a projection of the dataset onto a normative dictionary. Other popular unsupervised approaches use either clustering approaches such as fuzzy c-means [5] or heuristics on histograms of the T2W or FLAIR images [6]. While unsupervised methods should be preferred since not requiring a training set, in practice the free parameters need to be trained on each dataset to get optimum results.

Supervised methods for WMH segmentation typically involve machine learning methods at a voxel level with pre and post processing steps to improve the sensitivity and specificity of the results. Such machine learning approaches have included for example random forests [7], artificial neural networks [8] or multiatlas patch-based label fusion methods [9]. All these methods are trained on mono and multi-spectral normalized neighborhood voxel intensities within a standardized anatomical coordinates. Although the proposed feature involved neighborhood information (e.g., patch), these methods performed classification step at the voxel level. Therefore, by performing voxel-wise classification these methods ignore the inherent spatial correlation in lesions what results in lower segmentation performance.

To overcome the lack of local consistency of methods performing voxel-wise classification, we propose an automatic pipeline for FLAIR hyperintense lesion segmentation that performs patch-wise lesions segmentation in an over-complete manner. This pipeline benefits from some preprocessing steps aimed at improving the image quality and to locate it in a standardized geometrical and intensity space. Finally an over-complete Neural network classifier is used to segment the lesions. The proposed method is compared to related state-of-the-art methods and shows competitive results.

2 Materials and Methods

The aim of the proposed method is to automatically segment the hyperintense lesions visible on MR FLAIR brain images. The proposed method first preprocesses the images to improve their quality and to locate them into a standardized geometric and intensity space to take benefit of the redundant information among the images. Then preprocessed images and the corresponding label maps are used to train a neural network classifier.

Preprocessing

Denoising: The Spatially Adaptive Non-local Means Filter was applied to reduce the noise in the images. This filter was chosen because it is able to automatically deal with both stationary and spatially varying noise levels [10]. *MNI affine registration*: All the images have to be translated into a common coordinate space so the anatomy within the case to be segmented and the library cases is consistent. To this end, the images were linearly registered (affine transform) to the Montreal Neurological Institute (MNI) space using the MNI152 template. This was performed using the Advanced

Normalization Tools (ANTs) [11]. *Inhomogeneity correction and Brain extraction*: SPM12 was used to remove the inhomogeneity of the images and to provide a rough segmentation of the brain tissues [12]. A binary brain mask was estimated by summing grey matter, white matter probability maps and thresholding at 0.5. The resulting binary mask was further refined by applying an opening morphological operation (using a $5 \times 5 \times 5$ voxel kernel). *Intensity normalization*: The estimated brain mask was used to select only brain voxels. The resulting volume was intensity standardized by dividing all brain voxels by the median intensity of the brain region.

Supervised Classification. Once the images have been located in a common geometric and intensity space we train a neural network to automatically segment the lesions. This is done in two steps: (1) Region Of Interest (ROI) selection and (2) Network training.

ROI selection: After brain extraction, we can just focus on brain voxels to locate the lesions. However, the brain region has millions of voxels and only small amount of them belong to lesions. As lesions in FLAIR images are hyperintense a simple thresholding allows preselecting a ROI containing mainly voxels belonging to lesions. We used a global threshold of 1.25 as it was found to be optimal in our experiments.

Neural Network training: After ROI selection, the selected ROI contains a mixture of normal tissue and lesion voxels. To segment only lesion voxels a neural network was trained using a library of preprocessed FLAIR images and the corresponding labeled images only patches belonging to their corresponding ROIs were used as training set).

- *Features*: The features used to train the network are a 3D patch around the voxel to be classified, the x, y and z voxel coordinates in MNI space and a value representing the *apriori* lesion probability obtained from a map computed averaging all training label maps in the MNI space (convolved with a Gaussian kernel (5 mm)). We used squared patch intensities to enhance the contrast between the lesions and the surrounding white matter. In our experiments we used a patch size of $3 \times 3 \times 3$ voxel that leads to a total number of 31 features.
- *Network topology*: A classic multilayer perceptron was used. Two different settings were tested, voxel-wise and patch-wise. In the first case the network that we used had $31 \times 27 \times 1$ neurons (one hidden layer). In the second case, we used a $31 \times 54 \times 27$ network (labeling the whole patch rather just the central voxel). In this case an overcomplete approach was used so each voxel has contributions from several adjacent patches. This was done to enforce the final label regularity.

As a final step, the resulting lesion mask is mapped back to the native space by applying the corresponding inverse affine transform. Given a new case to be segmented, we first preprocess it following the previously described steps. Then, we apply the trained neural network over the ROI selection. Finally, the obtained the lesion mask is registered back to the image native space. The total processing time of the full pipeline takes around 3 min. We called the proposed method HIST (for Hyperintense Segmentation Tool).

3   Experiments and Results

All experiments were performed using MATLAB 2015a and its neural network toolbox on a standard PC (intel i7 6700 and 16 GB RAM) running Windows 10. For our experiments we used two different datasets consisting in T1 and FLAIR cases with their corresponding manual lesion segmentations.

Data Description

AIBL Dataset: In this work, we used a set of 128 subjects (including a wide range of white matter lesion severity, aged 38.6-92.1, male/female: 60/68) selected from the Australian Imaging Biomarkers and Lifestyle (AIBL) study (www.aibl.csiro.au) [13]. FLAIR scans were acquired for all the subjects on a 3T Siemens Magnetom TrioTim scanner using the following parameters: TR/TE: 6000/421 ms, flip angle: 120°, TI: 2100 ms, slice thickness: 0.90 mm, image matrix: 256 × 240, in-plane spacing: 0.98 mm. The ground truth for training and evaluating the proposed method was generated by manual delineation of the hyperintense lesions from all the FLAIR images by PR using MRIcro. Lesion boundaries were delineated on axial slices after bias correction and anisotropic diffusion smoothing.

MICCAI Dataset: To further validate our proposed method, we used a publically available clinical dataset provided by the MS lesion segmentation challenge at MICCAI 2008 [14]. As done in [3] we focused on the 20 available training cases. The data comes originally from the Children's Hospital Boston (CHB) and the University of North Carolina (UNC). Although there are available T1 and FLAIR images in this dataset we used just the FLAIR.

AIBL Dataset Results. The AIBL dataset (N = 128) was split in two subsets, one for training (N = 68) and one for testing (N = 60). Several neural network configurations were trained using the training subset and later applied to the testing subset. To measure the quality of the proposed method we used the Dice coefficient, sensitivity, specificity and volume correlation coefficient.

First, we measured the results using only the selected ROI as final segmentation to figure out how many outliers were included in the initial ROI. The average dice coefficient for our simple ROI selection procedure was 0.5960 ± 0.1597, a sensitivity of 0.7237, a specificity of 0.9995 and volume correlation of 0.9828. As can be noticed just a simple thresholding gives a relatively high dice coefficient although at the expense of having a large number of false positives.

Second we optimized the voxel-wise neural network (selecting randomly 20000 samples out of the full almost 1.000.000 samples training set). In this case, the average dice coefficient was 0.6447 ± 0.1477, a sensitivity of 0.9188, a specificity of 0.9995 and volume correlation of 0.9921. As seen, the neural network was able to leverage the results by removing many false positives (but also added some false negatives).

Finally, we also optimized the patch-wise neural network. In this case, the average dice coefficient was 0.7521 ± 0.1201, a sensitivity of 0.8171, a specificity of 0.9997 and volume correlation of 0.99. This overcomplete patch-wise version was able to further improve the dice results providing also very regular masks.

Table 1. Mean dice coefficient. Best results in bold.

Method	Lesion size*			
	Small	Medium	Big	All
LST-LGA	0.4518 ± 0.1531	0.6685 ± 0.0696	0.7668 ± 0.0406	0.6261 ± 0.1596
LST-LPA	0.4973 ± 0.1688	0.7102 ± 0.0983	0.7886 ± 0.0679	0.6637 ± 0.1669
HIST	**0.6441 ± 0.1449**	**0.7764 ± 0.0587**	**0.8423 ± 0.0399**	**0.7521 ± 0.1201**

Table 2. Volume correlation. Best results in bold.

Method	Lesion size*			
	Small	Medium	Big	All
LST-LGA	0.7712	0.8841	0.9732	0.9836
LST-LPA	**0.8178**	0.7690	0.9649	0.9736
HIST	0.7882	**0.8877**	**0.9849**	**0.9900**

*Small (<4 ml), medium (4 ml to 18 ml), big (>18 ml).

Comparison with Other Methods. We compared HIST method with related state-of-the-art methods to assess its quality. We compared the proposed method with the two methods included in the LST toolbox (http://www.applied-statistics.de/lst.html). The first was the LGA method that uses both T1W and FLAIR images [5] and the second was the LPA that only requires a FLAIR image to perform the lesion segmentation. In Table 1 the dice coefficient for these methods and for different lesion sizes is presented. In Table 2 the volume correlation is also presented showing that

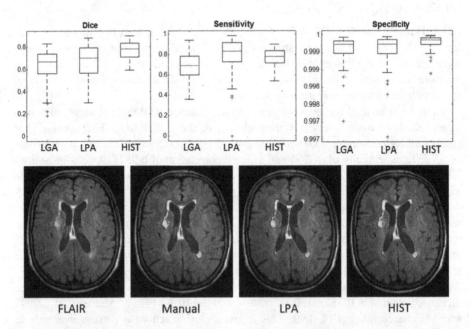

Fig. 1. AIBL dataset example results. In the upper row: dice, Sensitivity and specificity. In the lower row: a visual example of LPA and HIST segmentation results.

HIST method has a stronger volume correlation (0.99). Finally, Fig. 1 shows the boxplot graphs of dice, sensitivity, specificity and an example of the segmentation results.

MICCAI 2008 Dataset Results. We compared the results of the proposed approach with a recent method that was applied to the same dataset [4]. In this case we used the same metrics used in Weiss paper (i.e. True Positive Rate (TPR), Positive Predictive Value (PPV) and Dice coefficient). In Table 3 the results of this comparison are presented. As can be noticed, HIST method obtained the best results overall for the 3 metrics showing that the features learned on AIBL dataset were useful to segment lesions in other datasets.

Table 3. MICCAI 2008 train dataset results. Best results in bold.

Method	Weiss2013			HIST		
Case	TPR	PPV	Dice	TPR	PPV	Dice
UNC01	**0.33**	**0.29**	**0.31**	0.18	0.28	0.22
UNC02	**0.54**	0.51	**0.53**	0.39	**0.66**	0.49
UNC03	**0.64**	0.27	**0.38**	0.25	**0.32**	0.28
UNC04	**0.40**	0.51	0.45	**0.40**	**0.69**	**0.51**
UNC05	0.25	0.10	0.16	**0.62**	**0.31**	**0.41**
UNC06	**0.13**	**0.55**	**0.20**	0.09	0.20	0.12
UNC07	**0.44**	0.23	0.30	0.24	**0.72**	**0.36**
UNC08	**0.43**	0.13	0.20	0.30	**0.16**	**0.21**
UNC09	**0.69**	0.06	0.11	0.50	**0.37**	**0.42**
UNC10	0.43	0.23	0.30	**0.46**	**0.46**	**0.46**
CHB01	**0.60**	0.58	**0.59**	0.48	**0.68**	0.56
CHB02	0.27	**0.45**	**0.34**	**0.65**	0.20	0.31
CHB03	0.24	**0.56**	0.34	**0.48**	0.33	**0.39**
CHB04	0.27	**0.66**	0.38	**0.72**	0.49	**0.58**
CHB05	0.29	0.33	0.31	0.39	**0.50**	**0.44**
CHB06	0.10	0.36	0.16	**0.41**	**0.37**	**0.39**
CHB07	0.14	0.48	0.22	**0.51**	**0.50**	**0.51**
CHB08	0.21	**0.73**	0.32	**0.50**	0.47	**0.49**
CHB09	0.05	**0.22**	0.08	**0.40**	0.14	**0.21**
CHB010	0.15	0.12	0.13	**0.66**	**0.16**	**0.26**
All	0.33	0.37	0.29	**0.43**	**0.40**	**0.38**
All UNC	**0.43**	0.29	0.29	0.34	**0.42**	**0.35**
All CHB	0.23	**0.45**	0.29	**0.52**	0.39	**0.41**

4 Discussion

In this paper we presented a new method for hyperintense lesion segmentation based on an overcomplete patch-wise neural network strategy. We have shown that the overcomplete approach significantly improved the voxel-wise network by enforcing the regularity of the output masks and also by minimizing the variance of the classification error due to the aggregation of many patch contributions. The proposed method not only provided the best classification results in the comparative but also provided the higher volume correlation (0.99) which indicates that it can be used for fully automated lesion load assessment. Finally, HIST method was used on an independent dataset giving very competitive results demonstrating the generality of the proposed approach.

Acknowledgements. This research has been done thanks to the Australian distinguished visiting professor grant and the Spanish "Programa de apoyo a la investigación y desarrollo (PAID-00-15)" of the Universidad Politécnica de Valencia. This study has been carried out with support from the French State, managed by the French National Research Agency in the frame of the Investments for the future Program IdEx Bordeaux (ANR-10-IDEX-03-02, HL-MRI Project), Cluster of excellence CPU and TRAIL (HR-DTI ANR-10-LABX-57) and the CNRS multidisciplinary project "Défi imag'In".

References

1. Debette, S., Markus, H.S.: The clinical importance of white matter hyperintensities on brain magnetic resonance imaging: systematic review and meta-analysis. BMJ **341**, c3666 (2010)
2. Filippi, M., Rocca, M.A.: MR imaging of multiple sclerosis. Radiology **259**, 659–681 (2011)
3. Schmidt, P., Gaser, C., Arsic, M., Buck, D., Förschler, A., Berthele, A., Hoshi, M., Ilg, R., Schmid, V.J., Zimmer, C., Hemmer, B., Mühlau, M.: An automated tool for detection of FLAIR-hyperintense white-matter lesions in Multiple Sclerosis. NeuroImage **59**, 3774–3783 (2012)
4. Weiss, N., Rueckert, D., Rao, A.: Multiple sclerosis lesion segmentation using dictionary learning and sparse coding. Med. Image Comput. Comput. Assist. Interv. **16**, 735–742 (2013)
5. Admiraal-Behloul, F., et al.: Fully automatic segmentation of white matter hyperintensities in MR images of the elderly. NeuroImage **28**, 607–617 (2005)
6. Jack, C.R., O'Brien, P.C., Rettman, D.W., Shiung, M.M., Xu, Y., Muthupillai, R., Manduca, A., Avula, R., Erickson, B.J.: FLAIR histogram segmentation for measurement of leukoaraiosis volume. J. Magn. Reson. Imaging **14**, 668–676 (2001)
7. Ithapu, V., Singh, V., Lindner, C., Austin, B.P., Hinrichs, C., Carlsson, C.M., Bendlin, B.B., Johnson, S.C.: Extracting and summarizing white matter hyperintensities using supervised segmentation methods in Alzheimer's disease risk and aging studies. Hum. Brain Mapp. **35**, 4219–4235 (2014)
8. Dyrby, T.B., et al.: Segmentation of age-related white matter changes in a clinical multi-center study. NeuroImage **41**, 335–345 (2008)
9. Guizard, N., Coupé, P., Fonov, V., Manjón, J.V., Douglas, A., Collins, D.L.: Rotation-invariant multi-contrast non-local means for MS lesion segmentation. NeuroImage Clin. **8**, 376–389 (2015)

10. Manjón, J.V., Coupé, P., Martí-Bonmatí, L., Collins, D.L., Robles, M.: Adaptive non-local means denoising of MR images with spatially varying noise levels. J. Magn. Reson. Imaging **31**, 192–203 (2010)
11. Avants, B., Tustison, N., Song, G.: Advanced Normalization Tools: V1.0 (2009)
12. Ashburner, J., Friston, K.J.: Unified segmentation. NeuroImage **26**, 839–851 (2005)
13. Ellis, K.A., et al.: The Australian Imaging, Biomarkers and Lifestyle (AIBL) study of aging: methodology and baseline characteristics of 1112 individuals recruited for a longitudinal study of Alzheimer's disease. Int. Psychogeriatr. **21**, 1–16 (2009)
14. Styner, M., Lee, J., Chin, B., Chin, M.S., Commowick, O., Tran, H.-H., Markovic-Plese, S., Jewells, V., Warfield, S.: 3D segmentation in the clinic: a grand challenge II: MS lesion segmentation (2008)

Supervoxel-Based Hierarchical Markov Random Field Framework for Multi-atlas Segmentation

Ning Yu[1]([✉]), Hongzhi Wang[2], and Paul A. Yushkevich[3]

[1] Department of Computer Science, University of Virginia,
85 Engineers Way, Charlottesville, VA 22904, USA
ny4kt@virginia.edu

[2] IBM Almaden Research Center, 650 Harry Road, San Jose, CA 95120, USA
hongzhiw@us.ibm.com

[3] Department of Radiology, University of Pennsylvania,
3700 Hamilton Walk, Philadelphia, PA 19104, USA
pauly2@mail.med.upenn.edu

Abstract. Multi-atlas segmentation serves as an important technique for quantitative analysis of medical images. In many applications, top performing techniques rely on computationally expensive deformable registration to transfer labels from atlas images to the target image. We propose a more computationally efficient label transfer strategy that uses supervoxel matching regularized by Markov random field (MRF), followed by regional voxel-wise joint label fusion and a second MRF. We evaluate this hierarchical MRF framework for multi-label diencephalon segmentation from the MICCAI 2013 SATA Challenge. Our segmentation results are comparable to the top-tier one obtained by deformable registration, but with much lower computational complexity.

Keywords: Segmentation · Atlas · Supervoxel · MRF

1 Introduction

Accurate and efficient automated segmentation methods are highly sought in a range of biomedical imaging applications. The multi-atlas segmentation scheme, e.g. [10,18], has proven to be very accurate in a range of problems. Multi-atlas segmentation consists of two basic stages: *label transfer*, e.g., [8], and *label fusion*, e.g., [18].

Label transfer via affine registration to obtain global appearance matching is fast but has low accuracy in most applications. Label transfer via non-linear deformable registration, e.g., [3], leads to more accurate segmentation results by considering spatial variability of voxel-wise correspondence field, but at the cost of high computational burden. Recently, 3D supervoxels are introduced for cell segmentation by Lucchi et al. [12]. Supervoxel-based multi-atlas segmentation approaches [11,19] have eliminated the dependence of registration and have

---

This work was supported by the NIH grant R01 EB017255.

G. Wu et al. (Eds.): Patch-MI 2016, LNCS 9993, pp. 100–108, 2016.
DOI: 10.1007/978-3-319-47118-1_13

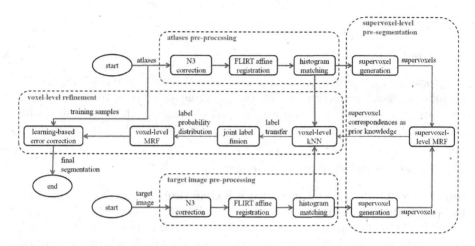

Fig. 1. Flowchart of the proposed framework. Three modules are indicated by the red titles. (Color figure online)

demonstrated comparative results in some segmentation applications. However, both kNN searching in [19] and the classification model in [11] ignore spatial relationships between supervoxels.

In order to combine the individual strengths of (1) the efficiency of affine registration; (2) the accuracy of local supervoxel matching, we propose a supervoxel-based hierarchical Markov random field (MRF) framework for multi-atlas segmentation.

Our study is inspired by the work of [7], who reformulated the problem of dense deformable image registration as an MRF model. Some similar works include [9], where Heinrich et al. use the minimum-spanning-tree-based graphical model of overlapping layers of supervoxels to represent the image domain and then use belief propagation to solve the discrete optimization.

In the label fusion stage, patch-based methods [6,16] outperform global methods due to spatially variable weight assignments, which better compensate local registration errors. Especially, [16] leverages PatchMatch algorithm [4] to approximate and accelerate kNN searching, such that label fusion becomes close to real time.

However, these methods consider each atlas weight independently and may ignore their correlations in between. Additionally, performing label fusion at the supervoxel level may not adequately capture spatial variations for optimal label fusion [19]. As a result, we derive the hierarchical MRF framework, where joint label fusion [18] and learning-based error correction [17] are incorporated into the voxel-level refinement. Joint label fusion is used to minimize bias from correlated atlases, while error correction is used to learn and compensate the systematic segmentation error made by the wrapped framework. The flowchart in Fig. 1 illustrates the framework.

2   Method

2.1   Pre-processing

All atlases and target images are pre-processed through the following pipeline: (1) inhomogeneity correction via N3 [14]; (2) affine registration to the ICBM152 template [5] via FSL FLIRT [15] with normalized mutual information similarity metric; and (3) global histogram matching [13] to the ICBM152 template [5].

2.2   Supervoxel-Level Pre-segmentation

Supervoxel Generation and Feature Extraction. We apply the same Simple Linear Iterative Clustering (SLIC) algorithm [1] as used in [11]. In SLIC two parameters are taken: (1) the region size is empirically set to 5 (in voxels) in our experiments, defining the sampling interval for initial grid-like supervoxel centers, and (2) the regularizer is empirically set to 4, defining the spatial regularization strength. As a result, ~ 5700 supervoxels are generated for the sub-region of each target and atlas MRI.

A feature descriptor for each supervoxel is constructed by combining the means, standard deviations, and histograms (with 8 bins) of voxel-wise intensity and gradient magnitude within each supervoxel. Each supervoxel is represented by 20 features.

MRF at Supervoxel Level. To implement label transfer, we compute a correspondence field between supervoxels in the target image T and in the atlas library. For a given atlas A, it can be formulated as a discrete multi-labeling problem on the supervoxel graph $\mathcal{G}_T = \{\mathcal{N}_T, \mathcal{E}_T\}$ of the target image, where each node in $\mathcal{N}_T$ corresponds to each target supervoxel and each edge in $\mathcal{E}_T$ connects two nodes that represent two adjacent supervoxels in T. A finite set of labels $\mathcal{L}$ is used to represent a discrete set of correspondence displacement vectors pointing from the center of the target supervoxel (Fig. 2, right). This set includes the zero displacement and the 26 3D lattice unit directions with lengths ρ and 2ρ, where ρ is the value of the region size parameter in SLIC (5 voxel lengths). Hence, the label set $\mathcal{L}$ contains 53 displacement vectors in total. Let $\mathcal{L}_T$ denote the set of all possible displacements spanned for all nodes in $\mathcal{N}_T$. The set of optimal labels L for all target supervoxels are simultaneously obtained by solving the second-order MRF [7], i.e., by minimizing a global energy function E taking the form: $L^* = \operatorname{argmin}_{L \in \mathcal{L}_T} E(L|T, A, \gamma) = \gamma \sum_{P \in \mathcal{N}_T} D(l_P|f_P, A) + \sum_{\{P,Q\} \in \mathcal{E}_T} V(l_P, l_Q)$, where P and Q are supervoxel indices; l_P is the displacement label at the node P; f_P is the supervoxel feature descriptor at node P; and the coefficient γ controls the relative importance of the two potentials.

We define the unary potential $D(\cdot|\cdot, \cdot)$ as the Mahalanobis distance in feature space between target supervoxel and atlas supervoxel pointed by a given displacement vector: $D(l_P|f_P, A) = dist_{Mah}(f_P, f_{A(c_P + d^l_P)})$, where the covariance matrix in the Mahalanobis distance metric is estimated by all the training

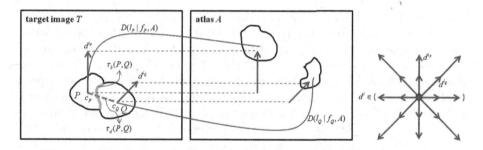

Fig. 2. A 2D diagram of the supervoxel-based MRF model.

features; c_P represents the center of target supervoxel P; d^{l_P} represents the displacement vector indexed by the label l_P; and $f_{A(c_P+d^{l_P})}$ represents the feature of the atlas supervoxel in A that covers the coordinate $c_P + d^{l_P}$.

We then define the pairwise potential $V(\cdot,\cdot)$ as the Manhattan distance in vector space, normalized by two factors, between the two displacement vectors indexed by the corresponding labels of two adjacent target supervoxels:

$$V(l_P, l_Q) = \frac{\tau_b(P,Q)}{\tau_d(P,Q)} \cdot dist_{Man}(d^{l_P}, d^{l_Q}), \tag{1}$$

where $\tau_b(P,Q) = \big|\{p \in P \,|\, \exists q \in Q, \, s.t.\, q \text{ is adjacent to } p\}\big|$ is the boundary overlap factor of P and Q, i.e., the number of voxels at the boundaries of P and Q; and $\tau_d(P,Q) = \|c_P - c_Q\|_2$ is the distance factor of P and Q, i.e., the Euclidean distance between the centers of P and Q. Figure 2 is a 2D diagram illustrating the formulation of the proposed supervoxel-based MRF model.

The proposed energy function is minimized by the Fast-PD algorithm used in [7]. After computing the correspondence field between supervoxels in the target image and in each of the atlases in the library, we assign to each target supervoxel the posterior probability of each anatomical label. This is done by simple majority voting.

2.3   Voxel-Level Refinement

Joint Label Fusion After kNN at Voxel Level. We define the relevant supervoxels are those with the posterior probability of any anatomical label more than a specified threshold (e.g., 0.1 in our experiments). Then in the following steps, we do not need to consider those irrelevant supervoxels, which greatly narrows down the search domain. For each voxel p inside the relevant supervoxels, we search its k nearest neighbors as corresponding voxels from all the corresponding atlas supervoxel domains. k equals 20 in our experiments. The distance metric is defined as the Euclidean distance between the two normalized intensity vectors (elements with zero mean and one standard deviation) over the patches with size $5 \times 5 \times 5$ centered at the two voxels respectively. The labels of the corresponding atlas voxels are transferred and fused into a consensus label for the target voxel through the joint label fusion (JLF) technique [18].

MRF at Voxel Level. JLF provides the probability vector v_p for each relevant target voxel p to belong to each label. Considering spatial smoothness, we apply the multi-labeling MRF model for the second time to satisfy voxel-wise labeling smoothness, where the label set $\mathcal{L}'$ includes all relevant anatomical labels. Mathematically, voxels inside all the relevant target supervoxels construct a graph $\mathcal{G}'_T = \{\mathcal{N}'_T, \mathcal{E}'_T\}$, where the edges $\mathcal{E}'_T$ are the four-connectivity lattice-like neighborhood system. Let $\mathcal{L}'_T$ denote the set of all possible labels spanned for all nodes in $\mathcal{N}'_T$. The energy function takes the form: $L^* = \arg\min_{L \in \mathcal{L}'_T} E(L|v, T, \mu) = \mu \sum_{p \in \mathcal{N}'_T} D'(l_p|v_p) + \sum_{\{p,q\} \in \mathcal{E}'_T} V'(l_p, l_q|T)$, where p and q are voxel indices and the coefficient μ controls the relative importance of the two potentials.

We define the unary potential negatively related to the JLF probability of a certain voxel to a certain label: $D'(l_p|v_p) = 1 - v_p(l_p)$.

We then define the pairwise potential negatively related to the absolute intensity difference of two adjacent voxels as long as they are assigned with different labels:

$$V'(l_p, l_q|T) = \begin{cases} 1 - \frac{|T_p - T_q|}{\max_{\{p', q'\} \in \mathcal{E}'_T} |T_{p'} - T_{q'}|}, & if \quad l_p \neq l_q \\ 0, & otherwise \end{cases}. \qquad (2)$$

MRF energy function at voxel level is minimized by the Fast-PD algorithm [7].

Learning-Based Error Correction at Voxel Level. As a final step, we correct systematic segmentation errors at voxel level by applying the learning-based error correction (ER) strategy [17] trained on the atlas library.

3   Experiments

We evaluate the proposed framework for multi-label diencephalon segmentation from MICCAI 2013 SATA Challenge [2], where there are 12 testing target images and 35 training atlases with 14 anatomical labels. The framework is implemented in C++ on a laptop with Intel i7 dual-core 2.40 GHz CPU and 8 G memory.

First, we test the proposed framework on the training atlas library based on the leave-one-out cross validation scheme. Accuracy is evaluated by the average Dice Similarity Coefficient (DSC) over all anatomical labels. Efficiency is evaluated by the running time per target image for each step. Results are summarized in Table 1. Here we set the optimal $\gamma = 3$ and $\mu = 2$ shown in the fine tuning curves (Fig. 3), which are not particularly sensitive to the results.

Second, we evaluate the effectiveness of MRF at supervoxel level before voxel-level refinement. We compare the proposed supervoxel-level MRF with (1) the supervoxel-level kNN method [19], and (2) the PatchMatch scheme [4] at supervoxel level. Figure 4 Left shows the boxplots of DSC over the training atlas library by the three methods. Supervoxel-level kNN completely fails on our dataset (mean DSC of 0.0093). The proposed supervoxel-level MRF obtains pre-segmentation results (mean DSC of 0.6336) that largely exceed those of supervoxel-level PatchMatch (mean DSC of 0.5516).

Table 1. Means and medians of the average DSC by each step and means of the running time (per target image) for each step of the proposed framework over the training atlas library in the leave-one-out cross validation scheme.

Steps	Mean (Median) DSC	Mean time
N3 correction	-	4 min
FLIRT affine registration	-	7 min
Histogram matching	-	1 min
Supervoxel generation	-	4 min
Feature extraction	-	1 min
Supervoxel-level MRF	0.6336 (0.6462)	1 min
Voxel-level kNN + JLF + MRF	0.8399 (0.8462)	2 min
Learning-based ER	0.8548 (0.8625)	1 min
Final DSC and total time	0.8548 (0.8625)	21 min

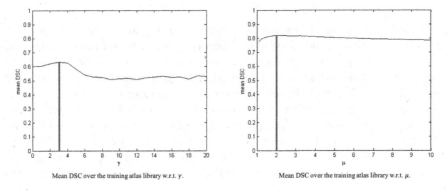

Mean DSC over the training atlas library w.r.t. γ.   Mean DSC over the training atlas library w.r.t. μ.

Fig. 3. Mean DSC over the training atlas library (in leave-one-out cross validation) with different settings of γ (Left) and μ (Right), respectively. Red lines indicate the optimal values which are also the settings in our experiments. (Color figure online)

Third, we evaluate the effectiveness of MRF at voxel level. We compare the voxel-level JLF segmentation with and without MRF. We also compare with the baseline segmentation provided by affine registration with voxel-level JLF. Figure 4 Right shows the boxplots of DSC over the training atlas library by the three methods. The proposed voxel-level MRF generates better segmentation results (mean DSC of 0.8399) than those of voxel-level JLF without MRF (mean DSC of 0.7844) and those of affine registration with JLF (mean DSC of 0.6828).

Additionally, over the testing images, we compare the proposed framework with one top-tier multi-atlas segmentation method [3] which includes the pairwise deformable registration. We also involve the random-forests-based atlas coding (Atlas Forest) [20], as another efficient method with single deformable registration (instead of several atlas-target pairwise registrations), for comparison. The implementation details and results of the compared methods are reported in

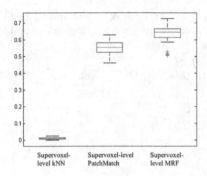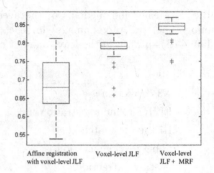

Fig. 4. Boxplots of DSC over the training atlas library. Left: by supervoxel-level kNN (left), supervoxel-level PatchMatch (middle), and supervoxel-level MRF (right), respectively. Right: by affine registration with voxel-level JLF (left), supervoxel-level pre-segmentation with voxel-level JLF (middle), and supervoxel-level pre-segmentation with voxel-level MRF (right), respectively.

[2]. Table 2 summarizes the overall performance on the same dataset. In general, our framework reaches better trade-off between accuracy and time complexity. Note that: (1) for practice consideration we use a global template for affine registration rather than perform atlas-target pairwise registration, which reduces the complexity by a factor of the atlas library size (35 in our experiment), and (2) the theoretical efficiency gain of the proposed framework is much higher than the "wall" time gain because the complexity of the registration problem over dense deformable registration is reduced by a factor of the supervoxel size ($\sim$125 in our experiment). Most of our time is spent in pre-processing and graph construction stages. **The actual time spent in FastPD is less than 5 s per target-atlas pair**.

Table 2. Means and medians of the average DSC and means of running time (per target image) by each method over the testing images. The results are reported in [2].

Methods	Mean (Median) DSC	Mean time
ANTs SyN [3] + JLF [18] + ER [17]	0.8663 (0.8786)	>1 h
Proposed framework	0.8343 (0.8421)	21 min
Atlas Forest [20]	0.8282 (0.8484)	20–25 min

4   Conclusion

In this paper, we proposed a supervoxel-based hierarchical MRF framework for efficient multi-atlas segmentation. In experimental validation, we showed encouraging performance: at the same rate of segmentation accuracy, our framework is much more efficient than one of top-tier state-of-the-art methods, enabling it more practical on large datasets or high-dimension images for clinical analysis.

References

1. Achanta, R., Shaji, A., Smith, K., Lucchi, A., Fua, P., Susstrunk, S.: SLIC super-pixels compared to state-of-the-art superpixel methods. IEEE Trans. Pattern Anal. Mach. Intell. **34**(11), 2274–2282 (2012)
2. Asman, A., Akhondi-Asl, A., Wang, H., Tustison, N., Avants, B., Warfield, S.K., Landman, B.: MICCAI 2013 segmentation algorithms, theory and applications (SATA) challenge results summary. In: MICCAI Challenge Workshop on Segmentation: Algorithms, Theory and Applications (SATA) (2013)
3. Avants, B.B., Epstein, C.L., Grossman, M., Gee, J.C.: Symmetric diffeomorphic image registration with cross-correlation: evaluating automated labeling of elderly and neurodegenerative brain. Med. Image Anal. **12**(1), 26–41 (2008)
4. Barnes, C., Shechtman, E., Finkelstein, A., Goldman, D.B.: PatchMatch: a randomized correspondence algorithm for structural image editing. ACM Trans. Graph. (Proc. SIGGRAPH) **28**(3), 24 (2009)
5. Collins, D.L., Neelin, P., Peters, T.M., Evans, A.C.: Automatic 3D intersubject registration of MR volumetric data in standardized Talairach space. J. Comput. Assist. Tomogr. **18**(2), 192–205 (1994)
6. Coupé, P., Manjón, J.V., Fonov, V., Pruessner, J., Robles, M., Collins, D.L.: Patch-based segmentation using expert priors: application to hippocampus and ventricle segmentation. NeuroImage **54**(2), 940–954 (2011)
7. Glocker, B., Komodakis, N., Tziritas, G., Navab, N., Paragios, N.: Dense image registration through MRFs and efficient linear programming. Med. Image Anal. **12**(6), 731–741 (2008)
8. Glocker, B., Sotiras, A., Komodakis, N., Paragios, N.: Deformable medical image registration: setting the state of the art with discrete methods*. Ann. Rev. Biomed. Eng. **13**, 219–244 (2011)
9. Heinrich, M.P., Simpson, I.J., Papież, B.W., Brady, M., Schnabel, J.A.: Deformable image registration by combining uncertainty estimates from supervoxel belief propagation. Med. Image Anal. **27**, 57–71 (2016)
10. Iglesias, J.E., Sabuncu, M.R.: Multi-atlas segmentation of biomedical images: a survey. Med. Image Anal. **24**(1), 205–219 (2015)
11. Kanavati, F., Tong, T., Misawa, K., Fujiwara, M., Mori, K., Rueckert, D., Glocker, B.: Supervoxel classification forests for estimating pairwise image correspondences. In: Zhou, L., Wang, L., Wang, Q., Shi, Y. (eds.) MLMI 2015. LNCS, vol. 9352, pp. 94–101. Springer, Heidelberg (2015)
12. Lucchi, A., Smith, K., Achanta, R., Knott, G., Fua, P.: Supervoxel-based segmentation of mitochondria in EM image stacks with learned shape features. IEEE Trans. Med. Imaging **31**(2), 474–486 (2012)
13. Rolland, J.P., Vo, V., Abbey, C., Bloss, B.: Fast algorithms for histogram matching: application to texture synthesis. J. Electron. Imaging **9**(1), 39–45 (2000)
14. Sled, J.G., Zijdenbos, A.P., Evans, A.C.: A nonparametric method for automatic correction of intensity nonuniformity in MRI data. IEEE Trans. Med. Imaging **17**(1), 87–97 (1998)

15. Smith, S.M., Jenkinson, M., Woolrich, M.W., Beckmann, C.F., Behrens, T.E., Johansen-Berg, H., Bannister, P.R., De Luca, M., Drobnjak, I., Flitney, D.E., et al.: Advances in functional and structural MR image analysis and implementation as FSL. NeuroImage **23**, S208–S219 (2004)
16. Ta, V.-T., Giraud, R., Collins, D.L., Coupé, P.: Optimized PatchMatch for near real time and accurate label fusion. In: Golland, P., Hata, N., Barillot, C., Hornegger, J., Howe, R. (eds.) MICCAI 2014, Part III. LNCS, vol. 8675, pp. 105–112. Springer, Heidelberg (2014)
17. Wang, H., Das, S.R., Suh, J.W., Altinay, M., Pluta, J., Craige, C., Avants, B., Yushkevich, P.A., Initiative, A.D.N., et al.: A learning-based wrapper method to correct systematic errors in automatic image segmentation: consistently improved performance in hippocampus, cortex and brain segmentation. NeuroImage **55**(3), 968–985 (2011)
18. Wang, H., Suh, J.W., Das, S.R., Pluta, J.B., Craige, C., Yushkevich, P.A.: Multi-atlas segmentation with joint label fusion. IEEE Trans. Pattern Anal. Mach. Intell. **35**(3), 611–623 (2013)
19. Wang, H., Yushkevich, P.A.: Multi-atlas segmentation without registration: a supervoxel-based approach. In: Mori, K., Sakuma, I., Sato, Y., Barillot, C., Navab, N. (eds.) MICCAI 2013. LNCS, vol. 8151, pp. 535–542. Springer, Heidelberg (2013). doi:10.1007/978-3-642-40760-4_67
20. Zikic, D., Glocker, B., Criminisi, A.: Atlas encoding by randomized forests for efficient label propagation. In: Mori, K., Sakuma, I., Sato, Y., Barillot, C., Navab, N. (eds.) MICCAI 2013. LNCS, vol. 8151, pp. 66–73. Springer, Heidelberg (2013). doi:10.1007/978-3-642-40760-4_9

CapAIBL: Automated Reporting of Cortical PET Quantification Without Need of MRI on Brain Surface Using a Patch-Based Method

Vincent Dore[1,2(✉)], Pierrick Bourgeat[1], Victor L. Villemagne[2],
Jurgen Fripp[1], Lance Macaulay[1], Colin L. Masters[3],
David Ames[4], Christopher C. Rowe[2], Olivier Salvado[1]
and The AIBL Research Group

[1] CSIRO Health and Biosecurity Flagship,
The Australian eHealth Research Centre, Herston, Australia
vincent.dore@csiro.au
[2] Nuclear Medicine & Centre for PET, Austin Health, Heidelberg, Australia
[3] The Florey Institute, Melbourne, Australia
[4] Mental Health Research Institute, University of Melbourne,
Melbourne, Australia

Abstract. Molecular brain imaging using Positron Emission Tomography (PET) is a robust diagnostic tool for which several tracers labelled with either ^{11}C or ^{18}F are available. For visual inspection of the images, cortical surface based display presents the advantage of providing a compact and more convenient visualization than volumetric scans. We have developed an automated reporting tool to display the semi-quantitative PET signal for the most common tracers without the need of a MRI. To project the PET uptake on the cortical surface, our tool uses multiple PET atlases selected by a local and dynamic patch-based method. The method was validated by comparing the surface signal computed with and without MRI. Our tool is available on-line to registered users and the processing is performed remotely (http://milxcloud.csiro.au/capaibl).

Keywords: Amyloid scan · PET-only · PET quantification · PET surface projection · CapAIBL · Patch-based

1 Introduction

During the last decade, developments in medical imaging have allowed the in-vivo examination of brain abnormalities associated with Alzheimer's disease (AD), such as β-amyloid plaques [1], cortical atrophy [2] and more recently, tau tangles [3]. ^{11}C-PIB Positron emission tomography (PET) imaging allows the detection of the neuropathology of Alzheimer's disease decades before the onset of clinical symptoms and provides invaluable insight into the development of the disease [1]. The logistical issues surrounding the short half-life of ^{11}C have paved the way for the development of ^{18}F tracers. These new ^{18}F PET radiotracers with a longer shelf life, will facilitate the use of Aβ imaging especially in remote areas. This technological advance raises the important issue of the standardization of PET processing.

© Springer International Publishing AG 2016
G. Wu et al. (Eds.): Patch-MI 2016, LNCS 9993, pp. 109–116, 2016.
DOI: 10.1007/978-3-319-47118-1_14

PET analysis typically consists in normalizing the scans to a normal scale and in quantifying the cortical uptake in specific regions. However due to the lack of anatomical information provided by the PET scan, visual reading and cortical quantification are tedious tasks that are often performed manually by a trained expert. PET images are then quantified using manual delineation of discrete regions of interest on same subject MRI scan after spatial registration with the PET.

The projection of the cortical PET uptake onto the individual cortical surface allows to better visualize and assess the patterns of targeted protein deposition or of glucose hypo-metabolism, and is then a very useful tool. However, cortical surfaces are usually extracted from individual MRI segmentation and the approach is then limited to the availability of a MRI scan which is not the case in standard clinical setups. Several PET Surface projection algorithm without the use of MRI scans have recently been developed. The advantage of these approaches is two folds; they allow to quickly assess possible pathologies but also due to the spatial normalization, individual scans can be compared with a normal population. Neurostat is widely used to assess glucose metabolism with FDG-PET [4]. However, this tool benefits from the fact that the FDG uptake in white matter (WM) is very low compared to the grey matter (GM) signal, allowing to extract the outer PET signal corresponding to the Gray matter easily. Another recent MRI-less Flutemetamol quantification was reported [5]. However, the selection of that single atlas remains an issue and affects the performance of the method. These two methods are specific to a unique tracer.

Despite varying levels of contrast and noise in PET images due to the different degrees of tracer binding affinity and pharmacokinetics, specific to each ^{18}F tracer, we have developed a tool that standardizes and universally displays the PET quantification on a brain cortical surface. The method uses multiple possible GM-WM surfaces, likely GM tissue maps, and PET scans to cover the whole spectrum of the elderly population. A subset of atlases is selected from the atlas pool using a local and dynamic patch-based selection technique. At each vertex of the cortical surface, 10 atlases are selected according to the closest "local" patch appearance [6]. Finally, we used a Bayesian framework to estimate the local weight of each atlas.

Our experiments revealed high visual concordance between PET only and MRI based surface projection; the surface projection is displayed using 8 standard views for consistent reporting. Across the 6 tracers tested, the average absolute error over the brain surface with and without MRI was 0.12, whereas the average variance was 0.018.

2   Method

2.1   Participants

Three hundred and thirty five participants from the AIBL cohort underwent a MRI and a PET scan. MR protocol has previously been described [7]. T1-weighted MRI were obtained using the ADNI magnetization prepared rapid gradient echo protocol at 3T, with in-plane resolution 1×1 mm and 1.2 mm slice thickness.

Aβ imaging was performed with six different tracers: ^{11}C-PiB (n = 113), ^{18}F-Flutemetamol (n = 66), ^{18}F-Florbetapir (n = 64), ^{18}F-NAV4694 (n = 15), ^{18}F-FDG (n = 54) and ^{18}F-Florbetaben (n = 43). PET methodology for each tracer has previously been described in detail [8]. A 20-min acquisition was performed 50 min post-injection of ^{18}F-Florbetapir (FBR) and 90 min post-injection of ^{18}F-Flutemetamol (FLUTE) and of ^{18}F-Florbetaben (FBB). A 30-min acquisition was performed 40 min post-injection of ^{11}C-PiB (PIB) or ^{18}F-NAV4694 (NAV) and 30 min post-injection of ^{18}F-FDG. A transmission scan was performed for attenuation correction. PET images were reconstructed using a 3D RAMLA algorithm.

2.2   Overview

Each new subject was processed as follow:

1. The individual PET scan was non-rigidly aligned to a common PET atlas in MNI space (Sect. 2.3). The spatially normalized PET scans was scaled using the recommended reference region for each tracers.
2. Local cortical PET profiles were extracted using the cortical surface of twenty different PET/MRI atlases in the MNI space. The construction of the atlases is described in Sect. 2.4.
3. The atlas tissue probability maps were used to estimate the cortical PET uptake for each points of each cortical surface atlas.
4. A subject-specific atlas selection was performed by dynamic and local weighting (Sect. 2.5).
5. The estimated cortical PET uptake from the selected atlases were combined under a Bayesian framework to improve the posterior probability of the estimation (Sect. 2.6).
6. PET scalars on the surface were smoothed using a Laplace-Beltrami at 6 mm.
7. The PET scalars on the cortical surface are finally compared to the distribution of healthy subjects (negative scans < 1.3 SUVR) to generate a Z-scores map for each SUVR corrected scalars surface (Sect. 2.7).
8. The final surface is used in visual reading (e.g. for clinical diagnosis) or used in population studies.

The final output from this approach is an external cortical surface (with atlas correspondence) in the PET resolution with each vertex encoding the raw cortical PET retention estimation for that particular location.

2.3   SUVR Normalization

Each PET image was spatially normalised to a PET atlas, and the AAL/IBSR templates were used to perform the SUVR scaling and neocortical quantification. The Aβ PET atlas was built using a separate subpopulation of 239 healthy controls who underwent ^{11}C-PiB and MRI as described in [7]. The population was divided in Aβ negative (N = 119) and Aβ positive (N = 118), and were used to build an Aβ negative (A_{neg}) and Aβ positive atlas (A_{pos}).

The mean atlas was first affinely registered to the target image. The Aβ PET atlas was then fitted to the PET image as a linear combination of an Aβ negative and positive atlas before non-rigid registration. The weight w was optimised by maximising the normalised mutual information between the adaptive atlas and the target.

$$A(w) = w * A_{neg} + (1 - w) * A_{pos}$$

2.4   Atlas Set Construction

Distinct atlases set should be used for different targeted molecules. Because the pattern of amyloid retentions are similar between all the different Amyloid tracers, a unique atlas was generated for all different tracers assessing amyloid deposition, while a specific atlas was used for FDGs.

Forty subjects with a PET (20 PIB and 20 FDG) and a MRI scan were visually selected based on their anatomical and PET patterns as atlases representing the population variability. The MR atlases were segmented into gray matter (GM), white matter (WM), and CSF using an implementation of the expectation maximization segmentation algorithm [7]. Furthermore, topological constraints were applied to enforce the GM to be a continuous layer covering the WM. PET and MRI atlas pairs were rigidly co-registered and all the T1w MRI were re-sampled using a non-rigid registration (nifty-reg) to a MRI atlas in the MNI space. Registration parameters were combined and used to propagate the PET scans as well as the tissue segmentations in the same normalized space.

Tissue segmentations were resampled in the PET resolution. The point spread function was first manually estimated on the PET scans and the associated smoothing kernel was further applied to all different tissue segmentations. These resulting segmentation were thresholded to the highest tissue probabilities. For each atlas, external surfaces of the WM and GM from the threshold coarse tissue segmentation were generated using an expectation maximization scheme. Due to the difficulty in getting a genus 0 coarse GM surface, we worked with the coarse WM surfaces. These surfaces were first topological corrected, using TAGLUT, registered to a common surface atlas, using a multi-scale non-rigid EM-ICP algorithm [9] and finally resampled for surface correspondence between the different atlases. These resampled WM surfaces were then iteratively inflated until intersection with the external GM surface. The resulting surfaces were 1 mm smoothed using CARET.

2.5   Local Subject-Specific Atlas Selection

For a given subject, not all of the 20 atlases were suitable for its estimation. Some atlases could be very different from the given subject due to the variation of individual brain shapes and of disease progression as assessed by the PET. Therefore, an optimal subset of atlases was selected specifically for each new subject to be processed.

The atlas selection in our approach was local and dynamic. "Local" because the selection of atlases was determined according to a local metric computed between small

PET image blocks. "Dynamic" because the optimal subset of atlases was different from vertex to vertex. In particular, for a given surface vertex, the PET image similarity between the subject and an atlas was assessed in a $30 \times 30 \times 30$ neighborhood by the normalized mutual information (NMI) [6]. The ten most similar atlas PET images were selected to generate the final estimation at the given vertex. This selection was repeated for all the vertices.

2.6 Surface-Based Measurement by Atlas Fusion

Given a PET image $I(x)$, where x denotes an image voxel, our aim was to measure the mean PET uptake in GM along the normal directions of the transformed atlas surface S^T. This is equivalent to estimating the expectation $E_{x \in \Delta}[\delta(I, x, l)]$, where $\delta(I, x, l)$ is an indicator function equal to $I(x)$ when $l = 1$. The symbol Δ denotes the intersection of the line along the normal direction of a surface vertex v and the PET image I. The symbol l is the tissue label at the voxel x, representing GM, WM and CSF with the values of 1, 2 and 3, respectively. Taking discrete x, we have:

$$E_{x \in \Delta}[\delta(I, x, l)] = \sum_{x \in \Delta} I(x) P(l = 1 | I, x) P(I, x)$$

Assuming that x is evenly sampled from Δ, the probability $P(I, x) = \frac{1}{|\Delta|}$, where $|\Delta|$ is the length of Δ. The posterior label probability $P(l | I, x)$ is estimated from the transformed atlases A_i^T ($i = 1 \ldots n$) with n the number of atlases selected in Section "Local atlas selection" by marginalizing the joint probability $P(l, A_i^T | I, x)$:

$$P(l | I, x) = \sum_{i=1}^{n} P(l, A_i^T | I, x) = \sum_{i=1}^{n} P(l | A_i^T, I, x) P(A_i^T | I, x)$$

Here $P(l | A_i^T, I, x)$ represents the GM probability at the voxel x in the atlas A_i^T which was obtained from the transformed atlas tissue maps. The probability $P(A_i^T | I, x)$ measures the chance to be well aligned at the voxel x between the target image I and the transformed atlas A_i^T. In our approach, $P(A_i^T | I, x)$ was set proportional to the reciprocal of the normalized mutual information metric estimated locally within the neighborhood $N(x)$ of x. That is, $P(A_i^T | I, x) = P(A_i^T | I, N(x))$. Due to the low resolution of PET images, the size of $N(x)$ should not be too small in order to avoid overfitting noise. In our approach, it was set big enough to cover all likely GM voxels along the line Δ. Therefore, $P(A_i^T | I, N(x))$ is constant with respect to the variable x ($x \in \Delta$).

Combining (1) and (2) gave:

$$E_{x \in \Delta}[\delta(I, x, l)] = \frac{1}{|\Delta|} \sum_{x \in \Delta} I(x) P(l = 1 | I, x)$$

$$= \sum_{i=1}^{n} P(A_i^T | \boldsymbol{I}, N(x)) \left(\frac{1}{|\Delta|} \sum_{x \in \Delta} I(x) P(l = 1 | A_i^T, \boldsymbol{I}, x) \right)$$

Equation (3) shows an additive property of our method: the estimation from multiple atlases can be attained by independent estimation from each single atlas and then linearly combined them using weights. This additive property was an advantage for our approach because the atlas set needed to be dynamically determined. The switch of selected atlases was facilitated by confining the changes to the affected atlases only.

When conducting individual estimation from a single atlas $P(A_i^T | \boldsymbol{I}, N(x))$, the PET value $\Delta(x)$ was weighted by the GM probability at x. This implicitly defined a GM region with a soft boundary, which reflected the variation observed in the training population.

2.7   Healthy Controls Distributions

For each radiotracer a set of twenty healthy participants were selected based on their neocortical SUVR. Selected individuals had a neocortical SUVR lower than 80 % of the SUVR cutoff value. Correspondence between the individual surface maps allows to generate smoothed healthy PET retention mean and variance surfaces map. Individual z-score map were computed against these distributions.

2.8   MR-Based Approach

Individual PET, MRI and coarse tissue segmentations were resampled in the MNI space. As described in Sect. 2.5, a cortical surface was generated from the coarse tissue segmentations and resampled to the common surface template. The surface resampling allows a direct vertex-wise comparison between the MRI-based and MR-less algorithms. The individual tissue probability maps were used to estimate the local PET uptake. MR-based healthy control distribution were computed using the same subjects as for the MR-Less approach.

3   Experiments and Results

To compare our method with the best case scenario, MRI-dependent method was applied on all subjects as ground truth. With the established surface correspondence, the estimates from these two methods could be directly compared.

Figure 1 shows four representative examples displaying the MRI-dependent (bottom row) and the PET-only (top row). The PET uptake map often appeared slightly smoother that the MR-based approach. Visual inspection revealed high concordance between PET only and MRI based surface projection; the surface projection was defined on 8 standard views for consistent reporting.

We also performed a quantitative analysis. The difference in PET uptake between PET-only and MR-based approached was estimated with absolute value and percentage

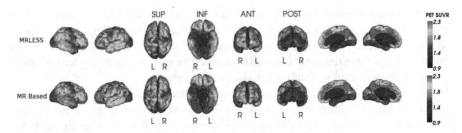

Fig. 1. Surface projection with the MR-Less and MR-based approach of the Flutemetamol cortical PET uptake

average over the total subjects undertaking a same PET scans. The two errors are defined as:

$$\varepsilon_{abs} = \frac{\sum_{i=1}^{N} \sum_{v=1}^{V} |E_{i,v}^{MRI} - E_{i,v}^{PET}|}{N \times V}$$

And:

$$\varepsilon_{\%} = \frac{2 \sum_{i=1}^{N} \sum_{v=1}^{V} \left| E_{i,v}^{MRI} - E_{i,v}^{PET} \right| / (|E_{i,v}^{MRI} + E_{i,v}^{PET}|)}{N \times V}$$

Where i is the index of a subject and $E_{i,v}^{PET}$ and $E_{i,v}^{MRI}$ are the corresponding estimations at the vth vertex.

In Table 1, "Mean MRI" and "Mean MR-Less" are the mean PET retention estimated by the MRI-dependent and PET-only methods respectively for the different radio tracers. The estimation differences were measured on the whole cortical surface. Across the 6 tracers tested, the average absolute error over the brain surface with and without MRI was 0.12, whereas the average variance was 0.018. The mean difference was always below the 5 %, which is in line with previously published results on PIB.

Table 1. Neocortical cerebellum SUVR values presented as mean +/− standard deviation for all six radiotracers.

Cb SUVR	FBR	PIB	Flute	FBB	NAV	FDG
Mean MRI	1.11 + 0.04	1.33 + 0.17	1.30 + 0.10	1.08 + 0.04	1.23 + 0.12	0.89 + 0.02
Mean MR-Less	1.13 + 0.03	1.33 + 0.15	1.32 + 0.09	1.12 + 0.03	1.25 + 0.10	0.89 + 0.01
Mean difference	0.09 + 0.01	0.11 + 0.02	0.12 + 0.02	0.11 + 0.02	0.09 + 0.01	0.06 + 0.01
Mean difference (%)	4.4 + 0.4	4.8 + 0.7	4.9 + 0.7	4.3 + 0.6	4.0 + 0.4	4.1 + 0.3

4   Conclusion

In the present study, we propose a new method to estimate PET uptake in the cortex without the use of individual MRI images. The approach has been validated on 6 different ^{11}C and ^{18}F tracers against conventional MR-based approach. The results were similar to published result of PIB quantification [6] and displayed similar accuracy for various ^{18}F labelled radiotracers. The validation was performed on a large cohort, more than three hundred participants, demonstrating the accuracy and robustness of the cortical PET uptake estimation. CapAIBL provides an efficient reporting tool for PET imaging easily accessed remotely through a web interface.

CapAIBL also allows an unbiased and standardize means of measuring the progression of Aβ accumulation and glucose metabolism. Moreover, given the current development and therapeutic trials of anti-Aβ treatments, there is a strong need for assessing their efficacy in reducing Aβ plaques in the brain as well as their effect over other markers, such as cortical thickness and tau aggregates.

Our algorithm is available on-line to registered users and the processing is performed remotely (http://milxcloud.csiro.au/capaibl).

References

1. Rowe, C.C., Villemagne, V.L.: Brain amyloid imaging. J. Nucl. Med. **52**(11), 1733–1740 (2011)
2. Acosta, O., Fripp, J., Doré, V., Bourgeat, P., Favreau, J.-M., Chételat, G., Rueda, A., Villemagne, V.L., Szoeke, C., Ames, D., Ellis, K.A., Martins, R.N., Masters, C.L., Rowe, C. C., Bonner, E., Gris, F., Xiao, D., Raniga, P., Barra, V., Salvado, O.: Cortical surface mapping using topology correction, partial flattening and 3D shape context-based non-rigid registration for use in quantifying atrophy in Alzheimer's disease. J. Neurosci. Methods **205** (1), 96–109 (2012)
3. Villemagne, V.L., Fodero-Tavoletti, M.T., Masters, C.L., Rowe, C.C.: Tau imaging: early progress and future directions. Lancet Neurol. **14**(1), 114–124 (2015)
4. Ishii, K., Willoch, F., Minoshima, S., Drzezga, A., Ficaro, E.P., Cross, D.J., Kuhl, D.E., Schwaiger, M.: Statistical brain mapping of 18F-FDG PET in Alzheimer's disease: validation of anatomic standardization for atrophied brains. J. Nucl. Med. **42**(4), 548–557 (2001)
5. Thurfjell, L., Lilja, J., Lundqvist, R., Buckley, C., Smith, A., Vandenberghe, R., Sherwin, P.: Automated quantification of 18F-flutemetamol PET activity for categorizing scans as negative or positive for brain amyloid: concordance with visual image reads. J. Nucl. Med. Off. Publ. Soc. Nucl. Med. **55**(10), 1623–1628 (2014)
6. Zhou, L., Salvado, O., Dore, V., Bourgeat, P., Raniga, P., Macaulay, S.L., Ames, D., Masters, C.L., Ellis, K.A., Villemagne, V.L., Rowe, C.C., Fripp, J.: MR-less surface-based amyloid assessment based on 11C PiB PET. PLoS ONE **9**(1), e84777 (2014)
7. Bourgeat, P., Villemagne, V.L., Dore, V., Brown, B., Macaulay, S.L., Martins, R., Masters, C.L., Ames, D., Ellis, K., Rowe, C.C., Salvado, O., Fripp, J., AIBL Research Group: Comparison of MR-less PiB SUVR quantification methods. Neurobiol. Aging **36**(1), S159–S166 (2015)
8. Villemagne, V.L., Doré, V., Yates, P., Brown, B., Mulligan, R., Bourgeat, P., Veljanoski, R., Rainey-Smith, S.R., Ong, K., Rembach, A., Williams, R., Burnham, S.C., Laws, S.M., Salvado, O., Taddei, K., Macaulay, S.L., Martins, R.N., Ames, D., Masters, C.L., Rowe, C. C.: En attendant centiloid. In: Advances in Research, vol. 2, no. 12. ISSN 2348-0394
9. Dore, V., Fripp, J., Bourgeat, P., Shen, K., Salvado, O., Acosta, O.: Surface-base approach using a multi-scale EM-ICP registration for statistical population analysis. 10.1109/DICTA. 2011.11

High Resolution Hippocampus Subfield Segmentation Using Multispectral Multiatlas Patch-Based Label Fusion

José E. Romero[1], Pierrick Coupe[2,3(✉)], and José V. Manjón[1]

[1] Instituto de Aplicaciones de las Tecnologías de la Información y de las
Comunicaciones Avanzadas (ITACA), Universitat Politècnica de València,
Camino de Vera s/n, 46022 Valencia, Spain
[2] University of Bordeaux, LaBRI, UMR 5800,
PICTURA, F-33400 Talence, France
pierrick.coupe@labri.fr
[3] CNRS, LaBRI, UMR 5800, PICTURA, F-33400 Talence, France

Abstract. The hippocampus is a brain structure that is involved in several
cognitive functions such as memory and learning. It is a structure of great
interest due to its relationship to neurodegenerative processes such as the Alzheimer's disease. In this work, we propose a novel multispectral multiatlas
patch-based method to automatically segment hippocampus subfields using high
resolution T1-weighted and T2-weighted magnetic resonance images (MRI).
The proposed method works well also on standard resolution images after
superresolution and consistently performs better than monospectral version.
Finally, the proposed method was compared with similar state-of-the-art
methods showing better results in terms of both accuracy and efficiency.

1 Introduction

The hippocampus (HC) is a complex gray matter structure of the brain located under
the surface of each temporal lobe. It is involved in many cognitive functions such as
memory and spatial reasoning [1]. It presents changes in its structure across the lifespan
related to normal aging [2] as well as to several dysfunctions like epilepsy [3],
schizophrenia [4] and Alzheimer's disease [5].

The HC is a three dimensional curved structure that has been linked to the sea
horse. The hippocampus is composed of multiple subfields that can be divided into
sections called the dentate gyrus, the cornu ammonis (CA) and the subiculum. The CA
is also subdivided in sub-sections CA1, CA2, CA3, CA4, layers alveus, stratum oriens,
stratum pyramidale, stratum radiatum, stratum lancosum and stratum moleculare. These
layers present a high neuron density and are very compact so high resolution imaging is
required to identify them.

Due to this morphological complexity and limitations of MR image resolution,
most of past studies have been performed over the whole hippocampus volume by
segmenting it as a single object [6]. These studies showed that the whole hippocampus

G. Wu et al. (Eds.): Patch-MI 2016, LNCS 9993, pp. 117–124, 2016.
DOI: 10.1007/978-3-319-47118-1_15

volume is a good biomarker for Alzheimer's disease [7]. However, hippocampus subfields have shown to be affected differently by AD and normal aging in ex-vivo studies [5].

Although high resolution MRI is becoming more accessible in certain scenarios, these data have been traditionally manually segmented. However, manual segmentation is a highly time consuming procedure which requires trained raters especially for complex structures such as hippocampus subfields. Taking about 50 h per case it is impossible to apply manual delineation to large cohort studies.

To avoid this problem automated solutions have been developed in the last years. The method proposed by Chakravarty et al. consists of a multiatlas method based on the estimation of several non-linear deformations and a label fusion step [8]. Also using a multiatlas approach Yushkevich et al. proposed a method where a multiatlas approach is combined with a similarity-weighted voting and a learning-based label bias correction [9]. In a different manner, Van Leemput et al. used a statistical model of MR image formation around the hippocampus to produce automatic segmentation [10]. Recently, Iglesias et al. pursued this work and replaced the model by a more accurate atlas generated using ultra-high resolution ex-vivo MR images [11].

In this work we propose a fast and accurate multispectral multiatlas patch-based method to segment the hippocampus subfields according to the atlas presented in [12]. The proposed method is an extension of a recently proposed segmentation algorithm called OPAL [13]. This extension integrates multispectral similarity estimation and a novel non-local regularization post-processing step.

2   Materials and Methods

2.1   Image Data

In this paper, we used a High Resolution (HR) dataset composed of 5 cases with T1-weighted and T2-weighted images to construct a library of manually labeled cases. The HR images are publicly available at the CoBrALab website (http://cobralab.ca/atlases). Both, the HR images used as input and the manually labeled validation dataset are the same as those used in Pipitone et al. [14].

To create the HR atlases, MR images were taken from 5 healthy volunteers (2 males, 3 females, aged 29–57). T1- and T2-weighted images were acquired for all subjects on a 3 T GE Discovery MR 750 system (General Electric, Milwaukee, WI) using an 8-channel head coil. High-resolution T1-weighted images were acquired using the 3D inversion-prepared fast spoiled gradient-recalled echo acquisition, FSPGR-BRAVO, in a scan time of $\sim$20 min, with the following parameters: TE/TR = 4.3 ms/9.2 ms, TI = 650 ms, $\alpha = 8°$, 2-NEX, FOV = 22 cm, slice thickness = 0.6 mm, 384 $\times$ 384 in-plane steps for an approximately isotropic resolution of 0.6 mm dimension voxels. High-resolution T2-weighted images were acquired using the 3D fast spin echo acquisition, FSE-CUBE, in a scan time of $\sim$16 min, with the following parameters: TE/TR = 95.3 ms/2500 ms, ETL = 100 ms, 2NEX, FOV = 22 cm, slice thickness = 0.6 mm, 384 $\times$ 384 in-plane steps for approximately isotropic 0.6 mm dimension voxels. Reconstruction filters, ZIPX2 and ZIP512, were also used resulting in a final isotropic 0.3 mm dimension voxels. All 2-NEX scans were then repeated three times and averaged for a total of 6-NEX. The hippocampi and each of their subfields were segmented manually by an expert rater including 5 labels (CA1, CA2/3, CA4/dentate gyrus, stratum radiatum/stratum lacunosum/stratum moleculare (SR/SL/SM), and subiculum). For more details about the labeling protocol please read the original paper [12].

2.2   Preprocessing

All the images (T1 and T2) were first filtered with a spatially adaptive non-local means filter [20] and inhomogeneity corrected using the N4 method [21]. Later, they were linearly registered to the Montreal Neurological Institute space (MNI) using the ANTS package [15] and the MNI152 template. Next, we left-right flipped the images and cropped them to the right hippocampus area so we have 10 right hippocampus crops. Note that after considering the flipped versions of the images only one of both hippocampi has to be considered otherwise we would have the same hippocampi twice. After that, we non-linearly registered the cropped images to the cropped MNI152 template to better match the hippocampus anatomy. Finally, we normalized the images to have the same mean and standard deviation as the MNI152 template and a sharpening operation (by substracting the laplacian of the image) was applied to the images to minimize the blurring introduced by the interpolation during the non-linear registration process.

2.3   Library

Multiatlas based segmentation methods are based on the use of a library of manually labeled cases. In our case, to construct the library, we processed the 5 HR images (T1 and T2 versions) as described in the previous section to finally have a 10 hippocampi library.

2.4   Labeling and Regularization

Multispectral Optimized PatchMatch (MOPAL). One of the most time consuming parts of non-local label fusion technique is the patch matching step. To reduce the computational burden of this process, we used an adaptation of the OPAL method [13] that is a 3D adaptation of the patchmatch technique proposed by Barnes et al. [16]. For more details, see the original OPAL paper [13].

In the original OPAL method, the probability maps from 2 different scales (patch sizes) were mixed using a late fusion scheme with equal weights for both scales. In this work, we learn a label dependent mixing coefficient to balance the different scale contributions per label using a gradient descend technique. Moreover, the maps returned by OPAL consist of a probability map for each label that is being considered. These maps are then processed to obtain the final segmentation by choosing the label with maximum probability for each voxel. When using a multiscale approach two probability maps are obtained for each label (one for patch size). Therefore a combination is required to generate a single probability map for each label. This step was done using a global mixing coefficient giving equal weight to every label. Given that different labels have different subjacent anatomy it is possible that different structures obtain a better segmentation from one scale than the other so we calculated an individual mixing coefficient for every label to maximize the segmentation accuracy.

We use multispectral distance computation taking into account information derived from T1 and T2 MRI in order to compute patch correspondences in a more robust manner. OPAL estimates the quality of a match by computing a distance as the sum of squared differences (SSD). This proposed multispectral distance is a balanced sum of •SSDs (one per channel) that we called multispectral sum of squared differences (MSSD):

$$MSSD = \frac{1}{M}\left((1 - \lambda)\left\|P(A_i) - P(A'_{s,j})\right\|_2^2 + \lambda\left\|P(B_i) - P(B'_{s,j})\right\|_2^2\right) \qquad (1)$$

Where A and B represent the target image for T1 and T2, A' and B' represent the libraries for T1 and T2 respectively, $P(A_i) \in A$ is a patch form image A centered on the coordinates i, $P(B_j) \in B$ is a patch from image B centered on the coordinates j, λ is a coefficient required to balance the different distance contributions and M is the number of voxels per patch.

Label Regularization. Automatic segmentations produced by MOPAL are performed at patch level. Even thou patchwise segmentation implies regularization it is not sufficient to produce smooth contours. Since hippocampus subfields are regular and layered structures, some extra regularization may help to produce feasible segmentations. To this end, the probability map (resulting from the combination of both considered scales) is regularized using a non-local means filter [17]. The final segmentation is generated by calculation the maximum probability for each voxel for all 5 structures probability maps.

3   Experiments and Results

In this section a set of experiments are presented to show the performance of the method and the effect of the proposed modifications. All the experiments have been done by processing the cases from the library described before in a leave-two-out fashion by removing the case being processed and its mirror counterpart (thus using only a library of 8 images instead of 10).

3.1   MOPAL Parameters

OPAL [13] was developed and evaluated for the segmentation of the whole hippocampus, so an optimization of the method parameters was performed. To measure the accuracy we used the DICE [18] coefficient for all the 5 structures. In all the experiments, we set the patch sizes to $3 \times 3 \times 3$ and $9 \times 9 \times 9$ voxels, for each scale respectively. The restricted search area was set to $7 \times 7 \times 7$ voxels. The number of independent Patch Matches was set to 32 and the number of iterations of OPAL to 4. The 6 scale mixing coefficients (5 structures + background) (alfa = [0.4711, 0.3443, 0.3826, 0.3900, 0.8439, 0.7715]) and MSSD balance parameters ($\lambda = 0.9$) were empirically estimated.

The multispectral proposed method was compared with the corresponding monospectral versions using the same parameters with exception of λ. In Table 1, it can be observed how the T2 based results are better than the corresponding T1 based results. This result is in line with previous studies [11]. However, T1 based performs better for CA2/CA3 while multispectral based segmentation benefits from both T1 and T2.

Table 1. Mean DICE and standard deviation for each structure segmentation using high resolution T1, T2 and Multispectral respectively. Best results in bold.

Structure	T1 HR	T2 HR	T1 + T2 HR
Average	0.6253 ± 0.0926	0.6762 ± 0.0716	**0.6957 ± 0.0651***
CA1	0.6752 ± 0.0254	0.7304 ± 0.0464	**0.7439 ± 0.0298***
CA2\CA3	0.6865 ± 0.0367	0.6468 ± 0.0642	**0.7015 ± 0.0398†**
CA4\DG	0.7129 ± 0.0319	0.7709 ± 0.0323	**0.7710 ± 0.0255***
SR\SL\SM	0.5085 ± 0.0960	0.5994 ± 0.0531	**0.6145 ± 0.0632***
Subiculum	0.5434 ± 0.0473	0.6336 ± 0.0485	**0.6476 ± 0.0406***
Hippocampus	0.8782 ± 0.0174	0.8880 ± 0.0171	**0.9011 ± 0.0097**

Significant differences between T1 and T1 + T2 are marked with * and between T2 and T1 + T2 are marked with † (p < 0.05).

3.2 Label Regularization

We performed also an experiment to measure the effect of the label regularization on the segmentation results. We optimized the non-local means filter parameters (patch size = $3 \times 3 \times 3$, search volume = $7 \times 7 \times 7$ and the smoothing parameter h = 0.02). In Table 2 improvements can be seen in almost every structure compared to Table 1. In Fig. 1 an example of the segmentation results is presented.

Table 2. Mean DICE and standard deviation for each structure segmentation using high resolution T1, T2 and Multispectral respectively. Values showing improvement with the regularization in bold.

Structure	T1 HR	T2 HR	T1 + T2 HR
Average	**0.6286 ± 0.0930**	**0.6775 ± 0.0704**	**0.6985 ± 0.0657**
CA1	**0.6788 ± 0.0252**	**0.7314 ± 0.0477**	**0.7487 ± 0.0287**
CA2\CA3	**0.6901 ± 0.0372**	**0.6491 ± 0.0638**	**0.7058 ± 0.0381**
CA4\DG	**0.7164 ± 0.0319**	0.7705 ± 0.0330	**0.7730 ± 0.0257**
SR\SL\SM	**0.5102 ± 0.0971**	**0.6032 ± 0.0558**	**0.6176 ± 0.0653**
Subiculum	**0.5476 ± 0.0483**	0.6332 ± 0.0488	0.6473 ± 0.0436
Hippocampus	**0.8806 ± 0.0178**	**0.8890 ± 0.0172**	**0.9032 ± 0.0104**

Fig. 1. Example of an HR MRI case. Figure shows T1w and T2w images and its corresponding manual segmentation.

3.3 Standard Resolution Vs High Resolution

As high resolution MR images are not widely available, especially in clinical environments, we analyzed how the proposed method performs on standard resolution images. For this purpose, we reduced the resolution of the HR images by a factor 2 by convolving the HR images with a $2 \times 2 \times 2$ boxcar kernel and then decimating the resulting image by a factor 2. As the library used in our method is located in the 0.5 mm resolution MNI space, the obtained down-sampled images were upsampled by a factor 2 using BSpline interpolation and a superresolution method called Local Adaptive SR (LASR) [19]. Results are shown in Table 3. As can be noticed, segmentations performed on images up-sampled with SR were better than using interpolation. Moreover, this experiment shows that the proposed method is able to produce competitive results when using standard resolution images.

Table 3. Mean DICE and standard deviation for each structure segmentation using the high resolution library and applying BSpline interpolation and LASR to the previously downsampled image to be segmented. Segmentation produced using the multispectral version of the method. Best results in bold.

Structure	BSpline	LASR
Average	0.6696 ± 0.0738	**0.6884** ± 0.0682
CA1	0.7247 ± 0.0382	**0.7420** ± 0.0286
CA2\CA3	0.6878 ± 0.0516	**0.7010** ± 0.0437
CA4\DG	0.7498 ± 0.0358	**0.7622** ± 0.0291
SR\SL\SM	0.5834 ± 0.0688	**0.6060** ± 0.0656
Subiculum	0.6023 ± 0.0495	**0.6308** ± 0.0442
Hippocampus	0.9001 ± 0.0102	**0.9042** ± 0.0095

3.4 Comparison

We compared our method with another recent method applied to hippocampus segmentation using the same number of structures and labeling protocol. The compared method is called MAGeT [8] and it lies on the estimation of a large number of non-linear deformations followed by a majority vote label fusion. Table 4 shows that

Table 4. Mean DICE for each structure. Segmentation performed by MAGeT and the proposed method. Best results in bold.

Structure	MAGET (0.9 mm)	Proposed (0.5 mm)
Average	0.526	**0.6985**
CA1	0.563	**0.7487**
CA2\CA3	0.412	**0.7058**
CA4\DG	0.647	**0.7730**
SR\SL\SM	0.428	**0.6176**
Subiculum	0.58	**0.6473**
Hippocampus	0.816	**0.9032**

the proposed method obtained higher DICE coefficients for all the structures. In terms of computation efficiency our method requires only a few minutes while MAGeT has an execution time of several ours per case. It has to be noted that MAGET results are computed in MNI space at 0.9 mm resolution while MOPAL results are computed at 0.5 mm resolution.

4 Discussion

In this paper we present a new hippocampus subfield segmentation method based on an extension of a recent method called OPAL. The proposed method achieves better segmentation results using an improved multiscale mixing strategy and especially a novel multispectral distance computation that enables to find better matches. Also, a post-processing step has been also added to regularize label probability maps.

The proposed method has been showed to perform well on standard resolution images, obtaining competitive results on typical clinical data. This fact is of special importance because it will allow analyzing a large number of retrospective data. Finally, it has been shown that the proposed method compares well to another related state-of-art method obtaining better results in terms of both accuracy and reduced execution time.

Acknowledgements. This research was supported by the Spanish grant TIN2013-43457-R from the Ministerio de Economia y competitividad. This study has been carried out with financial support from the French State, managed by the French National Research Agency (ANR) in the frame of the Investments for the future Program IdEx Bordeaux (ANR-10-IDEX-03-02, HL-MRI Project), Cluster of excellence CPU and TRAIL (HR-DTI ANR-10-LABX-57) and the CNRS multidisciplinary project "Défi imag'In".

References

1. Milner, B.: Psychological defects produced by temporal lobe excision. Res. Publ. Assoc. Res. Nerv. Ment. Dis. **36**, 244–257 (1958)
2. Petersen, R., et al.: Memory and MRI-based hippocampal volumes in aging and AD. Neurology **54**(3), 581–587 (2000)

3. Cendes, F., et al.: MRI volumetric measurement of amygdala and hippocampus in temporal lobe epilepsy. Neurology **43**(4), 719–725 (1993)
4. Altshuler, L.L., et al.: Amygdala enlargement *in bipo*lar disorder and hippocampal reduction in schizophrenia: an MRI study demonstrating neuroanatomic specificity. Arch. Gen. Psychiatry **55**(7), 663 (1998)
5. Braak, H., Braak, E.: Neuropathological stageing of Alzheimer-related changes. Acta Neuropathol. **82**(4), 239–259 (1991)
6. Chupin, M., et al.: Fully automatic hippocampus segmentation and classification in Alzheimer's disease and mild cognitive impairment applied on data from ADNI. Hippocampus **19**(6), 579–587 (2009)
7. Jack, C., et al.: Prediction of AD with MRI-based hippocampal volume in mild cognitive impairment. Neurology **52**(7), 1397–1403 (1999)
8. Chakravarty, M., et al.: Performing label-fusion-based segmentation using multiple automatically generated templates. Hum. Brain Mapp. **10**(34), 2635–2654 (2013)
9. Yushkevich, P.A., et al.: Automated volumetry and regional thickness analysis of hippocampal subfields and medial temporal cortical structures in mild cognitive impairment. Hum. Brain Mapp. **36**(1), 258–287 (2015)
10. Van Leemput, K., et al.: Automated segmentation of hippocampal subfields from ultra-high resolution in vivo MRI. Hippocampus **19**(6), 549–557 (2009)
11. Iglesias, J.E., et al.: A computational atlas of the hippocampal formation using ex vivo, ultra-high resolution MRI: application to adaptive segmentation of in vivo MRI. NeuroImage **115**(15), 117–137 (2015)
12. Winterburn, J.L., et al.: A novel in vivo atlas of human hippocampal subfields using high-resolution 3 T magnetic resonance imaging. NeuroImage **74**, 254–265 (2013)
13. Giraud, R., et al.: An optimized patchmatch for multi-scale and multi-feature label fusion. NeuroImage **124**, 770–782 (2016)
14. Pipitone, J.L., et al.: Multi-atlas segmentation of the whole hippocampus and subfields using multiple automatically generated templates. Neuroimage **101**(1), 494–512 (2014)
15. Avants, B.B., et al.: Advanced normalization tools (ANTS). Insight J. **2**, 1–35 (2009)
16. Barnes, C., et al.: PatchMatch: a randomized correspondence algorithm for structural image editing. ACM Trans. Graph. **28**(3) (2009)
17. Coupé, P., et al.: Adaptive multiresolution non-local means filter for 3D MR image denoising. IET Image Process. **6**(5), 558–568 (2012)
18. Zijdenbos, A.P., et al.: Morphometric analysis of white matter lesions in MR images: method and validation. IEEE Trans. Med. Imaging **13**(4), 716–724 (1994)
19. Coupé, P., et al.: Collaborative patch-based super-resolution for diffusion-weighted images. NeuroImage **83**, 245–261 (2013)
20. Manjón, J.V., et al.: Adaptive non-local means denoising of MR images with spatially varying noise levels. J. Magn. Reson. Imaging **31**, 192–203 (2010)
21. Tustison, N.J., et al.: N4ITK: improved N3 bias correction. IEEE Trans. Med. Imaging **29**(6), 1310–1320 (2010)

Identification of Water and Fat Images in Dixon MRI Using Aggregated Patch-Based Convolutional Neural Networks

Liang Zhao$^{(\boxtimes)}$, Yiqiang Zhan, Dominik Nickel, Matthias Fenchel,
Berthold Kiefer, and Xiang Sean Zhou

Siemens Healthineers, Malvern, USA
liangzhao@siemens.com

Abstract. MR water-fat separation based on the Dixon method produces water and fat images that serve as an important tool for fat suppression and quantification. However, the procedure itself is not able to assign "fat/water" labels to synthesized images. Heuristic physiological assumption-based approaches and traditional image analysis methods were designed to label water/fat images. However, their robustness, in particular to different bodyparts and imaging protocols, may not satisfy the extremely high requirement in clinical applications. In this paper, we propose a highly robust method to identify water and fat images in MR Dixon imaging using convolutional neural network (CNN). Different from standard CNN-based image classification that treats the image as a whole, our method aims at learning appearance characteristics in local patches and aggregating them for global image identification. The distributed and redundant local information ensures the robustness of our approach. We design an aggregated patch-based CNN that includes two sub-networks, *ProbNet* and *MaskNet*. While the *ProbNet* aims at deriving a dense probability of patch-based classification, the *Masknet* extracts informative local patches and aggregate their output. Both sub-networks are encapsulated in a unified network structure that can be trained in an end-to-end fashion. More important, since at run-time the testing image only needs to pass our network once, our method becomes much more efficient than traditional sliding window approaches. We validate our method on 2887 pairs of Dixon water and fat images. It achieves high accuracy (99.96 %) and run-time efficiency (110 ms/volume).

1 Introduction

The Dixon method is designed to separate water and fat signals in MR images. At least two images with different contrasts are acquired. By knowledge of the relative alignment of water and fat signal in the different complex-valued contrasts, water and fat contribution can then be separated [1]. Since "fat-only" and "water-only" images can be used for fat suppression and quantification, the Dixon method has shown values in the diagnosis of different diseases, e.g., adrenal adenomas and carcinomas, angiomyolipomas, focal fatty infiltration of the liver, etc.

© Springer International Publishing AG 2016
G. Wu et al. (Eds.): Patch-MI 2016, LNCS 9993, pp. 125–132, 2016.
DOI: 10.1007/978-3-319-47118-1_16

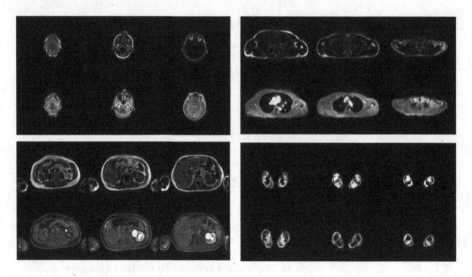

Fig. 1. Pairs of water (bottom) and fat (top) images.

Although the Dixon method provides images with different spectral properties, it is not able to identify those chemical components, i.e. label them as "water" or "fat". In order to display proper images to radiologists, heuristic physiological assumption-based approaches were designed to label fat and water images [2]. However, as those assumptions may be error prone, labels derived from physiological assumptions may not always be reliable. Although these wrong labels can be identified by radiologists, they may adversely affect the reading efficiency. (Radiologists have to search for the image with expected contrast in the entire MR study that often includes dozens of series.) More important, some automatic post-processing algorithms, e.g., Dixon-based PET MR attenuation [3], rely on the correct labels of fat and water images. These algorithms may have gross failures due to the wrong image labels.

Instead of relying on physiological hypothesis, fat and water images can also be differentiated by their appearance characteristics. Therefore, computer vision and machine learning technologies were also recently developed to identify water and fat images in MR Dixon imaging. A typical method starts from calculating some manually crafted features (e.g., intensity histograms) followed by a classifier that labels fat/water images [4]. Although these kinds of methods improve the image labeling accuracy, they may still not satisfy the extremely high request of real-world clinical applications. Note that since fat/water identification is the first step of many following manual or automatic operations on Dixon images, even 5 % of errors may affect the quality or efficiency of the workflow and cannot be ignored. Technically, however, it is very challenging to design a highly robust algorithm to deal with the large appearance variability (as shown in Fig. 1) from different body parts and imaging protocols (with or without contrast). The key challenge here is how to hand-craft a set of image features that work generically well on all different cases.

In this paper, we propose a fat/water image identification method using deep learning technology. Inspired by the tremendous success of convolutional neural network on natural image recognition (ImageNet competition [5]), we employ CNN as the backbone of our method. Thanks to the autonomous feature learning capability of CNN, hand-crafted feature design, which is extremely difficult for our problem, is no longer required. However, different from standard CNN-based image classification that treats the image as a whole, our method aims at leveraging appearance characteristics in local patches and aggregating them for global image identification. Specifically, our aggregated patch-based CNN consists of two sub-networks, *ProbNet* and *MaskNet*. While *ProbNet* learns the local appearance characteristics and generates a dense probability map of local patches, *MaskNet* further prunes and aggregates these local probabilities for volume-level classification. In this way, we essentially build a redundant and distributed recognition system that is robust to appearance variations. Since *ProbNet* and *MaskNet* are contained in a unified network infrastructure, we can conduct an end-to-end training to save the computational cost. More important, at the run-time, the testing image only needs to pass the pre-trained deep network once, which is much more efficient than sliding-window approaches.

2   Methods

2.1   Overview

Our system takes a pair of unlabeled fat and water volumes (V_1, V_2) as input. A pre-learned model (a deep convolutional neural network in this study) is applied to each of them to calculate their probabilities of being water images. The volume with higher "water probability" is labeled as water image, and the other is labeled as fat image. We define the volume-level water probability, $P_w(V)$, as

$$P_w(V) = \frac{1}{|S(V)|} \sum_{\boldsymbol{X} \in S(V)} \max_{\boldsymbol{X}' \in N(\boldsymbol{X})} p_w(\boldsymbol{X}') \tag{1}$$

Here, $p_w(\boldsymbol{X})$ defines the patch-level water probability of a local 2D transversal patch $\boldsymbol{X}$, $N(\cdot)$ is a neighborhood, $S(V)$ defines a sub-set of local 2D patches of the volume V.

The volume-level probability is, in fact, the average of water probabilities of a set of local patches. To avoid non-informative patches (e.g. local patches with homogenous intensities), we add some constraints to patches in $S(V)$.

$$S(V) = \{\boldsymbol{X} | \boldsymbol{X} \in V \ and \ Var(\boldsymbol{X}) > \theta\} \tag{2}$$

where, $Var(\boldsymbol{X})$ is the variance of intensities within patch $\boldsymbol{X}$, θ is a constant threshold.

A straightforward implementation of Eq. 1 is to train CNNs on local patches. At run-time, these CNNs will be invoked on informative patches and their outputs are averaged as the volume-level probability. This framework, however, is suffered from low runtime efficiency, since each patch is convolved independently without leveraging the overlapping information of neighboring patches.

Instead, inspired by [6], we adapt a fully convolutional network(FCN) as our first sub-network *ProbNet*. The output of this sub-network is a dense probability map of local patches. Since the convolution is shared by all local patches, the overlapping information across neighboring patches are fully utilized. Hence, the run time efficiency becomes much higher than patch-by-patch convolution. Our second sub-net, *MaskNet*, is designed to prune non-informative local patches. This sub-network efficiently calculates intensity variations of local patches. By implementing this calculation in a network, we can achieve higher run-time efficiency. Since the entire algorithm is now encapsulated in a unified network structure, we can conduct an end-to-end training by minimizing the following loss function.

$$L(\boldsymbol{W}) = \sum_{V \in T} \sum_{\boldsymbol{X} \in S(V)} (-\log(\max_{\boldsymbol{X}' \in N(\boldsymbol{X})} \mathcal{P}(l_{\boldsymbol{X}'}|\boldsymbol{X}'; \boldsymbol{W}))) \tag{3}$$

Here, T is the training data set, $\boldsymbol{W}$ is the model coefficient and $l_{\boldsymbol{X}}$ is the correct label, water or fat, of the patch $\boldsymbol{X}$. $\mathcal{P}(l_{\boldsymbol{X}}|\boldsymbol{X}; \boldsymbol{W})$ is the probability of the patch $\boldsymbol{X}$ of being correctly labeled with the model coefficient $\boldsymbol{W}$.

The overall network is shown in Fig. 2.

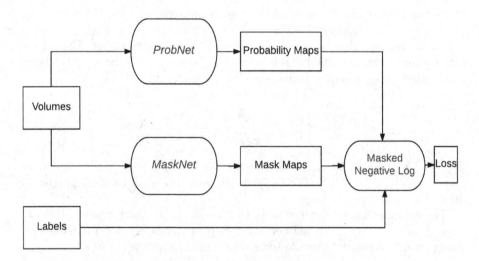

Fig. 2. Overall Network. With the input volumes, we use *ProbNet* to generate a map of patch classification probabilities $p_w(\boldsymbol{X})$, and use *MaskNet* (defined in Sect. 2.3) to compute maps of the boolean function $Var(\boldsymbol{X}) > \theta$.

2.2   Probability Subnet (*ProbNet*)

Our *ProbNet* aims at generating a dense probability map of local patches for each class. In typical deep learning classification methods, such as LeNet [7], AlexNet [8], and Caffenet [9], a CNN consists of a number of convolutional and max pooling layers followed by fully connected layers and a softmax layer. It takes a fixed-size input and outputs its class probabilities. Sliding window approaches are often employed to apply this standard network to generate a dense probability map.

As pointed out in [6], by converting fully connected layers to convolutional layers with kernels that cover their entire input region, we can get a fully convolutional network (FCN). It takes inputs of any size and outputs a probability map.

Let $CNN_{typical}$ be a typical network for binary classification of water/fat images, and CNN_{FCN} be its corresponding fully convolutional network. By setting the parameters properly, applying CNN_{FCN} to an image I is equivalent to extracting patches from I with a sliding window and applying $CNN_{typical}$ to the patches. A simple example is shown in Fig. 3.

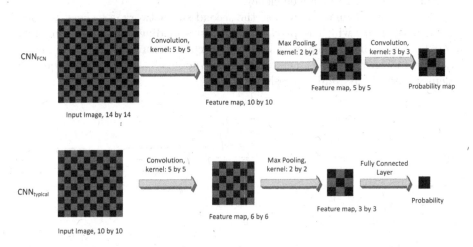

Fig. 3. A simple example of CNN_{FCN}. The red box is a sliding window on the input and its corresponding regions on feature maps. (Color figure online)

Generally, we can set the parameters as following:

1. $CNN_{typical}/CNN_{FCN}$ has n pooling layers (kernel 2×2, stride 2).
2. All convolutional and pooling layers have no padding.
3. The input sizes of all pooling layers are divisible by 2.
4. The input size of the network is $m \times m$ for $CNN_{typical}$, and $(m + k_1 2^n) \times (m + k_2 2^n)$ for CNN_{FCN}. m, k_1, k_2 are integers.

It is easy to see that, the size of the output probability map of CNN_{FCN} is $(1 + k_1) \times (1 + k_2) \times 2$, 2 is the number of classes.

We add the "no padding" condition to guarantee the translation invariance. Otherwise, some patches are padded with 0 s, but others are padded with pixels from neighboring regions.

Hence, computing the probability map of image I with CNN_{FCN} is equivalent to extracting patches from I with a stride 2^n sliding window and computing the corresponding probabilities with $CNN_{typical}$. But the computation cost is drastically reduced thanks to shared convolutional feature maps.

Our first sub-network, *ProbNet*, is defined as CNN_{FCN} followed by a stride 1 max pooling layer, M_L. We use M_L to select the locally most distinctive patches in the neighborhood $N(\cdot)$ defined in Eq. 1.

2.3 Mask Subnet (*MaskNet*)

MaskNet is designed to prune non-informative patches. As shown in Eq. 2, we simply use intensity variance to prune local patches that have homogenous intensities. Although intensity variance is easy to calculate, we still resort to a network structure for higher run time efficiency.

Given the input image I, we use the second sub-network, *Masknet*, to compute a mask map, which is pixel-to-pixel corresponding with the probability map. The mask map indicates that which patches are in $S(V)$ in Eqs. 1 and 3. As shown in Fig. 4, *Masknet* includes "Average pooling", "Elementwise Square", "Elementwise Minus" and "Threshold" layers.

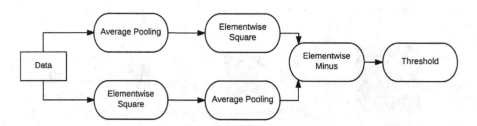

Fig. 4. *Masknet*: the "Average Pooling" layers are with kernel size $m \times m$, stride 2^n, and the "Threshold" layer is with the parameter θ

Masknet is designed based on the definition of variance, $Var(\boldsymbol{X}) = \overline{\boldsymbol{X}^2} - \overline{\boldsymbol{X}}^2$, and is easy to implement on deep learning systems with parallel computing, such as Caffe [9], Theano [10].

Note that, for each 2D feature map, we can generate its integral image in linear time, and compute the average of any rectangle region with its integral image in constant time [2]. Hence, the time complexity of *MaskNet* is linear to the input image size.

2.4 Implementation Details

In the first sub-network, *ProbNet* (CNN_{FCN} followed by M_L), we use $n=3$ max pooling layers in CNN_{FCN}, and set m to 72. CNN_{FCN} has 7 convolutional layers. The last 2 layers are fully connected layers in its corresponding typical network $CNN_{typical}$. M_L is with kernel size 5×5, stride 1, pad size 2.

We re-sample all training and testing volumes to the same resolution, and zero-pad the transversal slices to $(m+k_1 2^n) \times (m+k_2 2^n) = (72+8k_1) \times (72+8k_2)$. In training, we pad all the training slices to the same size. In the run time, we select the smallest k_1 and k_2 to pad each testing volume.

We implement our work on Caffe with stochastic gradient descent (SGD) training algorithm on Inter(R) i7-4710MQ@2.50 GHz CPU, GTX TITAN X GPU.

3 Experiments

3.1 Experiment Setup

Our dataset includes 300 pairs of water and fat MRI volumes, with different bodyparts, e.g., whole body, head, legs, etc. It is divided into training (200) and testing (100) subsets.

We re-sample training and testing volumes to $3\,\text{mm} \times 3\,\text{mm} \times 3\,\text{mm}$, and truncate testing cases to 2887 32-slice sub-volumes.

We also test two related approaches for comparison, with the same training and testing data.

1. **Random Sampling (RS):** To compare with local approaches with sliding-window, we use the typical convolutional network $CNN_{typical}$ on local patches, invoke them in a sliding-window fashion and aggregate the output. For a fair comparison, we use the same loss function Eq. 3 in training and the same probability definition in Eq. 1 in testing with the proposed approach. In the run time, $|S(V)|$ is set to 10, 50, 250 and 1250.
2. **Whole Slice (WS):** To compare with global appearance-based approaches, we also implement a CNN on whole slices. We pad all the slices to the same size, and use a typical classification network AlexNet to compute the probabilities. All slices that are not all 0 s are used for training or testing.

3.2 Training Time Comparison

In training, the convergence time of our proposed network is about 3 h and the convergence time of **RS** is about 24 h. The proposed network converge much faster.

Table 1. Comparative accuracy for truncated volumes

Methods	Identification accuracy	Classification accuracy	Inference time
Our approach	99.96 %	98.61 %	110 ms
RS (10)	95.42 %	90.30 %	54 ms
RS (50)	97.74 %	95.15 %	210 ms
RS (250)	99.96 %	97.92 %	705 ms
RS (1250)	99.96 %	98.96 %	3511 ms
WS	97.23 %	92.38 %	105 ms

3.3 Testing Results

Given the volume-based probabilities P_w with Eq. 1, we can identify a pair of unlabeled water/fat images (V_1, V_2) by comparing $P_w(V_1)$ and $P_w(V_2)$, and classify a single volume V_i by comparing $P_w(V_i)$ with 0.5. On the testing set of 2887 32-slice sub-volumes, the accuracy for the two tasks and the average inference time for a single volume are listed in Table 1. Our approach outperforms **WS**. And, to achieve a similar accuracy with our approach, the speed of **RS** is much slower.

4 Discussion

We design an aggregated patch-based CNN to learn the discriminative local information for a challenging image classification problem. The current system can provide volume-level identification for water/fat MRI images accurately and efficiently. In the future, we may further extend this technology to provide pixel-level identification as well.

References

1. WT, D.: Simple proton spectroscopic imaging. Radiology **153**, 189–194 (1984)
2. Lewis, J.: Fast template matching. In: Proceedings of Vision Interface (1995)
3. Ladefoged, C.N., et al.: Impact of incorrect tissue classification in Dixon-based MR-AC: fat-water tissue inversion. EJNMMI Phys. **1**, 101 (2014)
4. Ahmada, M., et al.: A method for automatic identification of water and fat images from a symmetrically sampled dual-echo Dixon technique. Magn. Reson. Imaging **28**, 427–433 (2010)
5. Russakovsky, O., et al.: Imagenet large scale visual recognition challenge. Int. J. Comput. Vis. (IJCV) **115**, 211–252 (2015)
6. Long, J., et al.: Fully convolutional networks for semantic segmentation. In: CVPR (2015)
7. LeCun, Y., et al.: Gradient-based learning applied to document recognition. In: Proceedings of the IEEE (1998)
8. Krizhevsky, A., et al.: Imagenet classification with deep convolutional neural networks. In: Advances in Neural Information Processing Systems, vol. 25 (2012)
9. Jia, Y., et al.: Caffe: convolutional architecture for fast feature embedding. arXiv preprint (2014)
10. Theano Development Team: Theano: a Python framework for fast computation of mathematical expressions. arXiv e-prints (2016)

Estimating Lung Respiratory Motion Using Combined Global and Local Statistical Models

Zhong Xue[1(✉)], Ramiro Pino[2], and Bin Teh[2]

[1] Houston Methodist Research Institute,
Weill Cornell Medicine, Houston, TX, USA
zxue@houstonmethodist.org
[2] Department of Radiation Oncology,
Houston Methodist Hospital, Houston, TX, USA

Abstract. In image-guided therapy of lung cancer, discrepancies between pre-procedural 3D or 4D-CT and patient's current lung shape could reduce the accuracy for guidance. While real-time imaging is often not available, it is necessary to estimate the lung motion from real-time measurable signals such as on-chest/abdominal fiducials or surface. Traditional regression models take the entire lung motion deformation as a whole and perform the estimation in a global manner. Given high dimensionality and complexity of the lung motion patterns, the correlation of lung motion in different local areas with the surface motion could be different. Therefore, we propose a combined global and local statistics-based estimation to improve the estimation accuracy because local deformations have similar patterns and could have higher correlation with the surface motion. Results with 37 4D-CT datasets suggest local motion estimation further improves the performance for lung respiratory motion modeling.

Keywords: 4D-CT · Respiratory motion estimation · High-dimensional data regression · Statistical model

1 Introduction

In image-guided lung intervention and lung cancer radiotherapy, due to poor reproducibility of respiratory cycles, discrepancies between pre-procedural static 3D-CT or 4D-CT images and patient's current lung shape could potentially reduce the accuracy for precise guidance. Lung motion estimation from chest and abdominal surfaces that can be captured during the procedure becomes an important task to help real-time monitor and track patient's motion during intervention and radiotherapy. It is thus necessary to study the relationship between real-time measurable signals such as on-chest/abdominal fiducials or surfaces and the lung motion. Recent works for computing lung motion include lung motion deformation modeling with image registration [1–3], using individual patient's 4D-CT dataset [4], and using statistical model to incorporate both group and individual information for motion modeling. In the latter methods, respiratory patterns are trained using existing patient's or population's data and used to estimate the dynamic images of individual patients [5–15]. The basic idea is to use the motion information of a patient's external features to compensate for internal respiratory motion based on an estimation model with prior knowledge.

© Springer International Publishing AG 2016
G. Wu et al. (Eds.): Patch-MI 2016, LNCS 9993, pp. 133–140, 2016.
DOI: 10.1007/978-3-319-47118-1_17

Previously, we studied this problem using principal component analysis (PCA)-based [11] and Kernel-PCA-based support vector machine regression models [14]. They estimate entire lung motion deformation as a whole and can be considered as a global estimation. The challenge is due to high-dimensionality of the lung deformation fields, which combine different motion directions and patterns at different locations. Given the very high dimensionality of lung deformation fields and high complexity of the motion relationships, we notice that regional or local deformations that are similar within that local area can have better correlation with the patient's surface motion, and hence, partitioning the entire lung area into different local regions can be beneficial because one does not need to model complex regression as a whole.

In this paper, we propose a combined global and local statistics-based lung motion estimation method. Specifically, the surface motion signals are not only used to estimate the lung motion as a whole, but also applied to estimate local deformations. Like the popular piecewise linear regression, local deformations defined on various regions or partitions are similar each other and potentially have higher correlation with the chest/abdominal motion, thus, can be estimated more accurately. The algorithm is composed of three steps: (1) after registering the longitudinal deformation for each subject onto the template space, the entire lung region is separately into a number of regions by using a spatial smoothness-constrained fuzzy C-mean clustering method on the deformation fields; (2) the joint statistical models of deformation and surface are then computed for the entire lung region and for each partition; (3) the global motion estimation is performed using PCA-based estimation and is further refined using the local estimation for each partition, constrained by the global estimation.

In experiments, we used 37 4D-CT datasets and evaluated the algorithm in a leave-one-out manner. First, the longitudinal deformation fields from exhale image to inhale image of each subject are registered onto a randomly selected template. Then, the template domain is partitioned into a number of local regions using a clustering algorithm on the normalized deformation fields. Both global and local PCA models are then constructed to model the joint statistics of lung motion and surface motion. For the left-out subject to be tested, its exhale CT and surface motion vectors from exhale to inhale were used as the input, and the inhale image/field was then estimated. The accuracy between the estimated deformation fields and those calculated from the original inhale image was calculated on the lung field area as the quantitative measure for the estimation methods. The results suggest local motion estimation further improves the performance for lung respiratory motion modeling.

2 Method

We formulate lung motion estimation as a generic regression problem. Specifically, suppose the lung motion vector is $\mathbf{u}$, and the corresponding chest/abdominal motion vector is $\mathbf{v}$, the task for the regression is to estimate $\mathbf{u}$ from $\mathbf{v}$, given a series of training sample pairs $(\mathbf{u}, \mathbf{v})$. Many methods can be used for this purpose, such as (general) linear regression, principal component regression (PCA), (kernel) ridge regression, and support vector machine (SVM) regression. In the previous studies, we showed that high-dimensional chest/abdominal surface data can outperform the fiducial point tracking-based methods [11].

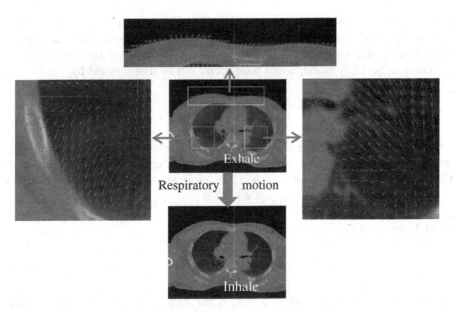

Fig. 1. Illustration of local variability of respiratory motion among different regions. Breathing deformations from exhale to inhale of a subject within the rectangular regions are enlarged.

However, given the very high dimensionality of lung deformation fields and high complexity of the motion relationships, different patterns can be observed at different lung regions. As shown in Fig. 1, when the lung moves from exhale to inhale, different areas move differently from the anterior surface motion (top image). Intuitively the lung regions close to diaphragm would mostly move in the inferior and superior direction, while the upper-front area will mainly move in the anterior and posterior direction. Clearly, if these regions can be separated to perform motion estimation locally, it will result in fewer burdens for a global motion estimation that needs to estimate different motion patterns as a whole. This indicates that it might be effective to consider estimation of deformation differently at different locations. In other words, the idea of recent patch-based analysis that splits the entire data into partial components is suitable for this purpose. This observation motivates us to study both global and local motion estimation in the lung motion modeling.

Specifically, if the entire lung deformation can be partitioned into the motion fields of different regions, the relationship between regional lung motion and chest/abdominal motion can be analyzed separately, and the final motion estimation is achieved by combining these models. More accurate estimation can be achieved since each regional deformation set is better correlated with surface motion.

2.1   PCA-Based Global Estimation

Given the respiratory motion field of subject s, $\mathbf{u}_m^s$, $s = 1, \ldots, N$ and the corresponding chest/abdominal surface motion $\mathbf{v}_m^s$, with $m = 1, \ldots, M$ represents the respiratory phase, we can construct the joint statistical model of them using PCA by rearranging them into column vectors (we still use the same symbols for simplicity). Thus, for any given phase (only inhale phase is used in this paper), without loss of generality, according to the PCA model, a new joint vector can be reconstructed by,

$$\begin{bmatrix} \mathbf{u} \\ \mathbf{v} \end{bmatrix} = \begin{bmatrix} \bar{\mathbf{u}} \\ \bar{\mathbf{v}} \end{bmatrix} + M \begin{bmatrix} \mathbf{b}_u \\ \mathbf{b}_v \end{bmatrix}, \tag{1}$$

where $\bar{\mathbf{u}}$ and $\bar{\mathbf{v}}$ are the average of all the N training samples, M is the matrix formed by the eigenvectors of the covariance matrix corresponding to K largest eigenvalues. Given a new set of motion vectors $(\mathbf{u}, \mathbf{v})$, its projected feature vector $\mathbf{b}$ on the PCA space can be calculated as $\mathbf{b} = M^T(\begin{bmatrix} \mathbf{u} \\ \mathbf{v} \end{bmatrix} - \begin{bmatrix} \bar{\mathbf{u}} \\ \bar{\mathbf{v}} \end{bmatrix})$, and $\mathbf{b}$ is subject to the following multi-dimensional Gaussian distribution,

$$p(\mathbf{b}) = \frac{1}{\sigma} e\left\{ -\sum_{k=1}^{K} b_k^2/2\lambda_k \right\}, \tag{2}$$

where b_k is the kth element of $\mathbf{b}$, and λ_k is the corresponding eigenvalue. σ is the normalization factor.

After obtaining the PCA model, given an input surface motion vector for a patient, denoted as $\mathbf{v}^P$, the corresponding lung respiratory motion field $\mathbf{u}^P$ can be estimated by solving the best feature vector $\mathbf{b}$ that satisfies two constraints: (1) the reconstructed vector $\mathbf{v}$ matches the input vector $\mathbf{v}^P$, and at the same time, (2) the feature vector $\mathbf{b}$ is subject to the prior distribution in Eq. (2), or $\mathbf{b}$ is subject to high pdf value constraints. Accordingly, the energy function is defined as [11],

$$E(\mathbf{b}) = \left\| \mathbf{v}^P - \bar{\mathbf{v}} - M_v \mathbf{b} \right\|^2 + \xi \sum_{k=1}^{K} b_k^2/2\lambda_k, \tag{3}$$

where matrix M is separated into upper and lower parts $M = \begin{bmatrix} M_u \\ M_v \end{bmatrix}$, corresponding to the dimensions of vectors $\mathbf{u}$ and $\mathbf{v}$. ξ is the weighting factor for constraining $\mathbf{b}$ with the prior distribution and is set so that prior constraint is about 50 % of the error term. After $\mathbf{b}$ is estimated by minimizing Eq. (3), the corresponding lung motion vector $\mathbf{u}^P$ can be calculated by $\mathbf{u}^P = \bar{\mathbf{u}} + M_u \mathbf{b}$.

2.2   Combining with the Localized Estimation

When the entire lung motion deformation $\mathbf{u}$ is partitioned into different patches defined on local regions, the relationship between the regional lung motion and the chest/abdominal motion can be analyzed separately. To partition vector $\mathbf{u}$ into C un-overlapping patches, each patch can now be represented as $\mathbf{u}_c = \phi_c \mathbf{u}$, with ϕ_c as the matrix to select elements that belong to the cth patch. On the other hand, given the motion for each patch, the whole motion vector $\mathbf{u}$ can be reconstructed by combining them. Similar to Eq. (1), the joint distribution of the cth patch can be modeled using the

PCA model, $\begin{bmatrix} \mathbf{u}_c \\ \mathbf{v} \end{bmatrix} = \begin{bmatrix} \bar{\mathbf{u}}_c \\ \bar{\mathbf{v}} \end{bmatrix} + \mathbf{M}_c \begin{bmatrix} \mathbf{b}_{c,u} \\ \mathbf{b}_{c,v} \end{bmatrix}$, with $\mathbf{b}_c = \begin{bmatrix} \mathbf{b}_{c,u}^T \mathbf{b}_{c,v}^T \end{bmatrix}^T$ as the feature vector

for the cth PCA model. Then, combining the global estimation in Eq. (3) and the local estimation of each patch, the final estimated lung motion vector $\mathbf{u}$ can be obtained by first calculating the optimal global vector $\mathbf{u}^P$ from Eq. (3), and then refining the final estimation by calculating $\mathbf{b}_c$ through minimizing the following energy function:

$$E = \left\| \mathbf{u}^P - \sum_{c=1\ldots C} \phi_c^T \mathbf{u}_c \right\|^2 + \sum_{c=1}^{C} \left\{ \left\| \mathbf{v}^P - \bar{\mathbf{v}} - \mathbf{M}_{c,v}\mathbf{b}_c \right\|^2 + \xi \sum_{k=1}^{K} b_{c,k}^2 / 2\lambda_{c,k} \right\},$$

(4)

where the first term is a global constraint to make sure that the reconstructed motion fields from different partitions are similar to the global vector. The second term is a combination of the estimation energy function for each partition. This energy function can be optimized for each $\mathbf{b}_c$ separately. In fact, there is an analytic solution for the optimization by setting the partial derivatives of Eq. (4) with respective to $\mathbf{b}_c$ to zero. After optimization, the estimated $\mathbf{u}_c$ is calculated by $\mathbf{u}_c = \bar{\mathbf{u}}_c + \mathbf{M}_{c,u}\mathbf{b}_c$, and the final motion vector is calculated by $\mathbf{u} = \sum_{c=1\ldots C} \phi_c^T \mathbf{u}_c$. For different regions, PCA model parameters ($\mathbf{M}_c$ and $\lambda_{c,k}$) are different, allowing for separate modeling for each local region. Moreover, the final reconstructed motion vector combined from different patches is also globally constrained by the global estimation. Finally the deformation across the boundary of neighboring partitions is smoothed, before a topological correction across the entire deformation field.

2.3 Partitioning Lung Region According to Respiratory Deformations

The proposed method is similar to the idea of a piecewise linear regression, and it is important to partition the entire lung region into a number of local regions, so that a PCA-based estimation works better for each region and so that the finally combined estimation can be more accurate. One solution for partitioning the lung region would be using clustering on the respiratory deformation fields. Superpixel-based methods are also good choices for partitioning. In this work, we use the spatially constrained fuzzy C-mean clustering method to partition the entire lung region into C different patches, each with similar in-group deformations. The objective function is defined as follows [16],

$$J = \sum_{i \in \Omega} \sum_{k=1}^{C} \mu_{ik}^q \| \mathbf{u}_i - \bar{\mathbf{u}}_k \|^2 + 1/\beta \sum_{i \in \Omega} \sum_{k=1}^{C} \mu_{ik}^q \sum_{l \in N_i} \sum_{j \in M_k} \mu_{lj}^q,$$

(5)

where N_i is the spatial neighbors of voxel i in the image domain Ω, and $M_k = \{1, \ldots, C\} \backslash \{k\}$. $\mathbf{u}_i$ is the respiratory deformation vector at voxel i, and $\bar{\mathbf{u}}_k$ is the clustering centroid for the kth region. The second term is the spatial smoothness constraints of the fuzzy membership functions μ, and β is the tradeoff coefficient between minimizing the first term (the standard FCM objective function) and the second term (the smooth membership function constraints). Notice that the performance of regression between each region with the chest/abdominal motion vector $\mathbf{v}$

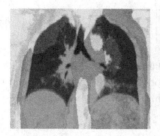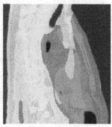

Fig. 2. Partitioning the lung region into six local areas, and motion estimation model is trained separately for these partitions.

could be considered during the partition. Herein, only clustering of respiratory deformation fields is performed to show the advantages of localized estimation.

Figure 2 shows the six partitions that were used in this paper, which were calculated based on clustering of all the normalized deformations between exhale and inhale phases of all the subjects. The chest/abdominal motion vector **v** could also be partitioned into local patches so that the most relevant portion of the chest/abdominal motion can be used to estimate relative local lung motion field. Partitioning **v** has the advantages of determining which part of the chest/abdominal motion is correlated with which part of the lung respiratory motion, and helps focus and locates the surface area that needs to be monitored during the procedure. For simplicity, we chose to only partition the lung motion field **u**, which has much higher dimension than **v**. Additionally, clustering does not converge well for large number of partitions, and superpixel-based method may be used for more detailed partitioning.

3   Results

The algorithms (Sects. 2.1 and 2.2) were implemented using C++ language and performed on a Dell PowerEdge C1100 workstation with two Intel Xeon X5650 CPUs and 24 GB memory. We used exhale and inhale images of 37 subjects in the experiments, where only small lesions are present so that the lung fields are mostly clear in order to eliminate the registration and training errors caused by pathology, for motion modeling. We used the exhale image as the baseline and constructed the motion between the exhale and the inhale images (the 5th phase from 4D-CT). The in-plane resolution is between 0.98 to 1.17 mm and the slice thickness is 3 mm. Leave-one out strategy was used for constructing the PCA model, and the left out subject was used for testing. For training, one subject was selected as the template, and all the subject images were the registered onto the template space by deforming their exhale CT onto that of the template. Longitudinal deformations were then deformed and re-oriented onto the template space [11]. For each test, it took less than one hour to construct the statistical model and 3 ~ 4 min for estimation. Global PCA-based estimation (Sect. 2.1) and the combined global and local estimation (Sect. 2.2) were compared to illustrate the improvement of motion estimation. Because chest and abdominal surface tracking signals were not available for out testing data, we used those extracted from the CTs, which only consists of the anterior part of the CT image surfaces. For proper correspondences of the surface across different images, after registration, a standard surface from the exhale image of the template was extracted, excluding the breast area. This surface was then deformed onto each subject's images and then locally adjusted so that each vertex matches the image boundary. Finally, a smoothing operation is performed to make sure the surface is smooth and topologically correct.

In the test, only the exhale and inhale surfaces, and the exhale image were used as the input and the resultant deformation field was then used to deform the exhale CT to generate the estimated inhale CT in order to match the input inhale surface signals. The inhale CT was only used as the ground truth. The errors of the deformation fields within the lung field area between the estimated deformation and the original one calculated between the actual exhale and inhale images were used to quantify the estimation accuracy. Among the subjects, the average of the maximal deformation from exhale to inhale was 17.5 mm with a standard deviation of 4.7 mm. In 36 leave-one-out tests, we got an average accuracy for global only estimation as 4.2 mm with standard deviation (std) of 1.1 mm. Further local estimation can improve about 20 % of the performance, with average 3.4 mm (std = 0.9 mm). We noticed that one of the obvious improvements is located around the diaphragm area, as illustrated in Fig. 3.

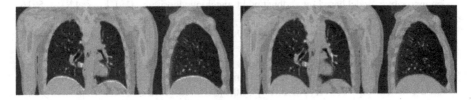

Fig. 3. Overlapping lung fields extracted from estimated inhale image on the original image. Left: global only; right: global + local refinement.

4   Conclusion

We proposed a combined global and local estimation algorithm for lung motion estimation using the chest/abdominal surface signals. The high-dimensional lung motion deformation is partitioned into different local regions, and motion estimation is performed using a PCA-based estimation method for each region and constrained by the global estimation. The partitioning decouples the complexity of lung motion and can better model the lung motion at different locations. Experiments by comparing with the global estimation confirmed the advantage using leave-one-out strategy on images of 37 subjects. In the future work, we plan to partition the chest/abdominal surfaces and perform an extensive validation using more clinical subjects.

Acknowledgement. This paper was supported by NIH grant 1 R03 EB018977 (ZX).

References

1. Handels, H., Werner, R., Schmidt, R., Frenzel, T., Lu, W., Low, D., Ehrhardt, J.: 4D medical image computing and visualization of lung tumor mobility in spatio-temporal CT image data. Int. J. Med. Inf. **76**(Suppl 3), S433–S439 (2007)
2. Sundaram, T.A., Avants, B.B., Gee, J.C.: A dynamic model of average lung deformation using capacity-based reparameterization and shape averaging of lung MR images. In: Barillot, C., Haynor, D.R., Hellier, P. (eds.) MICCAI 2004. LNCS, vol. 3217, pp. 1000–1007. Springer, Heidelberg (2004)
3. Vandemeulebroucke, J., Rit, S., Kybic, J., Clarysse, P., Sarrut, D.: Spatiotemporal motion estimation for respiratory-correlated imaging of the lungs. Med. Phys. **38**(1), 166–178 (2011)
4. Wu, G., Wang, Q., Lian, J., Shen, D.: Estimating the 4D respiratory lung motion by spatiotemporal registration and building super-resolution image. Med. Image Comput. Comput. Assist. Interv. **14**(Pt. 1), 532–539 (2011)
5. Klinder, T., Lorenz, C., Ostermann, J.: Prediction framework for statistical respiratory motion modeling. Med. Image Comput. Comput. Assist. Interv. **13**(Pt 3), 327–334 (2010)
6. Ehrhardt, J., Werner, R., Schmidt-Richberg, A., Handels, H.: Statistical modeling of 4D respiratory lung motion using diffeomorphic image registration. IEEE Trans. Med. Imaging **30**(2), 251–265 (2011)
7. Yi, J., Yang, X., Chen, G., Li, Y.R.: Lung motion estimation using dynamic point shifting: an innovative model based on a robust point matching algorithm. Med. Phys. **42**(10), 5616–5632 (2015)
8. Lu, B., Chen, Y., Park, J.C., Fan, Q., Kahler, D., Liu, C.: A method of surface marker location optimization for tumor motion estimation in lung stereotactic body radiation therapy. Med. Phys. **42**(1), 244–253 (2015)
9. Rottmann, J., Keall, P., Berbeco, R.: Real-time soft tissue motion estimation for lung tumors during radiotherapy delivery. Med. Phys. **40**(9), 091713 (2013)
10. Dong, B., Graves, Y.J., Jia, X., Jiang, S.B.: Optimal surface marker locations for tumor motion estimation in lung cancer radiotherapy. Phys. Med. Biol. **57**(24), 8201–8215 (2012)
11. He, T., Xue, Z., Yu, N., Nitsch, P.L., Teh, B.S., Wong, S.T.: Estimating dynamic lung images from high-dimension chest surface motion using 4D statistical model. Med. Image Comput. Comput. Assist. Interv. **17**(Pt 2), 138–145 (2014)
12. Lu, W., Song, J.H., Christensen, G.E., Parikh, P.J., Zhao, T., Hubenschmidt, J.P., Bradley, J. D., Low, D.A.: Evaluating lung motion variations in repeated 4D CT studies using inverse consistent image registration. Int. J. Radiat. Oncol. Biol. Phys. **66**(3), S606–S607 (2006)
13. Santelli, C., Nezafat, R., Goddu, B., Manning, W.J., Smink, J., Kozerke, S., Peters, D.C.: Respiratory bellows revisited for motion compensation: preliminary experience for cardiovascular MR. Magn. Reson. Med. **65**(4), 1098–1103 (2011)
14. He, T., Xue, Z., Xie, W., Wong, S.T.: Online 4-D CT estimation for patient-specific respiratory motion based on real-time breathing signals. Med. Image Comput. Comput. Assist. Interv. **13**(Pt 3), 392–399 (2010)
15. He, T., Xue, Z., Lu, K., Valdivia y Alvarado, M., Wong, K.K., Xie, W., Wong, S.T.: A minimally invasive multimodality image-guided (MIMIG) system for peripheral lung cancer intervention and diagnosis. Comput. Med. Imaging Graph. **36**(5), 345–355 (2012)
16. Pham, D.L.: Fuzzy clustering with spatial constraints. In: Proceedings of 2002 International Conference on Image Processing, vol. 62, no. 2, pp. II-65–II-68. IEEE (2002)

Author Index

Allard, Michèle   43
Ames, David   109
Arthofer, Christoph   84

Basham, Mark   17
Bobu, Andreea   60
Bourgeat, Pierrick   109

Cao, Xiaohuan   34
Chen, Geng   9
Coupé, Pierrick   43, 68, 76, 92, 117

Dalca, Adrian V.   60
Deledalle, Charles-Alban   43
Dong, Pei   1, 51
Dore, Vincent   109
Dossal, Charles   43

Fenchel, Matthias   125
French, Andrew P.   17
Fripp, Jurgen   92, 109

Gao, Yue   51
Giraud, Rémi   76
Golland, Polina   60
Guo, Yangrong   51
Guo, Yanrong   1, 34

Hao, Shijie   1
Hett, Kilian   76

Kiefer, Berthold   125

Lamecker, Hans   25
Liang, Peipeng   51
Luengo, Imanol   17

Macaulay, Lance   109
Manjón, José V.   68, 76, 92, 117
Masters, Colin L.   109
Mondino, Mary   76

Morgan, Paul S.   84
Mukhopadhyay, Anirban   25

Nickel, Dominik   125

Pino, Ramiro   133
Pitiot, Alain   84

Raniga, Parnesh   92
Romero, José E.   68, 117
Rost, Natalia S.   60
Rowe, Christopher C.   109

Saghafi, Behrouz   9
Salvado, Olivier   92, 109
Shen, Dinggang   1, 9, 34, 51
Shi, Feng   9
Shi, Yonghong   51

Ta, Vinh-Thong   76
Teh, Bin   133

Victoria, Oscar Salvador Morillo   25
Villemagne, Victor L.   109

Wang, Hongzhi   100
Wang, Li   1
Wang, Lin   34
Wang, Qian   51
Wu, Guorong   1, 34, 51

Xia, Ying   92
Xue, Zhong   133

Yap, Pew-Thian   9
Yu, Ning   100
Yushkevich, Paul A.   100

Zachow, Stefan   25
Zhan, Yiqiang   125
Zhao, Liang   125
Zhou, Xiang Sean   125

Printed in the United States
By Bookmasters